TOUCHING DISTANCE

KEVIN KEEGAN, THE ENTERTAINERS & NEWCASTLE'S IMPOSSIBLE DREAM

BY MARTIN HARDY

TOUCHING DISTANCE

KEVIN KEEGAN, THE ENTERTAINERS & NEWCASTLE'S IMPOSSIBLE DREAM

BY MARTIN HARDY

deCoubertin
BOOKS

First published as a hardback by deCoubertin Books Ltd in 2015.

deCoubertin Books, Studio N, Baltic Creative Campus, Liverpool, L1 OAH

www.decoubertin.co.uk

First Hardback Edition.

ISBN: 978-1-909245-25-9

A CIP catalogue record for this book is available from the British Library.

Cover design by Thomas Regan, Milkyone Creative.

Typset design by Allen Mohr.

Layout by Sabahat Muhammad.

Printed and bound by Standart.

FOR MATTHEW

CONTENTS

INTRODUCTION

AT THE START OF FEBRUARY 1992, NEWCASTLE UNITED WERE FACING relegation to the third tier of English football for the first time in their history. They were also facing bankruptcy. St James' Park had been neglected, the club's best players had been sold.

In a daring move, Newcastle appointed Kevin Keegan as manager. Keegan, the two-time European Footballer of the Year, had played for the club between 1982 and 1984. He had been out of football since. His appointment as manager was as big a shock as when he arrived as a player.

Exactly four years after Keegan's return to the north-east of England, Newcastle were top of the Premiership, nine points clear of Manchester United, having played a game less.

It would turn out to be one of the most memorable seasons in the modern history of English football. Keegan's side would play a unique brand of football and become known as The Entertainers. They would take part in a game at Anfield that was – and still is – widely recognised as the best the Premier League has ever seen. Keegan would also famously square up to Sir Alex Ferguson.

Touching Distance tells the story of that remarkable season, through the highs and the lows of a dramatic campaign. It also traces the seeds of the revival back to Keegan's first spell as a player, to his return and the dramatic impact he had on a football club, its supporters and an entire region.

Touching Distance talks to the people who made it happen, the players, the coaching staff and Newcastle's owner at the time, and relives a truly momentous period for the club.

It is a story of hopes and dreams and a time when, for Newcastle United, anything seemed possible.

KEVIN KEEGAN – BREAKING INTO HEAVEN

JUST A GOAL. THAT WAS ALL WE WANTED. A GOAL. NOT CUPS OR league titles. Not world dominance. Just a goal. Just one man scoring. Make this day better, Kevin. Make it even more magical. Give us a memory to take to the grave.

I'm ten, Kevin. Make me understand. Make me get what this club means to everyone, to every member of my family. Make me love it, Kevin. Truly love it. Make me crave it for the rest of my life. Set the bar in the gods. Score today. Just do that.

I don't understand why you're here. No one does, not really. It doesn't make sense, but it's beautiful and the ground is twice as full as the last time I was here. People are locked out. The excitement is something I don't know yet, but I will never forget it.

We had to get here in the morning, and the place was rammed with people. There were thousands of them, all desperate to get in. It still stands out.

Everywhere you looked there were Newcastle fans: happy, excited, expecting something special.

You don't forget magic. You don't forget falling in love, or seeing your children for the first time. That day was just as vivid. It was twelve o'clock, three hours before kick-off, and on Strawberry Place you couldn't move for people.

They had Kevin Keegan scarves for a pound and there were queues of supporters everywhere you looked trying to get in.

They tangled like boxed-up Christmas tree lights in the old West Stand car park. The stand had huge letters on that read out the name of Newcastle United FC. There were steps leading up to the entrance. It seemed perfect. Walking up to heaven. They were the steps you had to stand on when a cameraman asked you to wave a Kevin Keegan silk scarf.

There wasn't an inch of space in the ground. St James' Park has never been squeezed that full since. Crammed full of people, full of hope and dreams and men injecting their club into their souls.

You can't touch disbelief, but you could feel it.

You'd been European Footballer of the Year twice. They call it the Ballon d'Or now. You were Messi. You were at Newcastle. In Division Two.

It didn't make sense. It woke up a city.

Just a goal, Kevin. Score. Please score.

And on the hour, you were put through. The crowd inhaled. You can hear it if you go on YouTube. The crowd inhaled and hoped and prayed that once, just once, it would all make sense. And you hit a shot that you later claimed the sardine-packed terraces of the Gallowgate End sucked into the goal.

In the 60th minute a football ground exploded. It was like thunder. It could have woken the dead. You were engulfed. People were delirious. They had to drag you back to the Newcastle half to restart the game.

I watched men fall in love with Kevin Keegan that afternoon, on 28 August 1982.

'I didn't want to come out of the crowd,' you said. 'I just wanted to stay there forever.'

It was the perfect day.

Newcastle fans have never stopped believing in their dreams since.

17 MAY 1984

ALAN SHEARER – FLYING

THERE HAVE BEEN BETTER FIREWORK DISPLAYS, BUT FEW WATCHED with such genuine feeling. When the letters of 'Auf Wiedersehen, Kev' (in reference to the television programme featuring Geordie workers in Germany) sparked into fairly forgettable life at the Leazes End of St James' Park, the helicopter's whirring picked up.

Kevin Keegan really was leaving.

Twenty-two months after the signature that shocked football, not just Tyneside, it was over. Keegan had fulfilled his mandate – the club was back in the top division of English football after an enthralling promotion.

He wasn't just leaving Newcastle, but football.

For his retirement, and his testimonial, Liverpool had been invited. St James' Park was crammed full again. All proceeds were to be put towards buying new Newcastle players. It finished 2–2 and he scored.

Keegan was still in his black and white strip with the red number seven on the back when he jogged to the centre circle of St James' Park at the game's finish. There was a final bow on bended knees towards the Gallowgate End. Big hard men waved. It was night-time. Emotions were easier to hide.

The helicopter door opened. Tyneside gulped. Some people were in tears. Keegan was offered a hand and went on board.

A crowd of ball boys, with tight-fitting Co-op tracksuits, looked on in awe. A thirteen-year-old called Alan Shearer adjusted his sleeves and, like everyone around him, craned his neck backwards to follow the helicopter as it took Keegan from the centre circle, back to wherever he had come from.

'I was playing for the County Schools team and I was invited to be a ball boy,' says Shearer. 'I remember following him around like a pied piper in those stupid tracksuits we were in. I thought they looked great at the time.

'We found out a couple of days before the game. It was bedlam, just to be involved and to get the great pictures afterwards.

'I was there for his first game as well. I'd gone with all my mates. As soon as we got off the Metro and went to the ground there was just people everywhere. He scored and Newcastle won. It was a special day.

'I went flying when the goal went in. I was at the back of the Gallowgate End and I ended up near the front. It was chaos when he scored, it was euphoric, it was incredible, it really was.

'Then he left in a helicopter after the Liverpool match.

'It was his last game. We were all trying to get out there to see him. The helicopter was a special moment.

'He lifted the club up. It was pretty dull before he came. It was what was needed. As usual he didn't disappoint. He delivered what he said he was going to do. He gave the whole city a great buzz.'

ALAN PARDEW – HEAVEN KNOWS I'M MISERABLE NOW

FIRST THERE WAS THE PUSH, THEN THE SCRAPE OF OLD METAL, THEN came the clunk; the sound of decay, reluctantly letting you in.

The turnstiles at the Gallowgate End of St James' Park would spit you into the ground. It was a violent fight to get in, pushing against machinery, and logic.

The steps were crumbling, all toilets were open-air and in the concrete jungle that looked down on the city there was an uncomfortable mixture of shrubs and trees that had been planted to calm the mood of supporters.

The team was doing that.

At the very top of those stairs was a small opening, the only one, to the scoreboard end of the terrace.

There were just over 15,000 there that day, on 18 January 1992, when Newcastle faced Charlton Athletic. Newcastle had lost 20,000 fans in a decade. The mood of the football club at the time – and the club dictates the pulse of the city – was bleak.

Newcastle, relegated in 1989, had lost a Division Two play-off semi-final to fierce rivals Sunderland at St James' Park two years earlier. Supporters had invaded the pitch in what looked like an attempt to have the game abandoned.

It hadn't worked.

Sunderland had lost the final but still gained promotion, through the financial irregularities of Swindon Town, the team who had defeated them at Wembley.

The fragile hope that had followed the appointment of the World Cup-winning Argentinian Osvaldo Ardiles, by strange coincidence the man who had managed Swindon, as manager in 1991 and the young, local-born and club-produced team he had created did not last long.

Sir John Hall, a local businessman who had overseen Gateshead's MetroCentre development, a huge out-of-town shopping mall, had joined the club's board, but failed to ignite interest in a share issue that would have given supporters a footing in Newcastle United.

With the club fighting relegation to the third tier of the Football League, Charlton Athletic came to town.

St James' Park could not have presented a greater contrast to the moment when Kevin Keegan made his debut. The terraces he had filled stood largely deserted. The team's demise mirrored the ground. There were vast spaces wherever you looked.

St James' Park was most definitely half-empty.

Behind each goal, the two terraced ends now offered only decay. Still, by the 34th minute, the home side had scored three times, through Lee Clark, Andy Hunt and Kevin Brock.

By the 76th minute, the lead had gone. In the closing moments, Bob Bolder, the Charlton goalkeeper, launched a long ball that found Carl Leaburn on the edge of the Newcastle penalty area. Leaburn bundled the ball to Kim Grant, who in turn found a Charlton midfielder to his right.

The first goal-bound effort was cleared off the line by Steve Watson, then aged seventeen. The ball returned to the same player. From there, in the 89th minute, that man – Alan Pardew – struck for goal and a Newcastle player, Liam O'Brien, merely helped it in.

'We were getting a bit of a pasting off Newcastle,' says Pardew. 'Really and truly we didn't have a side that was good enough to come back. We got a goal and that changed the game. The ground wasn't full but coming to Newcastle was still intimidating. Newcastle were struggling but they were still a big scalp. I remember the goal, I hit it and it was cleared off the line then I scored on the rebound, right at the end.'

There was no way back. Not for Newcastle, and not for Ardiles, who was sacked on 3 February, following an FA Cup exit and another league defeat (5–2 at Oxford). Newcastle were second-bottom of the Second Division, the 45th-best team in England, and going down to the third tier in the English game for the first time in their 110-year history.

8 FEBRUARY 1992

SIR JOHN HALL – THE SECOND COMING

SIR JOHN HALL WAS IN LONDON BUYING TREES AT KEW GARDENS the first time he met Kevin Keegan. The Hall family had bought Wynyard Hall, a beautiful country house built in the 1820s, in 1987. It was set in 6,000 acres of land in Teesside. By 1992 Hall and his wife, Lady Mae, were eager to develop the land around the main building.

In the fight for control of Newcastle United, no one had won, save for those who held the existing shares, as the Magpie Group, with Hall and his family onside, fought for power with the existing board, led by Gordon McKeag, a Tyneside solicitor who made the mistake of referring to the football club as the 'Family Silver'.

Those previously worthless shares had been bought for more than £1,000 each in a bitter and bloody boardroom fight.

In the aftermath of the loss to Charlton and Bournemouth in the FA Cup, Hall had given an interview to the Mail on Sunday where he had backed Ardiles. Unbeknown to him, his son Douglas, chief executive Freddie Fletcher (who Hall had appointed from Glasgow Rangers) and Freddy Shepherd, by now a significant shareholder, had something far more dramatic in mind.

The penny was dropping that Newcastle were in serious trouble.

*

THEY HAD BEEN IN TROUBLE IN 1982 AS WELL.

When Queens Park Rangers headed south on 5 May that year, after a 4–0 win, Newcastle were wallowing in eleventh place in Division Two. There were just over

10,000 at St James' Park that day.

For the final home game of the season, against Wrexham, when Chris Waddle scored in a 4–2 victory, the attendance had fallen to 9,419. The average attendance in the 1981/82 season was just shy of 18,000, only the second time since the war that the club had dipped beneath 20,000. It was a sign of a deep malaise, and one that had been identified by those inside the club.

Only when attendances start falling does action at Newcastle follow.

In December 1981, Stan Seymour, then the chairman of Newcastle United, and Arthur Cox, who had been manager for eighteen months, met with Harry Swales.

Swales was Kevin Keegan's agent. Keegan did not even know that Seymour, Cox and Swales had met. He did not know that Cox and Seymour had said to Swales, if Kevin ever leaves Southampton – who he had unexpectedly joined after leaving SV Hamburg, where he had twice won European Footballer of the Year – Newcastle would be interested.

Keegan did not know that, and nor did anyone on Tyneside.

When his relationship with Lawrie McMenemy – a Geordie, a Newcastle fan, and the manager of Southampton – became strained, that foresight kicked in.

Within 24 hours of Keegan telling Southampton he wanted to leave, Newcastle secretary Russell Cushing was traveling with Cox and Seymour to meet Keegan and Swales at the Swallow Hotel in west London. Alistair Wilson had also travelled south with Cox and Seymour.

Wilson was the managing director at Scottish and Newcastle Breweries.

Five men – Cox, Seymour, Cushing, Keegan and Swales – met to talk about a deal that would alter the history of Newcastle United. In an adjacent room sat Wilson.

Cox told Keegan the team he would be joining was poor, but that he could be the spark. He told him attendances would double if he moved to the north-east. Keegan, who had been brought up on stories of the Newcastle support from his Geordie father, told Seymour he wanted 15 per cent of any increase in attendances.

On that innovative contractual detail dreamed up by Keegan, one from which neither side could lose, came the seeds of a bond between Newcastle United and Kevin Keegan.

Seymour agreed.

Keegan, the captain of England, was within touching distance of becoming a Newcastle United player. He met Wilson and told the man from the breweries that he would not advertise alcohol. He didn't tell him he was already intent on moving to a dormant football club. Wilson was honest and solid and trustworthy. Keegan liked him.

The Gosforth Park Hotel is roughly six miles from Newcastle International Airport, on the outskirts of the city, high up the A1. On 20 August 1982, Newcastle supporters were in its grounds, running around grass verges to try and peer in any window that didn't have its shutters down. Somewhere in that hotel was Kevin Keegan, and he was about to sign for their football club, for Newcastle United.

Nobody could believe it. There was a need to see if this was real. Seeing would be believing. Without visual evidence it still seemed footballing fantasy that England's most famous player was about to join a mid-table team in Division Two.

Keegan was stunned by the response from Newcastle fans. He would later use it as a gauge. 'I taught myself to anticipate it by imagining the most extreme reaction,' he said.

Keegan had sung the 'Blaydon Races' with his granddad when he was a small child. He said it was inevitable he would go to Newcastle.

It did not feel inevitable. It never felt inevitable if you were a Newcastle fan.

It felt like a miracle.

It felt like a once-in-a-lifetime lightning strike.

*

AS SIR JOHN HALL WALKED AMONG THE TREES OF THE ROYAL BO-
tanic Gardens ten years later, the board of directors of Newcastle United were trying their damnedest to see if lightning could hit the same place twice.

Keegan had spent seven years in the sunshine of Spain. Then the phone went. It was Alistair Wilson. He asked Kevin Keegan if he was interested in becoming the next manager of Newcastle United. Wilson was not optimistic. Keegan finished the call, put the phone on the receiver and turned to his wife Jean. 'I've just been offered the chance to manage Newcastle,' he said.

'You'll take it,' she replied.

On Monday, 3 February 1992, Keegan met Sir John Hall, Douglas Hall, Fletcher and Shepherd in the Hilton Hotel in London. The chairman of Newcastle United, George Forbes, did not know the meeting was taking place. Similarly, and obviously, Ardiles was also unaware that his position as manager was being offered to someone else.

'We were in London when I first met Kevin,' says Sir John Hall. 'I was in London with Lady Mae. We've always loved horticulture.

'The turnover of the club then was £3.2 million. It was just existing. You couldn't have bought players. Cash from the outside had to come in in order to support the club. We had put money in and we had to guarantee money in order to get this thing off the ground. It was a case of all hands to the pump.

'Keegan was ready to come back to the UK and we needed someone. If we'd been relegated we would have gone bust.'

John Hall was eight when he first went to St James' Park. He stood on a plank of wood on the opposite side to the West Stand, the Popular Side. His father was a miner and they travelled down from Ashington to watch Newcastle United play. 'If you got in early you stood on the plank of wood and watched the match,' he says. 'If you didn't they rolled you over their head to the front.

'I got this nose playing on St James' Park against the N's [the forerunner to Newcastle's Academy side]. Tot Smith was a centre-half and I played for East Northumberland in the Junior Cup. The ball came over my head and then Tot Smith hit me in the face.'

He lived in North Seaton, went to Bedlington Grammar and for four years worked as a surveyor in the mines after he left school, going underground. In the 1960s he saw an opportunity to start making money through renovating houses in Sunderland, a scheme backed by the government. His big break would come in 1979, when he raised £1 million to buy a plot of land in Gateshead.

Hall had seen the indoor American shopping malls first-hand. By 1982 the first stage of the MetroCentre was open. By the time it finished in 1985, it was the biggest in Europe. That year Hall bought 6,000 acres of land from the Marquess of Londonderry, which included Wynyard Hall.

In 1987 the MetroCentre was sold to the Church Commissioners for £272 million. By then Hall was being pressurised to get involved with Newcastle United. The Magpie Group had been formed with the aim of taking control of the club and, with the vigour of Malcolm Dix, were tracking down all existing shareholders.

'I said, "I'll tell you what I'll do, I'll pledge half a million,"' Hall adds. 'I don't want to own the club, it's a people's club. We needed about £2 million to challenge the board and put the shares on the market and try to democratise it.

'The story went in the Mail on Sunday. It was a call to democratise the club.' He enlisted the support of Tyneside's newspaper, the *Evening Chronicle*. 'Another two or three people came and pledged half a million each. It was Bobby Pattinson, Joe Robertson and Brian Reade.

'We carried the campaign and we fought the battle and Dix and the Magpie Group came in. He'd fought the board for years and years and hadn't been able to make the change. He joined us and I used him because he had all the information.'

Hall got a foot inside the door but it was a fractured board. There was a share issue for supporters, his initiative, but it failed dramatically.

'The fans didn't buy them,' he says. 'I felt let down. I never really wanted to own the football club. I'm a supporter. Only a few of the fans bought the shares because they didn't trust the board at the time.

'I was left with egg on my face. Initially I got a hard time in the boardroom afterwards. We'd bought the existing shares and we got up to 40 per cent. My son, Douglas, said, "Give me a million pounds and we'll go and get the shares."

'I said, "No, the families have been there for years, we have to respect them. We'll try and do this amicably." They put me on the board and I remember going along when Jim Smith was manager.

'Jim Smith didn't like us and when Gordon McKeag introduced me and Douglas to Smithy he wouldn't shake hands with us because I'd criticised him. He went to buy Roy Aitken and I felt he was too old.

'I went on holiday shortly after on a thirty-day around-the-world trip with Thomas Cook and there were eighty millionaires on the trip. We flew everywhere, it was tremendous, a wonderful experience. I got to Hong Kong and somebody shouted, "Is a Mr Hall here?" It was one o'clock at night. I said, "Yes, it's me, who knows I'm here?" It was Douglas.

'They were in the boardroom back at St James'. It was afternoon. Freddy [Shepherd] had been with him. Douglas said, "The club's going into receivership. The banks have pulled the plug." I said, "I've only been away a fortnight, what's happened?"

'I was on the phone for forty minutes and that call cost me £685,000.

'I had to put money in. I wasn't very pleased when I came back. I said, "What's been going on?" They explained to me the existing board still held the majority and had an overdraft with Barclays Bank for £1 million. They were not supposed to buy anyone but they went out and bought a player and Barclays pulled the plug and said, "Fund it yourself."

'Of course, that caused a lot of soul-searching amongst the shareholders. We had 40 per cent, 60 per cent wouldn't put their money in unless we put ours in. That's why I had to pledge the money.

'When that happened, I realised. I said, "We can't run a club this way." I decided to launch a takeover and it was a bloody takeover and that's where the Magpie Group came in. We eventually got control and we didn't know anything about football but I was lucky the brewery was here and Alistair Wilson was the prime mover. He was a tremendous support.'

Buying Wynyard had cost Hall an estimated £20 million.

'I had to stop the developments at Wynyard because we didn't have the cash to do the two,' he adds. 'Wynyard became the security for all the borrowings at the football club.'

Hall's home became the guarantee to the football club's debt, which was around the £7 million mark. Relegation and possibly going bust was put into a far greater context in light of where the funding had come from.

Talking to Keegan was the last throw of the dice.

Wilson was trusted by Keegan: he still worked for Scottish and Newcastle Breweries, who still sponsored Newcastle United. It seemed a perfect fit, but there was work to be done.

Keegan had to meet Sir John, but Sir John was not in London to meet the new manager of Newcastle United. He already had one of those. He wanted some new trees.

Instead, he found himself with a potential new manager. Keegan wanted guarantees and he was told there would be funding for new players. He turned down a three-year contract. That would have been another burden if the club did drop out of the division, he argued. Instead, Keegan signed a contract on a consultancy basis until the end of the season that would earn him £60,000 and another £60,000 if he kept the club up.

'We were ready to find someone,' adds Hall. 'It was a coming-together of willing participants. The one thing about Kevin is even though he'd been playing golf for nearly eight years, he never lost his appetite for the game and his knowledge of players.'

Keegan said yes. Ardiles was sacked.

Newcastle United called a press conference at the visitor centre of the Tyne Brewery, across the road from St James' Park. Hall picked up a microphone and said, 'Ladies and gentleman, I would like to introduce you to the next manager of Newcastle United. Mr Kevin Keegan.' At that point Keegan walked through a set of double doors. Jaws dropped. It could not have been scripted much better.

More crucially, Tyneside had not lost its appetite for Kevin Keegan.

There had been 15,663 at St James' Park for the final home league game of Ossie Ardiles' reign. The next time the ground hosted a Division Two match, the attendance had almost doubled, to 29,263.

Newcastle were playing Bristol City. The mood of everyone had changed. It did not feel like a day on which the club could lose. Bristol City were a poor team but they were swatted aside and Newcastle had forgotten how to do that.

A buzz had returned to the city. There was a roar when Keegan took his seat in the dugout; he was surrounded by photographers but in the wave came a realisation that he was joining a club in crisis. His debut as a player had been a dream. This was reality, harsh and cold.

Keegan's emotion that day came to the surface when David Kelly scored early in the second half. Then he punched the air. When Liam O'Brien added a second he raced on to the pitch. The real celebration came with the third, when Kelly swept in his second of the game. Keegan grabbed his number two, Terry McDermott, and both men looked ecstatic.

A caller phoned Danny Baker on Radio Five's 606 programme that night. 'The power has been unleashed,' he said.

The impossible once more seemed plausible. Keegan did that to Newcastle supporters.

By the time Newcastle won their third league game in Keegan's sixth game in charge (the last three victories had taken twenty games under Ardiles), at the Abbey Stadium on 10 March, they had climbed to nineteenth, three places outside the relegation zone.

To those on the outside, the new manager was once more working miracles. What they didn't realise was that Hall's relationship with Keegan was on the brink of collapse. Keegan believed promises had not been kept in terms of what he would have to spend; there was a problem over the permanent signing of Brian Kilcline, who had arrived on loan from Oldham.

Newcastle played Swindon on 14 March, won 3–1 and moved to eighteenth. They were now five points clear of being relegated. Keegan got in his car that night and drove to Hampshire. He did not intend to come back. Hall claimed he was unaware of the smouldering crisis.

'We played at St James' and Mae and I went back home to Wynyard,' he says. 'We got there and the telephone started ringing and ringing and we went, "What the hell's the matter here?" The press were on. "Keegan's walked?"

'I didn't know Kevin had gone. I said, "What's happening here?" Eventually I got the story.

'It was £300,000 for the Kilcline transfer and Mae and I were putting the cash up. We had to take the money off deposit and weren't keeping that kind of money in the current account. We said, "Yeah, we'll put the cash up but I've got to get it." When it came off deposit we put the money in the club.

'We didn't realise he had got up and walked away and in a sense was challenging us. I'm not the kind of person who takes kindly to being challenged. I said, "This is a nonsense." We were sitting in the house, the conversation was, "What are we going to do?"

'Mae spoke to me, she was the one who actually made me call. She said, "You're two silly men, you're two grown-ups acting like children. I think Jean will feel the same way I do. It's about time for you to call him."

'I said, "I'm not calling him."

'She said, "You've got to be big enough to call him. It's the club at stake." She said, "Do you want him?"

'I said, "He's a good manager. He knows the players."

'I picked the phone up. I said to him, "Kevin, there's only two men who can save Newcastle United and we're talking to each other. It's me and thee."

'He said, "Yes, chairman." He just wanted a call.

'He came back and we got on with it. We bought Killer Kilcline.'

The club was still buoyant. There was a draw at Grimsby and then a derby victory against Sunderland. Newcastle were still five points above a relegation place.

Then they lost five games on the trot.

DAVID KELLY – THIS IS THE ONE

THE 85TH MINUTE OF NEWCASTLE'S FINAL HOME GAME OF THE 1991/92 season had passed and the club was in a relegation place. They were drawing 0–0 against Portsmouth. The last game was away at Leicester, a week later.

Leicester were pushing for automatic promotion. They had lost just four of the 22 league games that had been played at Filbert Street. They had won their last five games there.

Oxford were drawing with Ipswich. That had moved them ahead of Newcastle on goal difference. Plymouth were losing at Swindon but were still a point clear. It was that tight.

St James' Park has rarely been that raw. Tension was palpable. Sir John Hall had painted an apocalyptic picture of what relegation to the third tier of English football would mean for the club. In his view it would be all over.

In the 86th minute Tommy Wright, the Newcastle goalkeeper, at the Leazes End of the ground, threw the ball to his right to Ray Ranson. Ranson hoisted a long, angled pass to David Kelly, who flicked the ball to Micky Quinn.

Quinn somehow hooked the ball back to Kelly. Kelly was less than fifteen yards from goal, at the Gallowgate End, his position strikingly similar to when Keegan had scored on his debut. The future of Newcastle United Football Club was now in his hands.

*

DAVID KELLY WAS FIVE WHEN HE WAS DIAGNOSED WITH PERTHES'

Disease. He fell out of a tree and broke his leg, and the reason he broke his leg was that the bone in his hip had not grown. That only became apparent when his leg would not set.

'I was in plaster and on crutches and in a wheelchair,' says Kelly. 'It's a disease that is still here today. There is no cure for it, you just grow out of it. The jumping out the tree and breaking my leg happened because I had no strength there.

'They'd have found out, it just happened quicker. That was that, it never held me back. I remember I had a double plaster cast to the end of my foot. I had a metal bar across the middle and my dad used to carry me up the stairs when I was little. I was on crutches for years. I used to hobble around with my three legs.

'That's just what it was. It wasn't anything different for me. Them are the cards and you just get on with it, don't you? I still played football.'

He played for Bartley Green Boys from when he was nine, then he went to West Bromwich Albion – his and half of his family's team – and was released. 'They said I wasn't good enough,' he adds. 'I was devastated.' He got a job at Cadbury's as a trolley porter in the factory and played in non-league Alvechurch's youth team.

'I used to work in the returns department,' he says. 'When pallets of chocolate break they get sent back to the factory, they unwrap everything and put all the different bits in the bins and it gets recycled.

'All the blokes who had had heart attacks and industrial accidents were there, it was low maintenance. You were just opening packets of chocolate. It was a really big department and I was the joey who looked after everybody and moved everything and made sure we had all the recruitment we needed.

'It was great, I really enjoyed it. It was a management course and you changed the areas you worked in. You went all round the factory.

'There was lots of older people in the offices who had loads of stories and I like listening to people's stories. I fitted in great. I was there for eighteen months. Did working there put me off chocolate? Oh God, no. Cadbury's chocolate is the best chocolate in the world. I'm very loyal, me.'

Kelly then had a trial at Walsall and got in. He was on £75 a week at Cadbury's. Walsall gave him £50 a week and a bus pass.

'There was a guy at Cadbury's called Arthur Hoey and when I told him I was signing he went, "You've got a career here for the rest of your life, son, it's a secure company. That football thing will never catch on." 'I said, "No, I've got to give it a go."'

That was in 1983. By the time he left five years later, to go to West Ham, he had scored 63 goals in 147 games, Walsall had been promoted and he had become an

Irish international, for which he qualified through his dad's side of the family.

'We'd played away at Rotherham and Tom Coakley, who was Walsall manager, said, "There's someone who wants to have a chat." I said, "What's that about?" He said, "It's Jackie Charlton." I said, "What the fuck does he want?"

'I went upstairs and he's at the bar. It was the old Millmoor and it was rammed. Maurice Setters and Jack are stood there and Jack is smoking a cigar, he turned around and said, "Do you want to come and play for me then, son?" I went, "Yeah, first team or under-21s?" He said, "First team." I said, "Yeah, I'm in," and I put my hand out.

'He said, "We'll write to you," and he put his back to me. That was my international call-up.'

He played in a European Championship and two World Cups for the Republic of Ireland. West Ham was less successful. 'I got slaughtered because I didn't play very well,' he adds. 'I found the dressing room difficult and we got relegated in my first season.

'I found it really hard, but I would still go back there if I had my time again. It's what gave me a really good career. It hardened me up.'

He was doing better at Leicester – although in the middle of a dry spell – when the new manager Brian Little suggested dropping to the reserves for a game.

'I went, "I ain't happy," and, as I did everywhere, I said, "I ain't playing reserve-team football." I just wanted to play first-team football. He said, "I'm only leaving you out for one game." I said, "That's not the point, the point is I just want to play first-team football."

'That was my attitude, I just wanted to play. He said, "Let's see how it goes."

'A week later I hadn't played again and I was still on the bench. I said, "Gaffer, I can't stay here, I'm too old." He said, "You're only mid-twenties!" I said, "I might not play for a month, and then another month, I can't have that. I want to play."

'He said, "OK, I've had Sunderland in for you."

'I went to see Denis Smith at Roker Park. He was saying this and that about the club and I said to Denis, "I need a bit of time to think about it." He said, "This is the biggest club you're going to play for."

'I said, "I don't deny it's a big club, but I want to have a think about it." I went home. Then Brian Little told me Newcastle were in for me as well.

'I phoned up my Uncle Ronnie, who, bless him, passed away a few years ago, after I'd spoken to my dad and told him and he said, "You've got to go to Newcastle. If you go to Newcastle and become a number nine, that's it, you'll have made it."

'He was an Irish-born Birmingham man. He said, "The number nine at

Newcastle is something special. Take the chance." It was purely and simply to do with Malcolm Macdonald, and the history of the shirt, and the importance of the number nine.

'I signed for Newcastle because of my Uncle Ronnie's words. "If you can do it at Newcastle and become their number nine," he said, "they'll never forget you."'

Kelly met Ossie Ardiles and his assistant Tony Galvin at the Holiday Inn at Scotch Corner. He signed the same deal that Sunderland had offered.

'What was the club like when I joined? Oh, it was a shambles,' he says. 'The training ground was up on that hill at Benwell. It was minus a million degrees and it was blowing a gale and the pitches were all boggy and the changing facilities were all scruffy and dirty.'

Still, he was overwhelmed by the passion for the club within the city.

'Newcastle has always had this thing throughout ever, really, that the support is different,' he adds. 'Until you have the time of living there or spending plenty of time there, you don't realise. People across the UK don't realise how big they are. I still think that sits today. Until you go there and turn up, then you don't realise. It's just a religion.

'Going and filling your car up on a Sunday morning, everyone wants to talk about the match. It was quite a shock. I remember my wife saying to me, "Can we not just go out and have a bit of food on our own?"

'It doesn't happen. "I'm sorry for coming over but, what do you think of such-and-such?" That was every time you went out.

'I embraced it. It was brilliant for me. I'm light-hearted and I see the positives in everything. They reminded me of me. They're all mad! I just fitted in and I fitted into the club straight away. Unfortunately, Ossie got the sack.'

Then Hall called a meeting with all playing staff at St James' Park.

'He came and spoke to everybody,' adds Kelly. 'He pulled us all in and said big changes were going to be made. He said, "We can't afford to drop and let this club go down, it's too big to go out of the league because it could be curtains."

'He said, "I'm not prepared to lose the money I've already put in. I want to give us a spark and a boost." I remember coming out of the meeting and thinking, "What a top bloke you are." I didn't know much about him.

'He said, "I will bring somebody in to rejuvenate everything." Then King Kev comes back in, it was like, woah, brilliant.

'Kevin came in and said, "This is all getting sorted, it's a dump. I'm going to make changes really quickly."

'He improved the training kit, he improved silly things like getting the boots cleaned. He improved little things that were being overlooked. He painted the dressing room. He tidied everything up. You walked into the club and thought, this is nice.

'The gaffer had a purpose. He changed it really quickly. That's why he was good. He saw the place was in the doldrums.

'The Bristol City game was one of the best games I've played in. It was all about him. There was a full house. The ground was jumping. You think, it could be like this every week.'

*

BY THE TIME NEWCASTLE WENT TO DERBY FOR THE THIRD-LAST GAME of the season, on 20 April, it was anything but brilliant. Newcastle had lost four games on the trot.

In the first half, Kevin Brock was sent off for handball. Then Kevin Scott was sent off for a second bookable offence, after flattening Marco Gabbiadini. The second half was still to start. Derby were 2–0 up.

The nine men of Newcastle rallied. A Kelly header was parried to Gavin Peacock, who scored from close range. There was a moment, a rare moment, of hope and against-the-odds delight for the travelling support.

There would, however, be no heroic comeback. Derby added a third before Liam O'Brien was sent off for kicking out at Tommy Johnson. A fourth followed. Terry McDermott was dismissed from the dugout too. Four thousand Newcastle fans refused to stop backing their team. David Kelly, who had run himself into the ground, threw his shirt into the away end at full-time.

'I remember the support that day,' he says. 'It was unforgettable. It was just relentless. The fans wouldn't let go.'

The Newcastle support kept singing, and shouting, and urging more. It was a call to arms in an apparently futile situation. It told people that Newcastle had eight men, and had conceded four goals, but that they were not defeated, at least not yet, anyway.

If nothing else, there was genuine defiance on the terraces.

'We were in the shit,' adds Kelly. 'I thought, we have to have a chase around, we can't give it up. I was really fit. Kevin said that if a crisp packet flew across St James' Ned would catch it. I'd always been called Ned. That's what he said and it came from that game.

'There were some bad decisions. The gaffer came on to the pitch afterwards with

Terry Mac. The fans just kept singing. You never forget that. It was one man and his dog on the pitch. We had no players left, but we had the fans.'

That defeat, however destructive it might have seemed – three players sent off, four goals conceded – was a rallying call. That call came from the support. Newcastle had two tiers of the Osmaston End of the Baseball Ground, and those there were not giving up.

None of them knew what was happening behind the scenes. Keegan was desperately trying to breathe life into their club. Nobody was sure if it would be enough.

'The change behind the scenes had to be seen,' adds Kelly. 'It changed completely when Kevin came in. Where there was no hope Kevin gave them hope, he gave everyone hope. He was positive in everything. He was always good in the press, and he was always doing things to include the community.

'Everything had quickened up in training. Derek Fazackerley is one of the best coaches I've worked for. I think he's really good. He knows his stuff but he's a miserable fart.

'That changed because Kevin came in and Terry Mac was the joker and even Faz was laughing with everyone. He was really good in his role then. Training was happier. Even though the results picked up and went back down, the stuff we were doing was really good.'

Keegan, McDermott and Fazackerley. They were the three men fighting to save a football club.

Finally, the dressing room at last understood quite how high the stakes of the game they were playing against Portsmouth that day, 25 April 1992, actually were: it was to rescue Newcastle United.

*

IN THE 86TH MINUTE, THE MAN IN THE NEWCASTLE NUMBER NINE shirt, there because his Uncle Ronnie from Ireland knew what it meant, steadied himself and hit a right-footed shot.

He shot to give a club a future and he struck a ball that flew past Alan Knight and into the net at the Gallowgate End and into the hearts of the club's supporters around the world.

The ground roared with relief. It was a different sound. It came from a different place. It was not ecstasy, or delirium. It was more primitive. When St James' let forth its emotion that day it was a deeper, more base emotion that rose from the people on the terraces that still surrounded the ground. The atmosphere had been febrile.

There was still chaos when the goal went in, but the celebration was as much for relief as it was for joy.

'The air changed,' says Kelly. 'It was as if, "We're safe." I played that goal in my head for an awful long time. You remember big goals. What happened after? Massive hugs. Relief. That's what you felt. You sit down in the dressing room afterwards and you're like, Yes! Thank fuck I scored!

'The feeling of relief was incredible. Of course you remember it. Your memories become fonder the older you get.

'You can't underestimate the value of Quinny there. In my head I was fifteen yards outside the penalty box! I struck it and it felt good. Then it was in. Just the noise. The feeling of relief was incredible. I didn't leave Leicester to get relegated. Newcastle United couldn't get relegated.'

History and the record books will show that Newcastle went to Leicester on the final day of the season and that they needed a victory to guarantee survival, but the significance of that goal from Kelly has never been lost.

At Leicester there was carnage and pitch invasions and fighting and in the bedlam of that ugly afternoon, a Newcastle supporter lost the sight in one of his eyes when a coin was hurled from the home end, into the section in which those from Tyneside were housed.

The home mood had become ever darker as the afternoon had progressed. Gavin Peacock had popped promotion balloons with a goal deep in first-half injury-time. By the time Steve Walsh headed an equaliser past Wright it was the last minute of the game and Leicester could not go up and Newcastle could not go down.

Everywhere around the side of the pitch were Leicester fans. Newcastle had a pocket in the corner of the ground, with gaps in the fencing to allow people to spill on to the pitch.

In injury-time, Wright cleared long, Walsh missed his header and tried to make amends with a left-footed back-pass that went into his own goal. For those travelling fans in the East Stand, it felt like the end of the road to hell, but as they celebrated and rejoiced that their greatest fears were unfounded, that their club had survived, and some spilled out of their end, Leicester's fans invaded the pitch for real.

Keegan, pitch-side, called to his staff to grab the players. 'They're going to get hurt, get them off,' he shouted.

By the time Peacock jumped into the arms of the substitute Steve Watson next to the visitors' dugout, Newcastle and Leicester fans were fighting in front of the away section.

When the referee David Elleray blew his whistle, early, to avoid more trouble,

David Kelly was chasing the ball as it headed towards the furthest corner flag from the dugout, right in front of the away support.

'I saw the Leicester fans and thought, where do I go?' he remembers. 'I jumped in the stand and sat down with all these Geordies going mental, celebrating. They were grabbing me and hugging me and going, "Yes, get in!" once they realised it was me.

'After a bit I've gone to get out to get on the pitch and the steward pushed me back in. I said, "Mate, I'm a fucking player!" I showed him my boots. He said, "Ah, Ned, come out," and he took me across the pitch. Although the fans were scrapping there was no one fighting near me. I wasn't worried about getting hit.

'It had all gone crazy in the dressing room before I got there. There was beers and all sorts and champagne bottles getting uncorked. It was bedlam. The gaffer went, "Where have you been?"

'I said, "I got stuck on the far side. I was chasing a crisp packet."

Within minutes of safety, Keegan put down a marker.

'It's the chairman and the board's job now to ensure the club does not get in this situation again,' he said. 'It's their job. I've told them what I think I need to turn the club round and they've got a meeting next week and if they come up with that I will certainly be Newcastle manager for the next three years.

'If they don't, they're going to have to find a miracle worker.'

BRIAN KILCLINE – FROM SAFETY TO WHERE?

THE TUXEDO PRINCESS WAS A NIGHTCLUB AND IT HAD A GANG-plank to get on it and the reason it had a gangplank to get on it was because it was a boat, and on the boat was a dance floor that used to go round in circles.

On the Tuxedo Princess, moored underneath the Tyne Bridge, it was not just the drink that made your head spin.

Kevin Sheedy, David Kelly and Brian Kilcline had been to York Races for the day, missed their train, jumped in a taxi to get back to the north-east (around 85 miles) and decided that going to the Tuxedo Princess would be a better idea than going home when they reached Newcastle.

Kilcline, who was six-foot-three and had a beard and a ponytail, was dressed in mustard cords and a mustard jumper when he went to the bar on the boat on the river. Kilcline was renowned for his drinking capabilities, but it had been a long day.

He ordered three pints, went to lean to his right, and unaware the flap at the bar had been lifted, fell straight through.

'It's one of the funniest things I've ever seen,' says Kelly. 'Killer went to put his arm on the bar, missed it and did the Del Boy, straight on to the floor. By the time he got up his mustardy-coloured outfit was covered in the dregs he'd just fell on. It was incredible. He was devastated. None of the bouncers knew what to do. He was the captain of Newcastle United.'

'Oh, I went right over,' adds Kilcline. 'I think it was that fucking dance floor that did it. I'll tell you what, though, I had the pint of Guinness in my hand I'd just bought and I didn't spill a drop.'

Brian Kilcline was not Kevin Keegan's first signing after taking over, but he was the first one that mattered. Without big Brian Kilcline, his beard, his ponytail and his mustard cords and jumper, the rest might never have happened.

He was stood on top of a conservatory fixing the roof when his wife Lynn shouted up that Kevin Keegan was on the phone. 'Kevin Keegan? Yeah, fuck off.'

He continues: 'I'm dangling off this roof and I took the phone from Lynn, Kevin went, "Hey, big man, do you fancy coming up to Newcastle and joining on loan?" I went, "Fucking right, do you want me coming up now?"'

'I remember driving up with my missus, I wasn't playing at Oldham at the time, I said to Lynn, "I have no idea what this is going to be like." I didn't even know where Newcastle were in the league. I drove up and stopped at Washington Services, and then I was driving into Newcastle, and then you come round the corner and you see them gates at St James' Park and I went, "Foookin hell!"'

'I pull up and the two of them [Keegan and McDermott] come running down the steps. "Big man, how are you?" They made me feel so at home.

'They went, "You look a bit stiff, I tell you what, we'll go to Benwell and you can have a run around." I went in and there's all these young lads sitting around. I managed to get some kit – Keegan had just cleaned it all out. I got the kit on and went out and trained with all these young lads.

'I came back in, and I was getting out of the showers and Keegan came over to me and said, "What do you think?" I went, "You've got some good young ones there, haven't you? The youth team must be doing all right." He went, "Killer, that's the first team." I said, "You're joking!"

'It was Steve Watson, Steve Howey, Lee Makel, Robbie Elliott, Alan Thompson, Dave Roche, all these kids.

'I remember the first game was at St James' Park. We got ready to go out on to the pitch and the lads went, "We're not going out to warm up." I said, "You what?" Apparently they were getting dog's abuse from the Newcastle fans because they were going through such a bad time and they didn't want to go out.

'I went out and warmed up and carried on and I think they took kindly to that. It suited me down to the ground. We had a lot of good young players and it was me who was just guiding them along.

'Their aggression was misled. I had controlled aggression, putting it in the right place and looking after the lads. They looked after me too, but every now and then I would look after them. "There's a big galoot here with us now," that's how it was. What I did notice was there was a great spirit in the camp. We were always laughing and joking.

'Liam O'Brien and Tommy Wright were absolute class, North and South Ireland, bickering all the time, best of mates but they would never stop arguing, like Tweedledum and Tweedledee. They were always on at each other.'

Newcastle had lost 3–1 at Ewood Park prior to Kilcline's arrival. It had been Keegan's first away game in charge and Newcastle fans flooded Blackburn. They were everywhere; it was a wild afternoon. David Speedie scored a hat-trick. 'I didn't play or I'd have kicked fuck out of him,' says Kilcline.

Kilcline had always been a size. He was put in goal when he first started playing because of it, in Nottingham. He was playing for St Margaret's Clitheroe against Arnold Vale. 'I was crying for letting four goals in and I wanted to come out but the teacher wouldn't let me,' he adds. 'Then I went in midfield and then I went up front. At secondary school I was a centre forward.'

Kilcline was very soon playing for the county. He broke goalscoring records for Nottinghamshire's representative side and scored twice in a final at the City Ground for Christ the King. 'We won three-two,' he says. 'Forest had played Sheffield United before we played and Cloughie came on to the pitch and he went, "Well, son, you didn't do too bad, did you?"

'I was like, "You think so? Great." Then I saw my dad and he went, "You were shite."'

Notts County asked him to sign first so he went there. 'I'm a loyal person. They were the first to ask. I could score goals for fun.'

Then the goals dried up in County's youth team.

'There was an injury to the first-team centre-half, the reserves' centre-half got an injury so they went, "Let's try him at the back, he's shit up front." They said, "Go and kick somebody instead of being kicked."

'Apparently I went out that day and had a blinder and kicked lumps out of Lee Chapman.'

He caught the eye of the Notts County manager, Howard Wilkinson. 'In the space of a month I've gone from getting bollocked for smiling like a Cheshire cat when I was a no-goalscoring centre-forward who wasn't playing in the youth team to playing in the youth team at centre-half, then playing for the reserves as a centre-half and then a first-team regular.'

He was a good centre-half and he was hard.

'As a fourteen-year-old I used to play Sunday League football. I was playing against these hard-as-nails bastards who'd been on the piss and I would get kicked to fuck and I would love it.'

Notts County won promotion and then Bobby Gould took him to Coventry. He faced Keegan early in his time there.

'[The coach] John Sillett said to me in the dressing room, "Kevin Keegan's come back to this country, let's show him what he's been missing, nail him." I went, "No worries, Sill."

'We lost. Sill came over and went, "Where the fuck were you?" I couldn't get near the bastard. Everything he did was one touch, it would get played into him and he was moving the ball all over the place. He was brilliant.'

Kilcline and his beard and his big hair would lift the FA Cup in 1987. He had a blood clot in his leg after fouling Gary Mabbutt, who had been a team-mate in the England Under-21s, and could barely walk up the steps at Wembley.

He went to Oldham, it didn't work out and then he climbed on top of a conservatory.

The Newcastle youngsters had a leader.

*

KILCLINE STARTED A PLAYERS' COMMITTEE. HE GAVE THE YOUNGER players confidence; they started to speak more. Personalities emerged outside of the obvious talent.

'I was a character and it brought the better sides of players' characters in the club out,' he says. 'Sometimes some of them were too scared to express themselves.

'I think all of them were waiting. It was about being in the right place at the right time, so much of life is like that. Everything is of a time. That little bit that might flick it off.

'They became less scared. It was frightening ability, just frightening. It was talent in abundance. You couldn't understand why they were down where they were. The young kids at Newcastle all wanted to do it but nobody was doing anything.'

Kilcline was fearless in the fight to stay out of the third tier of English football. He had seen the terror in the eyes of the Newcastle board on the morning of the final-day victory at Leicester.

'I remember walking out of the hotel on the morning of that game and all the directors were shitting themselves,' he recalls. 'To me I was going out for another game.'

That attitude was vital, but it was not just football leadership.

'The amount of times I was in places with the lads where they could have got battered and I've pulled soldiers, all sorts of people, out and said, "That's not happening," rather than my lads getting hit. I would defend them to the hilt.

'They would never know these things. They were plastered. I've been to places where they were out of their trees. I could take the drink and stand back and babysit them.

'It's the things they don't see that I'm most proud of. I looked after these young lads that came through and they looked after me on the field.'

Newcastle was becoming a different club. There was a stand-off between Keegan and the board after survival; it was a fraught summer. Keegan wanted assurances he would be allowed to buy Paul Bracewell, John Beresford and Barry Venison. Newcastle were still in debt. Hall was eventually persuaded that committing to an initial financial gamble would pay off.

'My philosophy was, if we are going to be big, let's be big,' said Keegan. 'If we aren't, then let's not wind fans up by pretending to be big. You can't pretend you're a big club and then run it on a shoestring. The one thing you know here is that if you get it right on the pitch, then you will fill the ground.'

Crucially, Hall had taken over the shares of director Bob Young. Now he had control and the remaining directors sold theirs and resigned. Douglas Hall, Freddy Shepherd and Freddie Fletcher met Keegan at the Los Monteros hotel in Spain. They, along with Sir John, were in control, as was Keegan. He said he would return.

'We had a crucial meeting at Wynyard in the summer of 1992 after I'd agreed to return,' Keegan added. 'Sir John Hall agreed to put up the cash to buy Beresford, Bracewell and Venison at a time when the financial picture was grim. It didn't take a lot of selling because Sir John is a businessman who understands risks, but he had to have his backstop and that was if we were struggling, we had to sell our best players, Gavin Peacock and David Kelly.'

It would never become an issue.

The new players made a huge difference. The feel of the club changed. There was confidence. The Second Division had battered them in 1991–92, when they fought for their lives to stay in it. Now, playing in the newly styled Division One in the first season of the Premiership era, they owned it. Newcastle won the first eleven games of the season. They were unstoppable. Kilcline as a player became peripheral but his personality was not. 'He got in amongst the players,' said Keegan. 'He helped turn the club around. He was brilliant. He doesn't believe the world owes him a living. He was the most important signing I ever made for the club.'

For Kilcline, it was one of the best times of his life.

'Christ, it's so important to be happy, in any walk of life,' he says. 'You see a lot of people walking around the streets and nobody is laughing. If you're lucky enough to go into a job that you love and you love the craic and you take the piss – and I never took myself seriously – then it helps get the best out of the people around you.

It makes them feel like a million dollars.

'It was very kind what Kevin and Terry McDermott said. Terry never got the credit he deserved. More than anything, it was the ride. It was such a special ride.

'In life you get on rides, if you're lucky enough it's a good one and you hold on.

'You've got to find the ride. Some people might not have gone to Newcastle, they were struggling at the bottom of the Second Division, I had a roof to fix and I fixed it rather quickly!

'It's all about the ride.

'People said before the cup final with Coventry, take it all in because it happens so quick. It was the same at Newcastle. I had such a good time there, there were so many good things, there were no bad things, even when I got injured.

'If you gave Kevin Keegan everything you had, he would give you the world.'

The team gave Keegan and Tyneside everything. When Newcastle played Grimsby, 8,000 fans were locked out.

There was a ride in town and everyone wanted on it.

*

BY BOXING DAY NEWCASTLE WERE TWELVE POINTS CLEAR OF second-placed Tranmere. The team had lost only three times all season and had scored more than any other side in the division.

They went to promotion rivals West Ham on Sunday, 21 February. The game was live on television. Newcastle were wobbling, having lost at Portsmouth and Blackburn. They fought hard in a goalless draw that kept the gap between them and second-placed West Ham at four points.

There was another draw at home to Bristol Rovers in the following game, their fourth without scoring, but then came a 3–0 win at Tranmere and in the following month Keegan signed Andy Cole from Bristol City for £1.75 million, smashing the club record.

Newcastle had fresh momentum. They won four of the five games played in April.

*

STEVE HARMISON WAS THIRTEEN WHEN KEEGAN RETURNED TO manage Newcastle. He would one day play for his country in a different sport, but Harmison was in the football club's centre of excellence as a centre-half who had been spotted at Ashington Juniors. John Carver was his development officer.

'Anybody that lives north of the Tyne has the dream of playing for the club,' says Harmison. 'Lots have them, few fulfil them. It was brilliant when he came back; it was, "Woah!" He got the whole place spruced up. He came in and said, "Make sure you give them three days off."

'They came back into a different, a more fulfilled atmosphere. It was a more buoyant club to be at. They didn't come into a dirty falling-down place.

'He was brilliant. Everyone thought it was going to take off when Kevin Keegan returned. The next season I remember going to watch them. I was lucky against Notts County when I think there was 5,000 people got locked out.

'Andy Cole scored for the first time and David Kelly scored two; luckily I got into the Gallowgate just before they locked the gates at twenty-five past two. Nobody else could get in, they were trying to climb over the wall.

'You knew then, something was happening, something special. It was crazy. It was a great time to be black and white.'

*

BY THE MORNING OF 4 MAY, KEVIN KEEGAN'S SIDE HAD 87 POINTS from 43 games. They had three to play. West Ham and Portsmouth, in second and third place, had just one. The two sides were two points behind the league leaders. The maths was simple. If Newcastle won their next game, they would be champions.

It is 161 miles from Newcastle to Cleethorpes. There are varying estimations of how many Newcastle fans made their way down to Blundell Park on that Tuesday night, but it was not less than 8,000. The official attendance was 14,402 and more than half were from Tyneside. Two points and Newcastle were promoted to the Premiership.

Sir John Hall was pulling into a service station so his wife, Lady Mae, could have a cigarette.

'We were going to get promotion,' says Hall. 'I had the Bentley then, I've always driven myself, I like driving. I've never bothered with drivers. My wife and I went down, she was desperate for a smoke. I wanted a coffee. We were a bit early so we stopped at the end of the M62, there's a Little Chef there.

'We went in and we had a coffee and she had a smoke. We got up to continue the journey to Grimsby Football Club. An old transit came in. It was battered. They parked across from us and the back doors opened and there must have been about fifteen of them in.

'They all jumped out and they ran to the hedge for a run-off [to go the toilet]. I was standing there horrified, and my wife was horrified. I shouted across, "Give me the number of your season tickets!"

'One of them went, "It's the effin' chairman!"

'They ran back into the van and some of them hadn't finished!

'A minute later they all came along and lined up. They went, "Sorry, chairman," and then they explained they'd driven down and had been drinking crates of brown ale. No service station would let them stop so they reached the point where they couldn't go on any further.

'I said to them, "Right, but if this happens again, I tell you, you're out, any of you!"

'My wife said to them, "I won't forget you either, but it won't be by your faces!"'

Wherever you looked in the streets of Grimsby there were Newcastle fans. It was sunny. Fish and chips and football and beer. Life was so good.

It felt great.

Newcastle were in yellow and green that night. A song tumbled down from the terraces: 'Champione'. It was new to everyone.

Two Grimsby players touched the ball at the start of the second half, then Rob Lee beat four men and slipped a pass through to Andy Cole. Cole took a touch and clipped a right-foot finish into the bottom corner of the Grimsby goal.

It was almost done.

In injury-time David Kelly went round Rhys Wilmot. The angle was tight and Kelly was almost on a bended knee when he hit a left-foot shot that sealed victory and the title, right in front of the main body of the travelling supporters, packed into the Osmond Stand.

You were just so happy to be alive and to be there and to be at the heart of Newcastle United. It was an enormous goal. It was symbolic of a new Newcastle United; getting it right when it mattered, going the extra mile.

Then the whistle went. Keegan punched the air. McDermott grabbed John Beresford, and then Keegan and McDermott hugged each other tightly. Newcastle fans came on to the pitch from all ends of the ground. The team joined them. Keegan was mobbed. He would be given a crown. The man was adored.

The players danced in front of the Newcastle support. The 'Blaydon Races' filled the Cleethorpes night air and you were blasting it out. People climbed the fences at the front, strips were waved in the air. You were so proud of your club. Keegan did that. You never wanted the feeling to end.

Newcastle were winners.

'It wasn't half of Newcastle down there,' recalls Keegan. 'It was all of Newcastle down there. They were even in our dressing room afterwards. It was absolute chaos in there, in a nice way. I remember the crown the fans gave me.

'We won the first eleven games with thirty-three points. We were virtually there after a quarter of the season, unless we did something really stupid. We knew we were going to go up, the defining moment came that night at Grimsby.

'What made it very special, and I know the players said this, was the support. The players didn't want to come back in. They wanted it to last forever.'

There was Oxford and then Leicester, for the final game of the season, at St James' Park. Newcastle had new strips that looked like Juventus. Lee Clark had shaved his head and looked like Gianluca Vialli.

'When we arrived a guy was putting something in the corner of the dressing room,' adds Keegan. 'I said, "What are you doing?" He said, "I'm putting a camera up." I said, "What for?" He went, "Well, Sir John Hall said we could." I went, "Take it down." He's the chairman, but he's got no right to put a camera in the dressing room. They took it down.

'I remember saying to Terry Mac before the game started, 'You know what's going to happen now, this is going to be a damp squib, we'll get beat one-nil."

Leicester were in the play-off places and they were destroyed. 'Terry nudged me after about half an hour, the scoreboard at the back was reading three-nil, I think, and he goes, "Some damp squib." He just gave me that cheeky little look he gives.'

By half-time Kelly had scored a hat-trick and it was 6–0. The whole ground was bouncing. There was joy wherever you looked. Everyone was singing the Andy Cole song. The strips looked great, even on supporters.

You were having the time of your life, and you knew it.

This, this is why you put up with so much, for so long. For a day like this.

It was like reaching the promised land.

Midway through the second half, Kilcline came on. He was the club captain by then. There was a huge cheer. Cole completed his hat-trick. Newcastle had won 7–1. The ground never stopped singing.

Brian Kilcline was presented with the First Division trophy and he roared as he lifted it into the air. Tyneside celebrated with him. Sir John Hall sang on the pitch. Lindisfarne played in the new Leazes End that was finally being built, sixteen years after the old one had been knocked down. The day had everything, absolutely everything.

'I would have paid money to have gone to Newcastle,' adds Kilcline. 'They didn't have to pay me. I would have gone for nothing, just for that, just for the ball, it was an absolute ball.

'Laughter is infectious, I found that more than any place in Newcastle. We got promoted and I loved it.

'Me and Lynn ask ourselves constantly, "What's it all about, life in general?" The Newcastle period in my life gave life a reason. It was that good.'

Lifting the trophy would be Kilcline's last major act for the club. Scoring a hat-trick and taking his tally for the season to 28 would be Kelly's.

'Kevin called me a couple of days later and I was driving down to Birmingham,' says Kelly. 'He said, "Where are you?" I said, "I'm driving." He said, "Go and sit yourself in a café, I need to have a chat."

'I said, "Am I going?"' He said, "I need to have a chat."

'I went off the A1 somewhere, sat down there and phoned him up. He said, "I've had a bid off the Wolves." I said, "Am I not going to play?" He said, "I'm signing one player and trying to get a few in."

'I said, "Who you signing?" He said, "Peter Beardsley." I said, "Decent!"

'I said, "Gaffer, I wouldn't want to stay if you're not going to play me."

'He said, "I know that because you've spoken to me about it before."

'I just wanted to play. That was my obsession. I scored twenty-eight goals that season. I went, "Right, I've got a year left, I want my money." He said, "Ned, don't worry, thanks for everything you've done."

'It's cut-throat and some people are horrible. He was brilliant with me. I've got nothing but respect for him. He told me what he thought and that was it. That was me gone.'

David Kelly would not return to St James' Park until 5 April 1997. He would be wearing the red and white of Sunderland when he did. When Kelly was brought on as a 61st-minute substitute for Allan Johnston, something unexpected happened. 'The whole ground stood up and applauded,' he says. 'It was a gulp moment. I've not had many of them in my life but it was humbling. I will never forget it.'

ANDY COLE – I (DON'T) WANNA BE ADORED

TIME DOES NOT STAND STILL, AT LEAST THE SCIENTISTS CLAIM THAT is the case, but when Andy Cole ran around Nigel Spink in front of the Leazes End, twelve yards from goal, it felt like everything in Tyneside stopped. It was a moment, like Kevin Keegan's goal on his debut, where you hoped that the script was right, and waited for magic, so you would never forget it, and in that instant football and life momentarily hit pause.

When Cole went around Spink in the 41st minute, he had the chance to become the greatest goalscorer in a season that the city of Newcastle had ever seen.

'Young, gifted and black and white'. Those were the words on the back of the T-shirt that had Cole, in his Newcastle strip, on the front.

Until that point, everything Cole had touched had turned to gold.

*

HE WAS PLAYING FOR BRISTOL CITY THE FIRST TIME A CONTINGENT from Newcastle turned up in early 1982. He had a hamstring injury but played on. Kevin Keegan turned to those with him: 'Sign him,' he said. 'He's got a hamstring injury and he's carried on. They're the kind of players I want at Newcastle United. Sign him.'

Newcastle signed him for £1.75 million. It was a lot of money. They lost on Cole's debut, at Swindon, but by the time the streets of Tyneside were awash with the celebration of promotion, the 22-year-old Londoner had scored twelve goals in twelve games. It was a warning of what was to come, but no one had quite grasped exactly how dramatic it would be.

The first game Newcastle played in the Premiership was at home to Tottenham. The excitement was overwhelming, but it was as much about seeing the new stand at the Leazes End as it was about the new world.

The Leazes End had been the home end at St James' Park until it was ripped down and never replaced in 1978. In its place was left a small, uncovered terrace. It was a sorry replacement and it became a true epitome of those in charge. By 1994, it was something special, you had watched it grow; a proper all-seater stand with a roof and vociferous support inside it. There was such anticipation that afternoon it was almost inevitable that Newcastle would lose. Ossie Ardiles of all people was in charge of Tottenham and Teddy Sheringham scored.

Then there was an away game at Coventry. David Kelly turned up in the Sky Blue Stand to sit with the traveling support and Newcastle, who did not have the injured Peter Beardsley, lost again. This was not the script. After two games Newcastle, who had warned Manchester United they were going for their title, were eighteenth in the table, joint bottom.

The third game of the season was away at Old Trafford, at the Premiership champions.

Everything changed after Old Trafford. Ryan Giggs scored with a free kick in the first half but Newcastle never looked frightened, and that was something completely new. A freshly promoted club, facing its third straight defeat, played their way back into the game and with twenty minutes remaining, Niki Papavasiliou slipped a ball through to Andy Cole. Cole accelerated to meet the pass without breaking his rhythm. Then he fired the ball past Peter Schmeichel.

In that moment, Newcastle became a Premiership team.

'In the first programme notes I put, "Watch out, Sir Alex, we're after your title,"' says Keegan.

'One of the directors said to me, "This puts so much pressure on everyone, Kevin." I said, "Good, rightly so." I remember saying, "That's the problem with this club, your expectations have always been, this is Newcastle, we don't do well. If you start stating what you want and you start believing, you might achieve it."

'There was a malaise about the club, right back to when I had played. "We're Newcastle, we're not quite good enough, we always fall back, we're not quite there." I wanted to change that.'

He did.

Cole scored four more in his next four games and then cracked a hat-trick against Notts County in the League Cup. He scored fourteen more in his next ten matches. Newcastle by then were fourth in the top division of English football, a point off second place. Keegan had been true to his word. Newcastle were becoming a genuine force in the top division of English football.

There would be another goal for Cole at home to Manchester United, a brace against Manchester City. It didn't stop. When he got the ball, he scored a goal. There was another burst of eight goals in six games and Newcastle by now were proving irresistible.

'Fans were coming to games believing, not only we'd win, but they'd see a good match,' adds Keegan. 'My management style was very simple. I said, "These people work hard all week, they'll come here on a Saturday and pay their hard-earned money and they want to see you die for the shirt. They like to see you win but more often than not, they want to be entertained. They won't complain if they see a three-three draw, but if they see a one-nil loss, and you can't run and you don't want to run, they will."

'We built it on exactly that. The players we got bought into that. We got better players and they improved it slowly. When we went up we were already a Premiership side, we'd bought when we didn't need to. We didn't need Andy Cole to get up, we bought him for the Premiership because we knew we were going to be there.'

There was a swagger about the team and the centre-forward, the fulcrum of life in Tyneside, was scoring more goals than anyone had ever done in a black and white shirt.

*

BY THE TIME NEWCASTLE FACED ASTON VILLA, COLE WAS SITTING on 39 goals in all competitions for the season. There were four minutes left in the first half when his chance came. Like most opportunities that season, Cole took it, and the roof was lifted. It was a phenomenal roar and it came from everywhere, from inside the stadium into which 32,216 were packed and from those around the world who had followed the club for decades. History was made and everyone celebrated with Andy Cole.

The player, with his long sleeves and his top button still fastened, made two fists to his sides, and wheeled away, spinning in complete delight.

Andy Cole was the king of Newcastle. That is what happens when you fill the number nine shirt properly.

He had scored 40 goals in 43 games. Cole had beaten the joint record of Hughie Gallagher and George Robledo; Gallagher had scored 39 goals in the club's title-winning season in 1927, and Robledo had lifted the FA Cup in 1952 with the club when he equalled the tally.

Cole would end his one and only full season as a Newcastle player with 41 goals in all competitions from 45 games. He was a folk hero. He was revered. He was also 22, quiet and from London with a girlfriend.

'That's when the Geordie fans basically said, "This kid's going to be our hero,"' said Cole.

'It was the toughest year and a half ever, in a good way, but not really knowing how to deal with it. It was like, oh my God, what is all this about to have all these fans who adore you the way they adored me? I was like, I'm not used to this.'

'That was a nightmare,' said his then girlfriend Shirley, who became his wife. 'If you walked into a supermarket to buy groceries, two hours later you'd come out with no groceries and he'd be stood there, signing autographs.'

The following season, however, things began to unravel. Keegan didn't think Cole was putting enough into training. The goals, by his high standards, began to dry up. He went eight games without one, which was unheard of. When Sir Alex Ferguson made a phone call to enquire about his availability, Keegan was about to test his relationship with the support of Newcastle United more than at any other time. He said Cole was available.

In a 2014 interview with Steve Harmison he described what happened.

The Andy Cole deal happened fairly quickly, once I'd made my mind up. I went to see the board about it and they went, 'You're kidding! You're selling Andy Cole?' I said, 'Yeah, it's the right time, and you have to trust me on this.' And they did, to be fair.

He had run his race for Newcastle United Football Club. Players come, players go. Sometimes players can give you something for two years, sometimes three years, sometimes, if you're lucky, for their lifetime. We had a big, big argument at Selhurst Park.

He didn't come back for three days. Terry Mac said, 'What are you going to do?' I said, 'I'm not going to do anything.'

On the Friday there was a knock on the door and he said, 'What should I do?' I said, 'You train, if you look fit enough I'll consider playing you tomorrow. If you're not, then you'll go on the bench and I might bring you on.' He went and trained properly, scored on the Saturday and at that point I knew – it didn't matter that nobody else knew – and my staff knew, and the players at

Newcastle knew, they'd seen what had happened, they knew Andy wouldn't be with us much longer. I got him a great move.

He went for £7 million, to Manchester United, with a young Northern Irishman called Keith Gillespie travelling in the opposite direction for £1 million.

The Cole sale caused chaos in the city. It felt too much like old times, selling the best players. Supporters turned up at St James' Park to voice their anger.

'Douglas said, "There's loads of them,"' added Keegan.

I said, 'There'll be more of them, Douglas, we've just sold Andy Cole.' He said, 'We'll have to get out of here.' We did the opposite, we went down the steps and Terry Mac was behind me.

As I went down it was almost like booing. I understood that. I got down to four or five steps in front of them. One fella said, 'What are you doing selling our best player to Man United, our biggest rivals?'

That's what he said and it was a fair thing to say. It was true. I said, 'You have to remember two years ago when I came here it wasn't Man United who were our rivals when we were in Division Two, you have to trust me.' Another guy at the back said, 'Well, he wouldn't sell him without someone lined up, would he?' All the guys went, 'Yeah,' and Terry Mac behind me went, 'Oh yes he would.'

I had no one lined up. I had an idea what I wanted to do.

I turned to Terry and I said, 'That's why this is such a great club, people sometimes say fans don't know what the game's about, but they sometimes know more than people in the club know.'

We moved it on again. We had to go to another stage. What was happening at Newcastle, we were never settling where we were. We were always trying to push the boundaries. We talked and after about five minutes the fans went, 'If he thinks he can improve it, you have to give him a chance.' We had an open board meeting, with Douglas, Freddy, me, Terry Mac and the supporters.

I learned more about Newcastle United Football Club than I could ever have learned in my office.

Keegan's parting shot could still not have been much more dramatic.

'If I've got it wrong, there's a bullet with my name on it,' he said.

LES FERDINAND – TRUE FAITH

WE WALKED DOWN THE TUNNEL. I COULD HEAR THE NOISE . . . THEN I stepped out. St James' Park. I looked around me. There was black and white everywhere. I thought to myself, I don't want to let these people down. I can't let these people down.'

*

1966 WAS A GOOD YEAR FOR NEWCASTLE UNITED. LES FERDINAND was born.

By 1995 St James' Park was ready. That was no small feat. It had taken more than a hundred years. Finally the four sides of the stadium were covered. Two new stands at the Leazes End and the Gallowgate End stood proudly at the top of the city.

The Milburn Stand had been built with the money from selling Peter Beardsley in 1987 but the roof had barely reached half of those in it. Now it did.

Even the East Stand had new seats. The capacity was still just over 36,000, the same as when Keegan had so memorably stepped out for his debut, but when Les Ferdinand repeated the attempt to dive into the hearts of Newcastle supporters, it was a different ground. It was a stadium. It was ready. So was the team, so was the city.

Four new players had arrived.

Warren Barton, David Ginola and Shaka Hislop walked into the home dressing room that day and did not see the number nine hanging on their peg. For some, the shirt has appeared made of chain mail. For the lucky few, the sleeves transform into wings.

It was a new shirt. The thickness of the black and white stripes was a statement. It was Adidas. It was quality; the granddad collar opened the gateway to a history that had seen Newcastle win three league titles and reach the FA Cup final five times within the space of seven years at the start of the twentieth century.

Scottish and Newcastle, now the biggest brewing concern in the country, were sponsors. The Brown Ale logo sat proudly on the shirt's front. The Tyne Bridge was on the front of the Newcastle strip. It was a shirt worn with pride. Symbolism matters. The team looked ready for business.

Les Ferdinand had the physique of a middleweight boxer. That made the task of filling the shirt easier. His succession was to Andy Cole. Cole was about speed and quickness of finish. Ferdinand was different. Ferdinand was raw power, like a supercharged steam engine.

He was also, very nearly, a Manchester United player.

'I'd been contacted by Man United in December of 1994,' says Ferdinand. 'If they had signed me in January I was eligible for the next stage of the Champions League. That's what Alex Ferguson wanted me for. They came to get me.

'It was let known to me that a bid had gone in so I was able to go to the [QPR] chairman, Richard Thompson, and he was like, "Look, who's told you?" I said, "I know quite a few people who work in the office and it was faxed through."

'He said, "Do you want to go?" I said, "They're winning everything at the minute, there's an opportunity for me to go." He said, "I can't lose Gerry Francis and in the same week sell my major goalscorer. Ray Wilkins is coming in, but he's coming in on the proviso you can't be sold for the rest of the season."

'Rumours were flying around at the time that I didn't want to move out of London, that I was a London boy. Someone made that up. That stuck. It was rubbish. Alex had been given a glowing report of what I was like in the dressing room but I couldn't leave.'

Manchester United instead bought Andy Cole.

'I'm a firm believer in what is meant to be in life will be,' he adds.

Aston Villa tabled a £6 million bid as soon as the season finished. Ferdinand was on his way to Birmingham to meet their chairman Doug Ellis when his agent's phone went.

'It was Kevin Keegan,' says Ferdinand. 'He said to my agent, "Look, can you please ask Les to allow me the favour of speaking to him before he signs for Aston Villa? The club will match the bid."

'Was my head turned by that? Oh yeah!'

Ellis made a valiant pitch. By the time he was finishing, Keegan was driving down from Newcastle to Cockfosters, in north London.

'I was sat in the hotel with my agent,' adds Ferdinand. 'Kevin came on his own, shook my hand and sat down. He started to sell the club. To be fair, just shaking his hand and saying hello did that. He'd come down and I'd made my decision there and then.

'I was impressed with what he said, where he wanted to take the club and how he wanted to take it there. I wanted to be part of that. There was no doubt in my mind that I was going to improve playing with the likes of Peter Beardsley in a team that had taken the Premier League by storm.

'I remember playing against Newcastle at St James' Park the season before. We'd won that game and I'd scored but the fans never stopped singing and they were clapped off even though they lost. We were in the changing room after, and I was going, "Imagine playing in front of that very week." My blood was already bubbling.

'Keegan said, "I'm going to be totally honest, Les. I tried to buy you to pair you with Andy Cole. I had Andy in my car one day and I took him to watch you play. I said, 'This is how centre-forward's play.' Andy went, 'I know all about Les!'"

'We were different types of player, me and Andy, but I would love to have played with him.

'Keegan said: "I'm going to give you the number nine shirt. It takes someone special to wear it but I think you have all the ingredients to handle it."

'I knew what he was talking about, the great players who had worn the shirt, Malcolm Macdonald, Jackie Milburn. I got all that. I understood it. I wasn't over-awed by it. I thought, if I play the way I know I can play, I'll be more than comfortable. It wasn't a burden to me.

'He said, "Look, I will give you time to consider it. We can't match what Aston Villa will pay you but we will give you a better brand of football." I said, "No problem." I was being diplomatic. I shook his hand and I knew I was going to join Newcastle.'

*

THE NUMBER NINE SHIRT WAS HANGING UP IN THE HOME DRESSING room at St James' Park on Saturday, 19 August. Ferdinand had already worn it in friendlies. Newcastle had played Gateshead at the International Stadium – albeit in their change strip of maroon and blue hoops. The ground was full to its 11,000 capacity. It was a sign something was happening.

Ferdinand had flown to Tyneside to sign his contract and complete the £6 million transfer from Queens Park Rangers. The first time he entered the city to stay he travelled in his car.

'I drove across the Tyne Bridge and I was like, it's the Tyne Bridge! And then I was like, there's St James' Park! You can see it from everywhere. It was like, bloody hell!

'It felt special coming over the bridge. Even when I flew up I'd gone in the stadium and thought, this place smells of football. It was just great. I walked round the ground and I just couldn't wait for the season to get started.

'We played Hartlepool in a friendly and then there was a full house at Gateshead in a friendly and I was like, whoa, and Steve Watson and Lee Clark were going, "If you think that's impressive, just wait."

'They took me under their wing. They said they would show me the sights of the city. They were brilliant with me. They brought me into Geordie life.

'I had come up but my family was still in London. We would train all week and then I would go back to London. During one week, they both went, "You can't go back to London this weekend. This is your initiation. You and all the new boys. We're taking you all out."

'We said, "No problem." We all stayed. It was pre-season and we all went out, and this was when you were still allowed to go out. We let our hair down. They showed us the sights, the Quayside and all that. They showed me Newcastle and let me tell you, they showed me everything! They had their line of restaurants and pubs we all went into and then we all went into a nightclub called Julie's.

'I just kept thinking, yes! Everything I had heard about Newcastle was absolutely correct. It was a great time. We had a real, good camaraderie. We were close as a squad. Then it was down to business.'

It was five minutes to three and Ferdinand was stood in the tunnel at St James' Park.

'Watto and Clarky had said to me, "Wait until the first day of the season, and you put that strip on. It will feel like you're floating down the tunnel."

'We walked down the tunnel. I could hear the noise. My heart started thumping. There was black and white everywhere. And then the roar. The hairs were standing up on the back of my neck. You float on to that pitch all right.'

The ground was awash with black and white shirts. Optimism seeped through the fabric. Robert Lee opened the scoring after seven minutes. In the 82nd minute Peter Beardsley fired in a penalty. Newcastle were cruising.

Just over a minute later Lee picked a pass that sent Ferdinand charging towards the Gallowgate End. He was further out than Keegan had been on his debut, thirteen years earlier, around forty yards from goal and near the touchline as well. John Filan, the Coventry goalkeeper, came racing from his penalty area.

'I went round him,' Ferdinand says. 'I saw the goal, I saw it open. I was at a bit of an angle and I was a long way out. I could have had another touch. It seemed like the moment went quick. As I've gone to the ball I thought: This is it, this is it! Put it in!

'The ball went into the back of the net. The way the stadium erupted! Peter Beardsley sprinted over and jumped on me. He was like, "Bloody hell, Les! Could you be more casual about your first goal!"

'Kevin Keegan, Terry Mac and Arthur Cox jumped off the bench. I realised what it meant, not just to me, but to all of them as well. I knew it was important for me, but I realised then what it meant to everyone else. The fans were going mad. I looked around and I realised.

'I was like, yeah, yeah, yeah, yeah, yeah! Now I know what it's all about. This is where I want to be. This is the arena I want to be in. This is why I play.

'At that moment I really understood it. I thought I knew what it meant, but I didn't really. Once the ball went in the back of the net, the elation, it was like, "We've got a new number nine here." That's what it felt like.

'I'd scored goals in pre-season. The first day of the season at St James' Park, when that shot went in, it was like I was born. I was born.'

*

FERDINAND HAD BEEN BORN IN PADDINGTON, LONDON, IN DECEMber 1966. When he was eleven he played in goal for the school team. That lasted for three years.

He played five-a-side on a Friday night. Then he was a striker. When the school centre-forward was injured for a game, the players he faced on a Friday told the year head, Mr Middleton, that Ferdinand was a forward. He scored a hat-trick. Mr Middleton said to him, 'Les Ferdinand, you will never play in goal again.'

He trained with Southampton twice but the journey, getting back after ten o'clock on school nights, was too long for the liking of his parents. He signed for non-league Southall and reached the FA Vase final. Then he moved to Hayes and combined that with working for a decorating company. At nineteen, Queens Park Rangers realised there might be a player there. He signed for £30,000. Then Jim Smith sent Ferdinand to Besiktas for a year when he was 21.

'It was probably the most important move of my career,' he says. 'Gordon Milne was in charge at Besiktas and he had a presence about him. I never did an apprenticeship. I probably didn't understand the professionalism of a footballer, having come from a non-league background, working part-time for a wallpaper shop, driving, stuff like that, doing a bit of decorating.

'I was still in that mindset. I went to Turkey and it was a year for me to just concentrate on football. No distraction, no mates knocking on the door going, "Les, you coming out?" Just football for a year. That was the making of me. It was the best thing I could have done. I scored twenty-one goals in thirty-three games. It was a successful year, I had a bit of a swagger when I came back.'

He scored sixty goals in the next three Premier League seasons before Keegan finally acted on his long-standing interest in the player.

The goal against Coventry changed his life.

'I always say to people it was one of the friendliest places I've ever been to. At no stage did I get fed up of it. I remember before I came, my first meeting with Kevin Keegan, the one thing he said to me was, "In London you can get lost, London is a big place and there's so many people. In Newcastle, football is the be all and end all. There is no hiding place. You will be in a goldfish bowl. Are you ready for that?"

'I said, "Yeah." I wanted to prove myself as a footballer and I was ready for it. He said, "OK."

'I'd been at the club for a couple of weeks when Kevin called me into the office at Maiden Castle and he said, "Is everything OK? Is there anything you want to do? I can imagine in the evenings you can't go out."

'I said, "Yeah, you know what, I need to learn how to cook. I'm going to enrol in a college in Newcastle to do some cooking at a night school." He said, "Mate, you're not going to college." I said, "Yeah, yeah I am." I was up for it.

'He was going, "Nah, nah, you can't go to a night class at college." I was going, "Yeah, I'm serious, of course I can." He just goes, "Les, you cannot go to college here in Newcastle to learn how to cook, you won't learn how to cook." I've gone, "What are you saying? I'm an idiot?"

'He said, "Nah, nah, you've got to understand. Arthur, you tell him." So then Arthur goes, "Les, Newcastle's number nine can't go to a cookery class at night school in Newcastle. You wouldn't get a minute's peace."'

In the end, Sir John Hall's butler taught Les how to cook.

The attention of the fans is an intrusion born of curiosity and affection. It can make or break a player in the north-east.

Ferdinand continues: 'Keegan said there had been problems with Andy because he was living out the way in an old mining village. He'd moved into a flat in Gosforth. He'd just had it fully furnished and interior designed and he left for Manchester United. He left me the shirt and the flat! I rented the flat off him.

'I used to live on my own and there was a big Asda across the road and I used to go there on my own and do the shopping. Everyone would be looking at me, going, "There's our number nine shopping!"

'I knew a fella called Andy, who worked for a production company. I met his wife, Alice, a Geordie girl. They're both Geordies. She said to me, "I always used to remember you in Asda, I used to follow you around in each aisle, seeing what you put in your trolley. You used to put in the blue Radox bubble bath."

'I went, "What!"'

You accept that or turn and run.

Ferdinand, stood, smiled and grew into the hearts of the people of Tyneside.

'I don't think there was a day when I left my house and didn't sign an autograph,' he adds. 'One day I went to training and I came back and hadn't signed one. There were always people at training so I'd signed them there, but in your ordinary life, this one day, I hadn't signed anything.

'I'd gone home, then on to Gosforth High Street. I walked to get to the Post Office. There was no one in there. There were two old women behind the counter. I'll never forget it. I got some stamps and some envelopes, and had some stuff to do and when I finished, I thought to myself, wow, this is going to be the first day I go back to my house and I haven't signed an autograph for anybody.

'The two old women were very professional in what they were doing: "Yes, you need to do this, yes, you need to do that." As I finished, I paid and she gave me my receipt. All of a sudden she went under the counter and picked up her Newcastle United mug and went, "Can you sign this for me please, Les?" I was like, "OK!" It was brilliant. That was brilliant. I had such an amazing time there.'

While he was at the club, Ferdinand started riding a motorbike.

'Me and Warren Barton decided we were going to do the bike test. I went to Keegan first: "Can I do this?" He went, "Yep, as long as you ride my Harley back." He'd had one built up past Gosforth. He goes, "Be careful." I went, "No problem, it's only 125s." They were like hairdryers.

'Warren said, "I'll go and buy some helmets." He ended up getting Harley helmets so they were open-faced, instead of closed-faced, like what Chris Eubank used to have.

'In the car park at St James' they did the CBT [Compulsory Basic Training] course and we were there on our hairdryers. Once you'd practised you got taken on to the road. We spent two or three hours on the bikes and it was freezing. I had jeans on and a leather jacket and a T-shirt underneath it. It started hailstoning for a while so my jeans got soaked.

'We went down a dual carriageway, it goes into a single road with pubs on either side. There were all these geezers stood outside one of the pubs. I had the helmet on and I was oblivious. All I heard was, "Hoo, Les, get off the bike, man!"

'I looked across, they couldn't believe their number nine was on a motorbike. I was that cold, I had a little wobble up! When we got to the car park Warren was pissing himself, he was going, "I nearly fell off as well, I was laughing that much." Then he goes, "No one was worried about me, just you!"'

Ferdinand could not ride his manager's Harley, though, even after he passed his test. The engine was too big.

He did, however, go one step further than Keegan after getting flying lessons. Ferdinand flew his own helicopter.

BLUE STAR SOCCER DAY

DUNSTON FEDERATION BREWERY, LANCASTRIAN
SUITE, 1983

GRAHAM FENTON –
BLUE (STAR) MONDAY

WHEREVER YOU LOOKED THERE WERE QUEUES OF CHILDREN, WEAV-
ing around the huge, rectangular tables. Earlier there had been a coaching session at
Newcastle's training ground.

'The Blue Star Soccer Day? Yeah, I went there, I was nine,' says Graham Fenton.
'It was at Benwell. My dad saw it in the paper and said, "Do you want to go?" I
remember little things, like doing different drills, shooting and dribbling.

'There was loads of kids there, and then at the end we played in a big game. It
was sunny and it was the summer of '83. We played a big game with some of the
players as well, Zico [Mick Martin] was there.

'After that we went to the brewery in Dunston. There was big tables and then
you would go to queue to get your picture taken with Kevin. He would sign things.
You were sat at the table then you joined this massive queue.

'That was my first experience of Kevin Keegan. I got my picture taken with him
and got my certificate. I got home and within days it was framed and up on the wall.
It stayed on my bedroom wall from then until when I left in 1990. It just stayed
there and it was still there when I came back at weekends to see my parents.

'I can't remember when my mam took it down. She redecorated when I bought
my own house. It might have been then. It will be in her loft somewhere now.'

STEVE HOWEY – THE BOY WITH THE WRONG PLACE IN THE SIDE

'I JUST REMEMBER STANDING THERE THINKING, I'M GETTING PAID for this!'

*

STEVE HOWEY USED TO DO A LOT OF STANDING WHEN HE WAS sixteen: at the bus stop near his home in Gilley Law; then at Sunderland station; then at Newcastle Central Station, as he waited for the bus to take him to Benwell, where Newcastle United trained.

'I used to get up at six o'clock when I lived with my mam and dad,' he says. 'My mam had to wake me. It would be pitch-black in the winter. I would get the bus into Sunderland city centre. I'd be standing at Sunderland station and back then the wind was brutal. I used to be standing there with about fifteen layers on, freezing. You just think, fuckin' hell, this has got to work.

'I'd get the train through to Newcastle and then the number 38 from Newcastle to Benwell. I would get there for eight o'clock. It was still freezing.

'The groundsman was a lad called Davey Orchard and he was wicked. He had two Alsatians called Max and Shadow. They used to leave dead rabbits and birds all over the place.

'He would be at the far side, where the pavilion was, and if Dave still had the dogs out – and he did it on purpose – the dog would hear you coming up the drive and it would be after you. You would have to sprint, and I mean sprint, and try to get in the door, with the dog trying to get you, snarling behind as you slammed the door shut.'

All that to get into the training facilities at Benwell.

'It was a shit-hole,' he adds. 'As you go in the door the apprentices were there. There was a corridor, a dressing room here and a dressing room there, the physio's room and the manager's room and then the laundry room.

'The boot room was outside and sandwiches would come in at lunchtime for the apprentices and you would try and grab whatever you could because, if you didn't, you could be left with beetroot. To this day I fucking hate beetroot.

'You would get a normal sandwich, a biscuit and a yoghurt. You would be sitting there hacky-black and you'd have something to eat, you knew you'd be training in the afternoon and you had to get something down you.

'You'd be doing your jobs because the pros would be finished. You'd put bins out in their dressing room and they would fling stuff all over the place, the bins were just full of crap. The bath was a communal bath. If we were lucky, and if there was any hot water left, we would try and fill it up.

'You had to leave in what the pros had been in so it was just full of mud and all kinds. You were actually dirtier when you came out. Then you would have to go in the boot room.

'I had four pros to look after and I had to clean their boots: Graeme Carter, Liam O'Brien – who was the miserablest man in the world – Rob McDonald and John Hendrie.

'John was quality, I got twenty quid off John at Christmas. I used to get a fiver off Graeme, he was a first-year pro. I used to get fuck all off Rob McDonald and nothing from Liam.

'We used to go in the gym and it was an old-fashioned multi-gym where everything was attached. The gym used to be carpet and the carpet would be up at the edges so you'd be running along and you could trip over. It was always freezing and always windy.

'If Suggy [youth coach Colin Suggett] was in a bad mood and he could hear the lads pissing about, he would wipe the light switch with his finger and find dust and say, "Do it again."'

This, in 1988, was the reward for being a standout young player in the northeast. Newcastle had only twelve apprentices spread over three years. These were the elite, the very best the region had to offer, scouted for years to make it to Benwell.

Howey had been coveted from when he was an eight-year-old playing for St Cuthbert's.

'I was a midfield player and we were a team that weren't bad,' he adds. 'Without being a tit, it was a one-man team, they used to give me the ball and it was a case of me dribbling through and scoring goals. I scored 126 goals in a season, which was a record for years.

'There was some great times there. I went to senior school at St Aidan's. We had an unbelievable team. In the five years we were there we lost four games. At every game every scout was there. My dad was inundated with scouts coming in. I didn't want to go anywhere.

'I went on a trial to Leicester when I was fourteen. I went down with Paul Kitson. He stopped and signed and I wanted to come back. It was always a choice between Sunderland and Newcastle.

'My family is red and white. I wasn't a major Sunderland fan to be honest. I used to go to both of them to train, Sunderland and Newcastle. I was thirteen when I started. I enjoyed both but I seemed to get on a lot better with all the Newcastle lads. Myself, Lee Clark, Steve Watson, Rob Elliott, Alan Thompson and Matty Appleby.

'There wasn't really that connection at Sunderland. In the dressing room at Sunderland I was on my own. Newcastle seemed a club where you had a better chance.

'At Newcastle there was a bloke called Peter Kirkley [the youth development officer], who was lovely. We were terrified of him, to be honest, but he was lovely.

'What made my mind up was when I met Lawrie McMenemy [who was in charge at Sunderland] at Cleadon, where Sunderland trained. He kind of came across as if I should be in awe of him, and I wasn't, I was only a kid. He was going, "So when are you going to sign?" and I said, "Well, I'm not, I'm just waiting. I'm at Newcastle as well."

'He then went and hammered me on the radio. He called me a cocky young kid and all this type of thing. Me dad was furious. Peter [Kirkley] sensed that. That was it. Plus it helped when Peter did his utmost, gave us boots and bits of kit, and I got nothing off Sunderland. That helped. In the end for me it was an easy decision to sign for Newcastle.'

Boots and a bit of kit meant the world.

'I was from absolutely fuck all to be honest,' he adds. 'I was from a council estate called Gilley Law in Sunderland. It wasn't exactly the nicest place in the world, lovely people, but it's not a great area.

'I always said if I ever made it I would buy my mam and dad a house to take them out of there. Once I got to the stage where I was doing quite well, I did. They still live in it now.'

To get out of there, Howey got out of bed every morning at six o'clock, when his mam woke him.

'They were long, long days,' he says. 'You would come away and you were knackered. You would finish at about four o'clock. I got the bus to Central Station, then the train, then another bus back home, the Six O'Clock News was on the telly with Sue Lawley and I used to sit in the kitchen and my head would be dropping in the middle of my tea.

'All the kids around the streets were knocking on the doors, going, "Are you coming out?" and going out was the furthest thing from my mind.

'I would go to bed not having had a great deal to eat and get up in the morning and do it all again. I got paid twenty-five pounds, plus twenty pounds to travel, and I think my mam got twenty for board, but I thought I was absolutely loaded.

'I definitely feel it helped that the lads got on so well, really, really well. Sometimes it was bloody tough. It made you realise how much you wanted it. It reinforced one hundred per cent that you wanted to make it. You'd be knackered the next morning at the train station, same platform on another bitterly cold morning and you'd think, this has to work, it has to succeed. I want to get a car. I want to drive there rather than arse around on buses and trains. At school I would get distracted so easily. There I was completely focused about trying to succeed.'

Howey was still a goalscoring midfielder. In his first game he got moved up front. 'It wasn't my choice, I was tall and there was no one else to play there. As a forward I'd be waiting for the ball and the centre-half was coming in front of me.

'We played Halifax at the Shay and the pitch was proper boggy. I remember sitting on the bus thinking, am I good enough? You have a couple of days when you're really down and then you go: You know what, it's Monday, let's work harder at it. It was surprisingly quick when I thought, I think I can do this.'

Howey was seventeen when Jim Smith picked him for the first time in the full Newcastle team, as a substitute against Manchester United in the last match of the 1988/89 season. That changed his life. So did Ossie Ardiles, and Kevin Keegan.

Howey did not play at first-team level for the entire campaign the following season after his debut. He nagged Smith – 'When I could see him in his office past the cigar smoke' – but another opportunity did not come. Smith was sacked the following season (1990/91) and Ardiles took over.

'Ossie was great for the young lads,' Howey says. 'But he put too many in and we struggled. It affected me because I was up front. The amount of grief I was getting off Newcastle fans at that time was just horrific. It was always, "Useless Mackem bastard", and all that kind of stuff. We didn't create anything.

'I was nervous against Plymouth for my home debut. My stomach was knotted up before the match. It was throughout my career but once the game started I didn't care less. I didn't care how many people were watching once it started. But on the first few times I was a bag of nerves. I had a chance and I rushed the finish. If it had gone in it could have been completely different.'

It didn't and instead Ardiles started watching training carefully. Howey would play at the back in five-a-sides.

'I could read where they were going,' he adds. 'I found it easy to intercept. You didn't have to be the quickest. I had a conversation with Ossie, he said, "I want to have a couple of games behind closed doors." I gave a couple of daft fouls away with sliding tackles and he said, "You're not ready yet, but I feel we'll work on it and we'll do it."

'It didn't happen because Ossie got sacked. When Kevin came in I think he automatically thought I was a centre-half. I think it was Colin Suggett who said to him, 'No, no, he's a midfielder-cum-attacker.' Again, it was a case of a couple of games behind closed doors. I was at centre-forward in the games. Kevin took me to one side and said, "If you want a future here, it's not as a centre-forward."

'We had another game and I played centre-half. He went, "Basically, I'll just reconfirm. I'm going to take this club to places you wouldn't believe. I would like you to be part of it but the only way you'll be part of it is if you're a centre-half. If not, I'll shake your hand and I'll wish you good luck."

'From that moment I was a centre-half.'

There was much to thank Keegan for.

'I was still at school when I initially signed for Newcastle. I was getting grief all the time, light-hearted grief. It was only when I got in the first team, because I was still living in Sunderland, that it changed.

'I was with my wife-to-be at that particular time and I would go out and get the most ridiculous amount of chew. I'd be going, "Hang on a second, I've been offered a job where it's better prospects than it is at Sunderland, if you were in the same situation would you not do it?" And they'd go, "Nah," and I'd go, "Well, you're an idiot."

'It would cause loads of grief. Me and Angela bought a house in Sunderland in Chester Road, it was called the Leazes.

'I remember Sir John and Kevin dropping me off one day and Kevin went, "You live here. Why do you live here?" I said, "It's all I can afford."

'I was on 125 pounds a week. I was in KK's plans but that's what I was on. He said, "You're not living here, come and see me on Monday." I got a better contract and ended up moving to Silksworth, which was a lot nicer, but it wasn't that long before word got round that I was living on that estate.

'What used to happen was when we played away, people knew I wasn't at home, they used to go round and terrorise Angela; we had Paige at the time, who was only a baby, and they'd throw paint all over the garden and across the house. Again I had to see Kevin and again I got another contract.'

Howey was earning those new contracts. The struggling striker had flourished to become one of the most accomplished central defenders in England. His composure and reading of the game was a feature of Newcastle's play.

He was driving home from training at Maiden Castle in November 1994 when his mobile phone went.

'"Hi, is that Steven?" I said, "Yes." He said, "It's Terry Venables." I went, "Yeah, fuck off," and put the phone down.

'All the lads had been winding me up and I thought, I'm not getting sucked into this. He called straight back and he went, "Don't put the phone down, it's Terry Venables, listen to the voice." I just went, "Oh, hello."

'He went, "How are you doing?" I went, "I'm fine." "Are you fit?" I said, "I'm good." He said, "I've been hearing loads of good things about you, not just from Kevin, from everyone involved and people who've been watching you. We've got a game coming up against Nigeria. I want to know if you're up for being involved?"

'I went, "You're asking me if I want to play for England!" He went, "Yeah." I said, "Of course! Best thing ever." He said, "Great, I'll send the details through but you're in the squad." It was over so quickly. It was surreal. I was in the car but I'd pulled over. There was no Bluetooth or anything.

'I was in shock. I can't remember getting home. I can't remember any of the traffic. My missus said, "What's the matter?" I said, "Terry Venables called," and we were just like, wow! From playing on the street to getting in the England squad all of a sudden.

'You dream about it but there's not many got in then. I couldn't believe it. I couldn't sleep and all the nerves came back again.

'The next day when I went into training I got absolutely battered off the lads. There was no, "Well done". It was, "How the fuck are you in there?"

'When I joined up with England we trained at Bisham Abbey. All the big-hitters came in and I was like, bloody hell, am I really supposed to be here? Paul Gascoigne, David Platt, Tony Adams and the whole surrounding of it. I was shaking their hands going, "Steve Howey", because I thought they'd be thinking, "Who's that?"

'Very quickly you bond and get on. We played Nigeria and it's a weird feeling when you're walking out at Wembley. I was pulling on the England strip and thinking, am I actually here? Is this really me? But the boys were absolutely brilliant and the manager was superb as well, best manager by far for tactics, frightening, absolutely frightening.

'I probably wouldn't have got into that dressing room without Kevin Keegan in my career. At the same time I was playing well, we were really high-profile. It was because of him we were high-profile. The club wouldn't have been in that situation but for Kevin, one hundred per cent.

'He kept saying I would play for England. We were playing Norwich one week and he said, "If you play well, I'm phoning the England manager up." That did the power of good for you. I did well. Kevin was absolutely all over me. My nickname through Barry Venison was "The Boy" because I was a boy when I first got in the team. I was the young lad.

'I came off and Kevin was all over me. He went in the papers, saying this and that about me. The lads were all like, "Aye, Boy, is he your fatha?"

'I remember when Kevin came as a player. We were up in Scotland in 1982. Obviously Arthur Cox was the manager then and I remember it being on the radio. Me dad is a massive Sunderland fan, he was going, "Keegan going there? He's finished. He'll do nowt."

'Kevin completely turned it round with Peter [Beardsley] and Chris Waddle. Of course, it changed the mindset of Newcastle fans. Keegan gets a lot of plaudits for things he did. You had to think how much work Arthur Cox did. He has to be thanked for that. If it wasn't for Arthur getting Kevin, then none of this would have happened.

'Arthur is one of the maddest men in the world. He's also one of the best blokes I've ever met in football, proper old school.

'He'd say, "Who did you go to bed with last night, son?" I'd be like, "What?" He'd say it again, "Who did you go to bed with last night?" "The missus." "Does she pay the bills, son?" "What do you mean?" "Does she pay the bills?" "No." "What pays the bills, son?" "Me." "The ball, son. Kick your missus out of bed, son, and take the ball to bed. That pays the bills."

'We would see him on the far end of the training ground. You know the old-fashioned exercise routines you'd see in a Carry On film? He was like that. You'd see him in the distance doing these mad stretches.'

Howey was there when Keegan came back and fumigated the training ground he had spent his youth in. He was there when the club moved to Maiden Castle. He was there when Warren Barton walked in for the first time.

'I had my tracksuit on. I said, "Where the hell are you going?" He said, "What's the matter?" I goes, "I don't even get that dressed up when I'm going out!"

'He looked a million dollars. I said, "You're coming to bloody training, man." He came to training every morning that smart. I'd go, "It's training, man, not a fucking model show."

'It was a case of we'd go in and say, "Who have we signed? How much for?" Another one and another one. Kevin must have been like a kid in a sweet shop with Sir John or Freddy: "There you go," and they got everybody together.

'The new signings came in and straight away we introduced them to the culture, the fans and they picked it up very quickly. That was because of myself, Watto and Lee Clark.

'We made them understand what it meant to us, as north-east lads, and what it means to the area and to the fans, and the fans had been unbelievable.'

*

NEWCASTLE WORE THE SECOND OF THEIR GRANDDAD SHORTS FOR the first time, the maroon and blue hooped version, that night at Burnden Park, where one half of the away end was filled with a supermarket and the other with optimism that for once seemed justified. There was a spring in everyone's step. Newcastle had a team to show the country.

'It was a lovely, balmy August night,' adds Howey. 'They were proper good strips.

'Bolton were up for it and it was at Burnden Park but we were unbelievable.

'I was standing back and watching us play and thinking, this is the easiest thing ever. I'm actually on the pitch, I'm getting paid to be on the pitch and I'm doing bugger all and I'm watching David Ginola tear the arse out of their full-back and whip balls in for Les.

'That was the first time I realised how good Les and David were. We used to test the new players out in training and we'd proper wrap it into them. Small-sided, fast games. We had Steve Guppy and Darren Huckerby, and they were good players, but the ball would be bouncing all over the place off them. I played with Hucks at Manchester City and he said to me that he just couldn't cope. Training was really quick and some people couldn't get it. Dave was just like, bang, in there straight away.

'He still goes mad about it now. Every time I'm talking to him I'm going, "Dave", and he goes, "It's Daveed." And I would go, "It's Dave. You're in Newcastle, it's Dave. When we're in France I'll call you Daveed."

'Before you would get the ball in training you would have six or seven options in your head. By the time the ball got to you, two of them would be gone. They could all go pretty quickly and you'd have to get another picture pretty sharpish and make your mind up because when the ball came sometimes you couldn't even take a touch, it was that quick. You had to have a back-up.

'You were seeing that in the games. We were just playing so well. It was an amazing cross from David for the first goal and what a header from Les. He wasn't the tallest but we used to call him Zebedee because of how high he would get up. I remember a bit later David was on the right and he curled one past the post with the keeper beat with the outside of his right foot. It was ridiculous.

'They equalised, Rob Lee got the second and then Les just powered through for the third and people were bouncing off him.

'I remember speaking to Alan Thompson, who was at Bolton by then, afterwards, and he went, "Oh my God. How good are you?"

'How good were we? We were frightening.'

DAVID GINOLA – LOLA

THERE WAS A STUMBLE INTO THE MIDDLE OF THE ROAD, A RIGHT hand was raised towards the car bonnet. It was night-time in the Quayside. Traffic to the man's right had stopped. He took a further step forward and, buoyed by the initial success, raised his left hand to the opposite side of the road. The man had drunk a bit too much. Again, cars came to a halt. He turned around, smiled, and waved the six-foot-two Frenchman across the street.

David Ginola could not quite believe what was happening – he was bringing Tyneside to a standstill.

It was not quite like this in Sainte Maxime, where he had grown up, in the south-east of France, along the Cote D'Azur. His dad, who worked in a factory that made torpedoes for submarines, had played right-back for ASM, the local team. His son would play on his own at their small stadium, the Stade Gérard Rossi.

At home he played in the street. In tournaments he was catching the eye. Scouts from AC Milan and Nice arrived at his house. At thirteen he moved to Nice, an hour from his home. He was there for three years but did not get offered a professional contract – he was too thin. 'It was a hell of a knock-back,' he said.

It opened a door to Toulon though. Ginola flourished, and made his debut as a substitute against Metz. His full debut came when he was eighteen, against Bordeaux, then he played away to Nice and scored one and made one, from the right side of midfield. Ginola was on his way.

He signed for Matra Racing after impressing against them, moving from the sea of Toulon to the centre of Paris. 'For a southerner to move to the capital is something else,' he said in his autobigraphy. 'When I signed for Matra it was like changing country. I imagine it is the same for Geordies going to London.'

Ginola was twenty and barely missed a match in his first season, when he was doing his military service. In his second year the finance at Matra was pulled (they became Racing Paris). They still reached the final of the Coupe de France in 1990 (as huge underdogs), where they faced Montpellier, who had a forward called Eric Cantona. Ginola scored in extra-time, but Paris still lost, 2–1.

He moved again, to Brest, and became a full international, the first player from the club to do so. The call came from Michel Platini. 'My heart just went boom,' he said. Brest, however, were besieged by financial problems, and despite finishing sixth were relegated. The players were allowed to leave for nothing after a tribunal. David Ginola chose Paris St-Germain. He was called a traitor for turning down Marseille and the south.

'I may have been dubbed a Judas, but according to the fans the real enemy of Marseille is Eric Cantona,' said Ginola. 'He once threw his white shirt to the ground and trampled over it when he was substituted, which was seen as being utterly sacrilegious and unforgivable. The fans worship that shirt. You can kiss the shirt, you can clasp it like a flag or a trophy, but you can't do something like that with the shirt of Marseille. Anyone who did the same with the shirt of Newcastle would be construed as the ultimate traitor.'

He was there for three-and-a-half years. He won the French Cup twice, the league title once and the League Cup once. He was voted French player of the year in 1993 and Ligue 1 player of the year in 1994. He scored in both legs of a victorious UEFA Cup tie against Real Madrid in 1993.

Ginola, in the capital of France, became a huge star.

That he did so despite giving the ball away in a World Cup qualifier against Bulgaria in 1993 was no small achievement. The clock read 89:44 when Ginola fired over an inaccurate cross from the Bulgarian by-line. By the time the clock had ticked to 89:58, Emil Kostadinov had scored and France would not go to the 1994 finals in America. Didier Deschamps left the field in tears. Ginola slumped to his knees over an advertising hoarding.

Gerard Houllier was manager of the French team by then. 'David Ginola is a criminal,' he said. 'I repeat, he is a criminal.'

Ginola offered his own explanation in his autobiography:

> *This is what happened. Make up your own mind. There was a free-kick, someone passed me the ball out wide and I crossed the ball to Eric Cantona, who was unmarked in the 18-yard box.*

There was no one around him. There were nine players in our half. Bulgaria intercepted my cross and five passes later they had scored and France had lost the game. They said it was my fault.

Did this warrant the manager branding me a criminal? I am not a criminal. I have never stolen anything in my life. I have never killed anyone. I try to be honest. Everybody makes mistakes and people should be honourable enough to forgive them. Houllier's words caused national hysteria.

Ginola scored in his next game against Toulouse. 'If Houllier was there in front of me I think I would have wanted to smash him to bits,' he said. 'I have not spoken to him since and I never will.'

He was jeered at every ground in France. He went to see Michel Denisot, the PSG chairman, and told him he wanted to leave French football. Luis Fernandez took over as manager of PSG; the pair, who had played together at Matra Racing, did not get on. Arsenal made a move and it was rejected, but the clock was ticking.

In the summer of 1995, Ginola spoke to Inter, Real Madrid, Bayern Munich, Arsenal and Celtic, but it was Barcelona who led the chase. He spoke to them for six weeks. The transfer was delayed because the Catalans had six foreign players on their books and, because of restrictions, they could only play four. The Ginola transfer could not be completed until two of those had been sold.

Ginola was getting nervous when Newcastle made their move. In contrast, Newcastle moved with incredible speed. Three days after the agent Franklin Sedoc called Ginola's representatives to confirm Newcastle's plans, the deal was being finalised.

Terry McDermott was stood in a caravan park up the north-east coast when he spoke to Ginola. Keegan was in America. The line was poor.

'Some people we knew had a caravan,' says McDermott. 'The signal kept going. He was probably thinking, what the fuck?

'I talked to Ginola but not just about money; we can't do this or we can't do that. I can't remember the figures but I told him what a place it was and how he would love it. I said, "Will you be able to come over tomorrow?" He went, "Yeah, I'm coming tomorrow." The deal was done in no time.

'Kevin was back home the next day. We knew he was a great player and that he would be something special.'

'Terry was very impressive in selling Newcastle United to me,' said Ginola.

He painted a purely positive picture. He told me about their meteoric rise in the last five years. He stressed the possibilities for the club to evolve were excellent, given the amount of money the chairman, Sir John Hall, was pumping in. This would allow Newcastle to realise its potential as one of the best clubs in Europe.

What won me over was the positive way everyone from Newcastle spoke to me, and their unbreakable belief they would fulfil the club's ambitions. I chose Newcastle because they gave me the guarantees I was looking for at every level; financial, professional and personal. It was all fixed very quickly.

The verbal agreement meant Arsenal's eleventh-hour move, when David Dein finally caught up with Ginola, was too late.

'All the journalists at a press conference at St James' asked me what I'd come to Newcastle for,' he added. 'My reply? I've come to win the English championship.'

Nobody inside the Newcastle dressing room knew a great deal about the £2.5 million signing from PSG. Scott Sellars was a lovely footballer, all left foot, with great vision. His place on the left wing was immediately in doubt after the transfer.

'We didn't know much about David Ginola,' says John Beresford. 'Then we saw him in training for the first time. Scott, who was playing left-midfield at the time, turned around and went, "Shit, that's me screwed!"'

The Maiden Castle training facility that Keegan had moved Newcastle into was owned by Durham University. It meant Newcastle's players were not the only people using it.

'We were showering with lads from the university,' says Steve Watson. 'Ginola couldn't believe it. He said, 'Who are these fucking people?'

'There'd be some lads with towels the size of a flannel and Ginola would be there with ten different body sprays. He'd be going, "Who are they?" We'd say, "We don't own this place David. It's owned by them actually."

'The pitches were great and that's all the players cared about. We didn't know any better. We didn't want hydrotherapy pools. You wanted a dressing room that was warm, you wanted a really good pitch and you wanted a shower.

'Poor Scott, he watched David Ginola train and then he got undressed in the changing room for the first time and took his top off and he looked like Tarzan, and Scott went, "Fucking hell, that's all I need."'

By the time Newcastle faced Middlesbrough, Ginola had already scored his first goal in English football, at Sheffield Wednesday in a 2–0 victory, a strike that cemented Sellars' early concerns. It was a fine goal. He had caught people's attention.

Ginola sat in the visiting dressing room at Hillsborough in the glow of victory, pulled out a packet of cigarettes and lit one.

Ginola recalled what happened next in a TV interview for the Time of our Lives series for Sky Sports, in 2009.

> After the game I relax and I have a cool down, I was sitting in the bathroom, I lit a cigarette and started smoking. All the lads said, 'David what are you doing?'
>
> It was my first goal. It was a fantastic game. I just wanted to chill a little bit, the players shout, 'Gaffer!'
>
> Kevin came to see me and he said, 'Listen, I don't mind if you're having a cigarette if it can make you more relaxed but in England we have traditions and we don't smoke.'
>
> I said to Kevin, 'I don't know everything about this country so you have to teach me,' there was no shouting.
>
> Keegan was the guy who looked after that [the potential egos]. He didn't want any trouble. He would help keep the players in a good mood.
>
> I came to England for a different life. It was a challenging moment, as a player for Newcastle. Just to discover a different football, a different life, a different everything. I discover most of all the passion. Without passion you can't do anything. The main thing is the passion. It's a passion on the pitch and off the pitch. It was a delight, not the training ground though. I was quite surprised at the time.
>
> It was not a fantastic training ground but the atmosphere was just made by people, not by material things, it was people. For me it was very important. That's why we played so well on the pitch. We weren't concerned, we want to win together, the football we played, we were together.

As Ginola made use of the halted traffic to cross the road, it felt like a city was united.

'When I was in Paris it was not the same,' he said:

> We have fans, but not that much. The game at Sheffield, they didn't see me playing before that. The first game away, we came

back, we decided to have a drink in town straight after.

We went to the Quayside and I remember walking in the street. People were on their knees kissing my feet and I couldn't cope with that. No, I don't want that. 'Ginola, Ginola'. It was very emotional. Everybody was concerned about the results of the team, and the football club.

Everything was about watching or going to the game. After they would celebrate in town or they were crying and laughing together. It was all together. We were sharing the same emotions.

It would be a Wednesday evening, when the Match of the Day cameras rolled into Tyneside, that the nation would discover what Newcastle had already learned, that they had a player of unique talent. It was a night no one would forget, least of all Neil Cox, the Middlesbrough right-back, who was ill-equipped to stop the Frenchman's dancing feet.

It would be as torturous for Cox as it was mesmerising for the St James' Park crowd. Beresford saw Cox two weeks later at a sports shop. 'He was still untangling himself,' he says.

'I showed a few tricks on the edge of our own box, bamboozling their full-back Neil Cox, to get the ball out of defence and into attack,' said Ginola. 'It was analysed again and again on the television.'

Finally, in the 67th minute of a particularly one-sided game, Ginola jinked his way down the right side of Middlesbrough's defence once more. By now Nick Barmby had moved over to help his struggling team-mate. It made no difference, Ginola crossed deep and with bend and Les Ferdinand demolished Derek Whyte to head in his fourth goal in his fourth game in a Newcastle shirt.

A new song echoed around the streets of Tyneside later that night, to the tune of the Kinks' 'Lola':

'We've got the best team and we've got the best fans, and we've got the best player and he comes from France, Ginola, la la la, Ginola.'

DARREN PEACOCK – MISSION IMPOSSIBLE

NEWCASTLE HAD PLAYED SIX LEAGUE GAMES BY THE TIME CHELSEA arrived at St James' Park on a Sunday afternoon. They had conceded three goals in those six games; there had been three clean sheets. All of those goals had come in the second half. Only one had been of significance, that scored by Jim Magilton in the only defeat, at Southampton.

The defence was rarely letting in goals. Nobody mentioned it.

*

THE NOISE IN THE HOUSE AT THE END OF THE STREET IN WHITCHURCH, a small village in Somerset, was becoming familiar and maddening: an eighteen-year-old with a shattered leg in a cast up to his thigh jumping up and down the stairs to make sure the good leg did not go the same way. It was a terraced house. The noise was shared with equally unimpressed neighbours. Thankfully it was on the end of the row.

In the front room, parents Janet and Henry sought inspiration to bite their tongue. It was easily found. When Darren Peacock had his right leg shattered in a challenge with Carlisle's Mick McCarthy, and when it didn't set properly and his body rejected the bolts that were trying to keep it together, they were told something by his surgeon that their son was not. He would not play again.

They opined the news would be more shattering to their boy than the tackle. They said nothing. When Darren Peacock hopped relentlessly up and down stairs to keep even the most basic level of fitness in his battered body, his mum and dad counted down the days to when the conversation would come. It never did.

Darren Peacock was a swashbuckling centre-forward when he was on Bristol City's books as a schoolboy, until he was fourteeen. He was powerful and he scored goals. He went to Bristol Rovers and played against Chelsea and Tottenham. They said he wasn't good enough.

'That was when Tony Pulis offered me a trial at Newport,' says Peacock. 'He was a coach there. I played in a triallists' game. People don't believe this but I scored five goals in the trial.'

The only out-and-out defender Newcastle had in 1995 was originally a forward.

'My old man used to give me ten pence a goal,' he adds. 'I played for two teams at the weekend and I scored sixty-eight goals in one season, believe it or not. I was fourteen.

'Tony organised it and got me the trial. They put me in midfield. I was sixteen. It was the day I left school. I was in limbo for a couple of days. Like most people, there was no plan B whatsoever. There was so much on it.

'My parents drove me back home to Bristol. A guy call Bob Smith was manager of Newport with Colin Addison. I got a letter in the post and I was in. From July I was off to digs in Newport. I was offered a two-year apprenticeship on sixteen pounds a week with my digs paid for. It was a great letter. That was it. I left home at sixteen, it was 1985. It was most probably the best thing that ever happened to me.

'I played in midfield at Newport with a guy called George Woods, who moved me back to centre-half within about eight weeks. He didn't give me a reason, he just said, "You're not a midfielder." I never asked the question why, I wasn't very talkative back then. I just took it. I was just happy to be playing football. Come the October I was playing in the first team at centre-half.'

In the space of six months Peacock had gone from being a centre-forward at Bristol Rovers youth level, to being released, to going to Newport on trial, to scoring five goals in midfield, to getting a deal with Newport at youth level, to being moved back to centre-half, to making the first XI of a Football League team.

Then came a tackle that took three-quarters of an inch off the length of his leg and very nearly took his dream.

'I went home and I put loads of weight on through my mam's cooking,' he adds. 'My leg was in a cast up to my hip. I was in it for thirteen weeks. The first six weeks I came out and it didn't set.

'Then I had pins in place and my body rejected it. Then I had a bone graft from my hip. That made it stronger than it was before, apparently. Then came rehab. When you're at home you're doing nothing, kicking around, doing a thousand leg chops a day, like.

'I was jumping up the stairs on my left leg with my pot on, bored out of me head. Bouncing up and down, again and again. The next-door neighbours must have been going potty. I didn't know what the doctors told my mam and dad. I never knew.

'By the time I came back I had problems with my back because my leg was shorter. I had a special thing made on my boot to raise it up. Adidas did it for me. When I got the rehab at Lilleshall [the National Recreation Centre], they knew all the people. They did it for me. It was brilliant but it caused all kinds of problems to my back, my back was out. It was eighteen months of hell.

'I spent six weeks in Lilleshall and that was good, there was competition. You worked harder with people around you. I used to go up there in an old white Ford Capri. You'd park up on the Monday and go home on the Friday. This one time it wouldn't start and there was rugby players there. Thing was, I was pointing uphill. Shaun Edwards and a few of them pushed me up a hill to bump-start it. That sticks out in my mind.'

Uphill jump-starts were becoming a theme. In February 1989, within months of his return, Newport folded. Bob Smith, who by then had moved to Hereford with Colin Addison, signed him. He was back in Division Four.

'Hereford was great, brilliant,' he says. 'I was there for sixteen months. I was centre-half and played a few games up front. They were good times. We had a good side there.

'I appreciated it more because of what I'd been through. I had a bit more independence. I was driving so I wasn't relying on my parents to take me everywhere. They were a really good bunch. Just getting back working in that sort of atmosphere, it was great to be back. I'd been jumping up and down stairs, remember.'

He started leaping them. A move to Nottingham Forest was mentioned in the papers. Then from nowhere in 1990 came Queens Park Rangers.

He adds: 'I was in the manager's office and Colin Addison said, "QPR have come in for you." Bobby Gould was working with Don Howe there. Bobby was briefly at Bristol Rovers. He had this black book of good lower-league players. At the same time he brought Rufus Brevett in from Doncaster.

'What was my first reaction when I was told QPR were in for me? Go. Go. My mum and dad were chuffed, more so my mum. They said, "You deserve this, you've worked so hard." You don't realise how much they do, driving you everywhere when you're young. My brother ferried me around as well on the back of his motorbike when my old man wasn't around.

'Bobby lived in Bristol as well so I got myself back to Bristol and the next day he picked me up to take me to London. By Bristol City's ground there was a bus station. My old man dropped me there with one bag, a collar and no tie. I just had a shirt on.

'I got in the car with my future assistant manager, I was always on my best behaviour. That time I was especially very respectful. I answered his questions. I just nodded my head at the right time. We got up to QPR and the PFA had a representative for me.

'There was me, the PFA and Bobby, and he was sat in his chair and he put us on a lower sofa and he told us the offer. The PFA said, "That's a bit disappointing." I said to Bobby, "I want to think about it." He wasn't very pleased with that.

'I got on the phone to Colin Addison. He said, "Come back here if you want, we're playing Scunthorpe in a couple of weeks. Who have you got? Liverpool. Don't be an arsehole, son."

'That put me in my place. The next day I went in and signed. As soon as I signed Bobby went nuts with me for not wearing a tie. He said, "If you ever dress like that again I'll come down on you like a ton of bricks." I liked Bobby. The fee was £270,000. You're so young you just don't think about it. You just want to play football, don't you?

'I was a bit nervous. Players like Ray Wilkins and Kenny Sansom were there and then Les [Ferdinand] came back for a bit. Again, it was great times. It seemed like from coming back playing after breaking my leg I was always going up a level every fifteen months.

'The facilities were different. The football was getting higher. How you got treated as a player, plus the financial situation. The professionalism and everything that goes with it. It was great. At Newport we were scratching around for somewhere to train. We finished fifth at QPR and we were the top club in London.'

Peacock played against Newcastle at St James' Park and QPR won. He man-marked Andy Cole. 'Wherever Coley went, I followed him,' he adds. 'Gerry Francis [the QPR manager] would put me on the goalscorer and that was my job. I followed him everywhere.'

Cole did not appreciate the attention. He told Keegan Peacock was a handful, and Peacock got wind Newcastle were interested. QPR had gone back on a contract agreement to start negotiations on a new deal.

The timing was right. It was 1994. Peacock did not speak to anyone from Newcastle but those close to him were made aware that the interest was genuine. He was told a transfer request would open the door. 'What was my first reaction?' he says. 'I put a transfer request in straight away! I got a call from the gaffer and I didn't believe it was him, obviously.

'He goes, "Hi, Darren, I'm interested in bringing you up." I think I said, "I'll call you back," just so I could check it was him. How long did I wait? About a minute, it was as long as I could manage. It was Kevin Keegan. It was all sorted very quick and I got a flight up the next day.

'Did he sell the club to me? He didn't have to. Newcastle were playing Ipswich. The gaffer came to see us after the game, I think Newcastle won two-nil. He didn't have to sell it at all. He breezed in, he was so enthusiastic after the win. He had done his pitch. Whatever he had said I would have signed.

'That was it, deal done. I think I signed the next day. Then we went to the ground and the press conference.

'I had never been to Newcastle before in any other capacity except as a footballer. To be fair to the gaffer, he did really well because he would get players to meet you, like Andy Cole and Peter Beardsley. It was a fantastic idea. He introduced me to the press, a few questions and it was great the players were there. It was brilliant. It was like joining a family. He did it with everyone.'

Peacock did not open his wings. The £2.7 million transfer fee, a club record, weighed heavy.

'It didn't take off for me,' he adds. 'I had a poor start, to be honest. The price always got brought up and it was just a big change for me. I don't think I was ready for it.

'There was one time quite early in my Newcastle career on a night out a couple of supporters went up to Barry Venison and started talking about me, "He's shit," and all that, "He's not worth £2.7 million." I went up to them and said, "Come and say that to me." It got a bit heated. I got used to it. I wasn't one of the stars, like Pedro [Beardsley] or Ginola. Coming from where I'd been seven years prior, playing for one of the biggest clubs in England, you take everything.

'We would get four or five thousand in training and because I had a bad start you would get stick from the supporters in training as well as the games. It was a bit of a shock.'

It took time for Peacock to settle but the second season was significantly better. By then he was getting used to the huge change in training sessions.

'We would spend hours at QPR, day after day, on defending, every player,' he says. 'We would do it live on the pitch in the pouring rain. We would spend hours on it, doing set-pieces. I went to Newcastle and it was five-a-side. It would be so quick.

'Get warmed up, all with the football, games and competitive games, three or four against each other, then up to five-on-five for forty-five minutes and then a bit of shooting and then all the while the gaffer and Terry Mac would be involved. It was great. Without doubt it improved me as a player.

'As a defender it worried me. I asked if we could do a bit of defending and we did it once. We did it once before we played Southampton and we lost and we didn't do it again. I think it was '95.'

Yet within that lay a fierce ambition. Those four new players arriving – Ferdinand, Barton, Ginola and Hislop – told the dressing room that this was the time.

'It seemed like every couple of weeks the record was being broken,' adds Peacock. 'The gaffer had a vision of what he wanted to play. Not just players, it was just building momentum all the time. It was relentless. Every single week it got cranked up another notch. That excited the players and it excited the supporters as well.

'You could feel it on the terraces and in training when there are four thousand there, and hot-dog stands, and ice-cream vans and people selling shirts. It was great.

'At the time you wanted to walk through the fans signing autographs. At that point I can't imagine it happening anywhere, even Man United. That reaction to it, the players coming in, the fever that was throughout Newcastle, you couldn't really see it ending.

'Some of the football we played in training was even better than in games. There was no pressure. Things click in. It was so quick and so accurate. It was breathtaking.

'Those first six games we had fifty per cent clean sheets. Our strategy was to batter teams for thirty minutes; take the game to them and take them out of the game. Teams would surrender. They couldn't come back from a two-goal lead in the first half-hour.'

In September 1995 Newcastle played Bristol City at Ashton Gate in the League Cup. Peacock was made captain. He scored with a glancing header. 'It felt brilliant, brilliant,' he says. 'It wasn't in my mind at all that they didn't take me back when I was sixteen!' Newcastle won 5–0. The fifth goal was one-touch excellence.

And then came Chelsea. Chelsea had Mark Hughes, Dennis Wise and Ruud Gullit. It didn't matter. Newcastle were on a different plane. Ferdinand was once more unplayable, scoring in each half. He had scored eight goals in the eight games since his move to Tyneside. 'We were in control that day,' Peacock adds. 'We weren't troubled at the back and they had Hughes and Mark Stein up front.

'What stands out for me was that "Toon, Toon" song going on for twenty minutes. Just relentless. It was like a wall. No break. Twenty, twenty-five minutes of "Toon, Toon, black and white army". Non-stop. Things like that stand out.'

Newcastle went back to the top of the Premiership, ahead of Manchester United, who had conceded eight goals. Newcastle had conceded three times in seven league games.

Still, nobody mentioned the defence.

31 MARCH 1982

MARTIN HARDY – FOOLS GOLD

'CAN I GO TO THE MATCH?'

'No.'

'Why not?'

'Because you can't. You've got school in the morning.'

'What if he scores a goal? Can he go then?' (This from a helpful team-mate.)

'Go on, take me to the match if I score.'

'I'll see.'

'Please.'

'OK, OK. You can go if you score a goal.'

We played Christ Church on Preston playing field and I scored twice.

Newcastle played Crystal Palace. It was a Wednesday night. Two Newcastle fans tried to fight each other on the Metro. I raced up the steps, round the corner into the West Stand paddock when we got in the ground. The benches looked freshly painted against the brightness of the floodlights. It was a night game. You never forget night games. The grass seemed greener. It was so vivid. Anything seemed possible.

The game finished 0–0.

Newcastle's forwards didn't have as much to play for as me.

WARREN BARTON – ON TOP OF THE WORLD

KEVIN KEEGAN LOOKED DOWN THE WIMBLEDON TEAM-SHEET. 'I'VE got the one I wanted,' he said. Then he crumpled the team-sheet up into a ball and threw it on the floor. 'Just go out and beat them.'

*

WARREN BARTON WAS SIXTEEN WHEN FRANK CLARK CALLED HIM into his office at Brisbane Road. The Orient manager had played 457 games for Newcastle between 1962 and 1975, the third highest total for a player in its history. He helped Newcastle lift the Inter-Cities Fairs Cup in 1969, played in an FA Cup final and a League Cup final (both were lost) and in 1975 was handed a free transfer.

Brian Clough took Clark to Nottingham Forest, where he won the league and the European Cup.

In 1982 Clark became the manager of Orient. Three years later he took Barton to one side and said to him, 'You're too small, son. You won't make it.'

Barton was released, as he had been by Arsenal and Watford for the same reason. 'I was devastated,' he says.

He signed for non-league Dagenham and Redbridge. Aged just sixteen, Barton walked into his first dressing room full of men.

'There was a policeman, a builder and a plumber,' he says. 'The builder went, "If you don't help us win this game, and we lose our £25 bonus, you'll get your head knocked off." That was a wake-up call.'

By then, Barton had a job himself, working in the mail room at Arthur Andersen.

'I used to go across London on a moped,' he adds. 'I used to take all the mail up to the secretaries and the bosses. I had to make sure the signatures were OK. It was a real change from being a professional footballer. That was my job. It was nine to five in a suit, going to work on a moped or jumping on the underground tubes.

'I was going to work, going home on the moped and then going to training at seven o'clock in east London – and that was three days a week – for Dagenham and Redbridge. If I had to get off work early I would ask my boss. I'd do a day's work and then go and play, just like everyone at Blyth Spartans or any other non-league club. That was the real world.

'I was at Orient and then two of us got released as apprentices. We knew someone at Dagenham and Redbridge so we went down and trained.

'Dave Andrews was the owner. He got us a trial. I went there as a skinny little blond kid and suddenly you had these men telling you what to do and that you had to do it. You have to grow up. You don't have a choice.

'Then I went to Maidstone and John Still was there at the time. When we got promoted [to the Football League] he didn't want to go full-time, he wanted to stay part-time. They had three players who had really good jobs who didn't want to go to a league club.

'I wanted to take that chance. I wanted to be a professional footballer. I was earning more money working and playing non-league but I wanted to be a player. I sacrificed that.'

Then came the call from Bobby Gould at Wimbledon in 1990.

Wimbledon and Gould paid Maidstone £300,000. It was a record for a player from the Fourth Division.

'It was a bit daunting meeting Vinnie [Jones] and Fash [John Fashanu]. I think because of my background, because I had worked and the effort I had shown to get there, they welcomed me in.

'I hit the ground running. I was [Wimbledon's] player of the season and I got in the England set-up as well. It went really well for me. That's where I went from being a youngster to being a man. I went from being a boy to a young man at Dagenham and Redbridge and then straight up to Wimbledon and coming off the back of an FA Cup final win, it was made aware I knew what was expected.

'There was all sorts went on there. When I got picked for England, Sam Hammam, the owner, slashed all the tyres on my Saab car.

'We had [Elizabeth] Emanuel, the designer for Lady Diana's dress, come down before we played Manchester United. I got in there and I knew something was up. Fash called a meeting just outside the room where we used to get changed.

'All the press were there and the players grabbed me and stripped me naked. I had to walk past Emanuel with a police cone over my privates. Typical Wimbledon, I said, "Good morning," shook her hand and walked into the changing room.'

His form when in a strip, rather than being stripped, was catching the eye.

Kevin Keegan was not the only Premier League manager whose attention had been grabbed by Barton's form. Arsenal were also keen. Keegan, John Hall and Douglas Hall met Barton and his agent in a London hotel.

'I sat down and the first thing Kevin said was, "Come and join a big club,"' he explains.

'I was on a sofa with my agent. Within minutes, you couldn't help but want to go and play for him.

'It was a tough call because Arsenal were my team. I'd supported Arsenal, but once you met Kevin, particularly at that time, you were taken away by how buoyant and enthusiastic he was. He was telling me about Shaka, and Les and David. He told me what he was trying to do and I'd obviously played with Rob Lee at England.

'It was an easy decision to make in the end. It was just that: "Come and join a big club."

'I said, "Yeah, that's where I want to be." They agreed the fee. Arsenal were still waiting. Sam Hammam was a very good businessman. He said, "This is what I want." Kevin being Kevin and Sir John and Douglas, who were there as well, with their ambition, just went, "Yeah, we'll pay it."

'If they wanted something, they went out and got it.

'The wages and what have you were easy, you were going there because you wanted to win something. It was the place to be.'

Four months after his £4 million transfer, a then Premiership record for a defender, the texts started arriving. 'We're going to break your leg', 'We'll do you', 'Watch your back'.

On 21 October 1995, Newcastle played Wimbledon at home.

'Kevin just stood there in the dressing room,' says Barton. 'He would put the opposition team-sheet on the board. He went through it and said, "I've got the one I wanted. Just go out and beat them."

'He knew it was an important game for me. I had a lot of people there. I had respect for all the staff and players from Wimbledon. Kevin being Kevin, he just crumpled the team-sheet up and said to me, "There was only one player who I wanted from them, and I've got him. Go and do it." Of course it made you feel special.'

Barton still had friends to face.

'Sam came up and punched me,' he adds. 'It was like seeing old mates, my family were there, Robbie Earle was best man at my wedding. I'm godparent to his kids. We spent a lot of time together so we were as close as brothers.

'The whole game was special. Les patted me on the back and gave me a little punch in the kidneys. I just remember walking out and I looked across as I did. That was me a year ago and now I'm here wearing black and white.

'I looked at Robbie and he said, "Do you remember last year when we were stood in the centre circle here doing our stretches after the game saying what it would be like to play for Newcastle? You're here now."

'I admit I had a little bit of apprehension. It was against my mates. We got off to a good start. I think we did that to a lot of teams, Les getting goals.'

Wimbledon had been a long-term nuisance to Newcastle United. There had been a late League Cup victory for the Dons at Plough Lane in 1987, there had been the squeezing of Paul Gascoigne's privates by Vinnie Jones on 6 February 1988 and then an FA Cup tie two weeks later at St James' Park. Gascoigne was nullified, Newcastle lost, and Mirandinha, the first Brazilian to play in England, was so annoyed he did a karate kick into Dave Beasant when the game had finished and ran along the side of the pitch to escape.

In the north-east, they did not share the romantic notion of brave Wimbledon.

On 21 October, Newcastle finally put Wimbledon to their sword. It was a destruction. The visitors held out for half an hour. Then the rout started, when Steve Howey looped a Keith Gillespie cross past keeper Paul Heald.

The second came four minutes later, Ginola beating three men by a corner flag at the Leazes End before crossing to Ferdinand, who smashed his header into the bottom corner. It was the seventh straight game he had scored in. Ferdinand was within one game of equalling Newcastle's record. Five minutes later a cross came from the other wing, from Gillespie, and this time Ferdinand looped a second header into the visitors' goal.

Early in the second half, Ferdinand went charging down the right, touched the ball past Heald and was then flattened by the Wimbledon goalkeeper, who had already been booked for time-wasting. Heald was dismissed and Jones went in goal.

On the hour Lee Clark cracked a left-footed shot into the top corner. Marcus Gayle's header was brief respite. Moments later another Gillespie cross was headed to Ferdinand by Robert Lee and his hat-trick was complete. The sixth came with six minutes left and was everything Newcastle were about. Philippe Albert, the central defender, picked the ball up midway inside the Wimbledon half, did a one-two with Scott Sellars and curled a shot with the outside of his left foot past Jones.

It could not have gone much better for Barton.

'We were just on a high,' he remembers. 'The football, with Vinnie going in and Philippe chipping it in. Vinnie was helpless, he let it go wide and it floated in.

'At that time no one could live with us. No one could play against us. We were such a good team, everything was going for us. Everything was easy. Nash [Lee Clark] was going box to box, and Les was doing his bit. It had a special feeling. We thought we were never going to get beat.'

Two teams' worth of Warren Barton's family sat in a Tyneside restaurant that night.

'It was a goldfish bowl at Newcastle,' he says. 'It can suffocate you, or you can embrace it, and we embraced it. I remember after the game twenty-two members of my family had come up to watch, my mum, my dad, my brother, everyone was there in a restaurant and you had couples banging on the restaurant window given you the thumbs-up, coming over and shaking my brother's hand.

'My family, being from east London, just embraced it. They loved coming up, getting on the train with all the fans. They still support Newcastle now.

'I remember going to the MetroCentre with my wife. Everywhere was black and white. You had the kids wearing the black and white, the wives wearing it and the grandparents wearing something with Newcastle on. It made you realise what you were playing for.

'The shops were black and white, even if they were a women's clothes shop. There were black and white balloons and cakes in food shops and it wasn't even a cup final. Everything had a football theme to it. Obviously, with making the stadium bigger, we knew it was a special time.

'There was such a rapport with the fans, they appreciated what we were doing. The city was building. Apartments were going up everywhere on the Quayside. The nightlife was unbelievable. It was in the top ten in the world. There was a real good vibe about what was going on.

'We were going to win having fun. It wasn't work. You had fun in training. Kevin and Terry would be sat on the top of the hamburger stall and they'd be having a cup of coffee watching us train.

'It was easy. We had the link-up with the brewery. We'd lunch with the fans, there was a real togetherness. You knew something was happening that will never happen again.'

KEITH GILLESPIE – PRETTY GREEN

'WE WERE TRAVELLING BACK ON THE COACH AFTER A ONE-ONE draw at Spurs and Ginola had scored, and Kevin was talking to Peter Beardsley and he pointed at me and said, "He could be the best player in the country at this time,"' says Keith Gillespie.

'I'd just lost forty-seven grand in one day, because my spare time was always took up with gambling. It never affected me, the gambling. I remember on the Friday, after I lost the £47,000, I was out training – that was me getting away from gambling.

'It didn't have any effect on me. Obviously two days prior to when I lost the money was the Stoke game, when I had the £500 double on Peter Beardsley first goal to score and two-nil, two-one and three-nil and three-one.

'We were three-nil and up you're thinking, I'm going to win over fifty grand here. It wasn't really talked about whether you could bet or not. To me, you're not betting on your team to lose, you'd never do that.

'To be a player and I'm playing in the game, and we're winning three-nil, and I'm near enough counting the money, with six minutes to go. Then Darren pops up. I wouldn't have minded if it was Les or someone, but Darren Peacock!

'Gambling was something I got into. Some people enjoy the gambling, some just do it. It was a buzz for me. Gambling was part of my life. Obviously, you have a lot of money at your disposal and you knew you had a good wage coming next week as well.

'It was easy to get involved in, especially when I moved up here and I was living in the Gosforth Park Hotel for five months. I was going home to an empty hotel room every day. Other players were going home to their family, their wives, their kids. I'm going home to nothing. It was easy to get into.

'Terry sort of heard a few whispers. I denied it and said, "Nah, nah." If I had said it then, things might have been different, but it was hindsight.

'The club was brilliant with me. Kevin was brilliant, he really was. They sorted everything out for me. Kevin was very supportive. It was February before it all came out. It was snowing at that time. I had a day off and there was a report. It must have been a photographer there because he got me when I had just got out of bed with my hair all over the place!'

Only two good things came from a wild night in Stoke, where cars were overturned and a town wanted to fight anyone from Newcastle; the visitors won 4–0 and were outstanding, and Les Ferdinand scored for the eighth consecutive game, equalling the club's all-time record.

24 MARCH 1983

JOAN BRADSHAW –
WAKE UP, LITTLE SUSIE

LUDVIC WAS A CARTOON CAT, AND IT WAS A CAT THAT REPRESENTED something huge, and Joan Bradshaw was intent on making two of them; two stuffed cuddly toys to help with the heartache her family had endured in 1981.

Joan and her husband John's daughter Susan was a baby when they spoke to a doctor who would change their lives forever; when they were told their child had a rare liver disease.

'It was very painful,' says Joan. 'When she was first diagnosed I wanted to look behind to see who they were talking to because you don't believe these things happen to you.

'We coped with it because after you're told, you hoped and you just kind of don't really believe it. It's amazing where you get your strength from.

'As long as she was there and I could get up and look after her every day everything was fine and she progressed very slowly up to twelve months and then she started to deteriorate.

'I still kind of hoped that something wonderful would happen. Liver transplants hadn't come along but there was talk of them in the press and I wrote to the professor who was doing liver transplants and asked what the possibility was and he said it was early days and it was very unlikely. People didn't accept the thoughts of babies giving livers.

'You've always got hope. All these hopes you have don't work but you keep on trying. Nobody cured her but everybody gave a little bit of something.'

Susan Bradshaw was twenty-two months old when she died.

It was a life not lived. For Joan and John Bradshaw it was twenty-two months of love and anguish and gut-wrenching pain, and brief joys that can still cushion some of the crushing sadness of the time.

By the following year, 1982, Joan Bradshaw had become heavily involved in the Liver Disease in Children charity.

'You have this huge void in your life and that's what fills the void, doing something for other children who are the same,' she adds. 'I did it for ten years and we raised £100,000 in that time.

'I met some amazingly nice people and we raised most of the money in the poorest parts of the north-east.'

The Great North Run became a massive event. One year 200 people ran the race for the charity.

In 1983, a letter was sent to Newcastle United. John Cunningham called Joan. He was Kevin Keegan's friend. Keegan was prepared to come and do a talk-in as long as there was no publicity and it wasn't in a pub.

On 24 March, the hall of Harton Comprehensive School bristled with expectant men, women and children.

In the headmaster's office, a thirty-second walk from the hall, a photographer from the Shields Gazette aimed his camera at six wide-eyed children, the former captain of England and a cheque for £400 for children with diseased livers.

Five minutes later the hall stood as one and cheered as Keegan entered. He told stories, answered questions, played football and signed the autographs and posed for the pictures that everyone in the room wanted.

'The people there were enthralled by him,' adds Joan. 'He started the chat show and he was fantastic. Afterwards he played with the kids and he had loads of photographs taken, he stayed for as long as people wanted him to.

'He wowed the audience. To be in a school with Kevin Keegan on the stage and Kevin coming off the stage and having photographs taken with all your kids, yeah, he wowed everybody.

'We made him tea in the staffroom afterwards. There was probably John and me and a few others. He asked about the charity and he talked about his horses.

'At the time the charity had a cat called Ludvic - I get a bit upset but don't worry Martin, I don't mind, I want to tell you this - which had a question mark for its tail, and it had the letters of LDC in its name, and I made him two of them for his little girls.

'He was really touched by it. I don't get upset about it often now, but when I think about that, and people like him, he was so sincere and he was really, really moved. I made them for him and he was just lovely. He was a lovely man.

'I don't talk a lot about Susan nowadays. I probably get more upset now than I used to because you get soft as you get older.

'He was quite emotional when I gave them to him for his little girls.

'He asked for no publicity and he didn't get very much publicity. You find with some famous people they take a lot of publicity out of it and give nothing back. Kevin Keegan was the exact opposite.

'He did it to raise money for our charity and he didn't expect anything back from it. I think he chose us because it was local and a child and it was a sad story.

'He was probably there until after half-ten. He gave John a handshake and me a hug and then he was off. We just felt really warm, you just thought, "What a lovely night it's been."

'He was a man of the people, he really was.'

ROB LEE – THE HEAD TENNIS RITUAL

'GET YOURSELF A PARTNER.' THOSE WERE THE FIRST WORDS KEVIN Keegan said to Rob Lee on his first day at training as a Newcastle player. 'You're playing against me and Terry Mac.'

Rob Lee had never played head tennis in his life.

'I teamed up with Franz Carr,' says Lee. 'He was the player I was replacing in the team. We got battered. Kevin and Terry Mac would do this thing where they'd cover their mouth with one hand in mock embarrassment if you were no good. They did it a lot that day.

'They were brilliant at it and they were piss-takers. It was my first day, Kevin was going, "Terry, how much did we pay for him? He can't even play head tennis." I was getting absolutely hammered.

'This was the first time I'd played head tennis. I didn't play it at Charlton. It was a badminton court with a badminton net and a football, and you were allowed one touch with any part of your body and you had to get it back over the net. They were so good, they must have been playing it for twenty bleeding years.

'Every day I went I was trying to find a new partner, until I found Bez [John Beresford] and then we started playing head tennis properly. It wasn't until I met Bez – and it still took us months – but we started beating them.

'Keegan was getting really pissed off with the fact we used to beat them, Bez did his ankle and Kevin went, "You can't play head tennis any more."

'Honestly, training didn't used to start until half-ten, I used to be in at nine o'clock. You'd want to get in there first and get on the court, winners stay on. All the players would be queuing up in their twos, it was brilliant, and that was before training started. That would go on for over an hour. Kevin would eventually go, "I've got to go in the office, I've got to make some phone calls!"'

The first time Lee had spoken to Kevin Keegan during a call, he was sat on his couch with his wife, Anna. 'I put the phone to my chest and I started giggling. I mimed to her, slowly, "It's Kevin Keegan!" She was like, "Wow!" We were both trying not to laugh.'

Rob Lee's granddad had taken him to buy his first pair of boots at the Bobby Moore Sports Shop when he was a child, opposite Upton Park. Rob Lee was London.

The first time his friends came to watch him play at St James' Park, they were taken aback.

'My mates went, "We were in a pub and these guys came over to us and spoke to us,"' he says.

'I said, "What did they say?" They went, "Well, they were talking about football and stuff and about our accents. They were really friendly, like."

'My mates couldn't believe it, they were, like, woah! They said to me, "We thought we were going to get beat up."

'No one knew they were my friends. That's what I noticed when I walked down the street in the north-east, people talk to you, it's not like that in London. That's what I found was the difference, they're just a friendlier bunch of people in the north.'

First Lee had to get there.

*

HE PLAYED FOOTBALL AS A KID UNTIL IT WENT DARK ON THE PARK opposite his home in Rainham , after his family moved from Plaistow in east London. When it went dark they moved under street-lights. He played for a team called Pegasus.

'I went to Tottenham and [youth coach] Robbie Stepney said I wasn't good enough. I've never seen him since. It was devastating. I said, "I'm not going to do this any more.' I was fifteen. I hadn't been there long. I played one game.

'It's devastating for someone to hear that. I thought, I'm not enjoying this. I went back and played with my mates. A friend of mine called Ray Underhill ran Pegasus and all my mates played from school. I went and played with them.

'It happened that Ray was friends with Martin Robinson, who played for Charlton. He came over and watched a game and a massive fight broke out. He must have seen something and then Les Gore, the chief scout at Charlton, came to watch me and Les liked what he saw. I started playing for their youth team.

'My dad was working in America so it was Ray who used to drive me to all the Charlton games. He used to work on the papers, he was a printer, he finished at five a.m. and he had two hours' sleep and then he would drive me to all these Charlton games.

'Then I was playing for my future father-in-law's team in the afternoon. I couldn't let him down either. It was Park Heath. Anna's brother, who was four years older at twenty-one, played, they were big guys, I would come in at half-time and I was battered. I was quicker and stronger than them, and then I played for Pegasus on a Sunday morning. I loved it.

'I was centre-forward in those games. I played a few games for Charlton's youth team and Les called me and said, "Do you want to be a footballer?" I went, "Yeah!"

'He said, "We want to sign you for a year." They offered me one hundred pounds a week and I was on a hundred and ten at work. I just thought: Give it a go.'

'Work' was in the office at the shipping company that employed his dad, for eight months. 'I was doing clerical work, making cups of tea, things like that and I hated it. I absolutely hated it. I despised it. It was awful.'

He was sixteen then and seventeen when he started a quick jump from reserves to first team at Charlton (having worked three games on the turnstiles at the Valley because of his dad's close affiliation with the club). He scored four goals in ten games and was offered a three-year deal.

The last time Kevin Keegan ever played in the capital was on 7 April 1984, at the Valley. Rob Lee, then eighteen, played against him.

'I was like, fucking hell, Jesus Christ, it's Kevin Keegan,' he adds.

'I was a West Ham supporter but I liked Liverpool because he'd played for them. It's a bit embarrassing really. I had pictures of Kevin on my wall.'

Eight years and fifty-nine goals later, Lee turned down his old Charlton manager Lennie Lawrence and the chance to go to Middlesbrough, who were then in the Premiership.

'I was waiting for West Ham to come in for me,' he says. 'I admired Lennie and he helped me throughout my career but Middlesbrough didn't feel right then. I went to meet him. They were in the Premiership and he was going to play me behind the front man, I just didn't feel it was the right thing for me to do.

'I came back after meeting him and went to Curbs [manager Alan Curbishley], "I'm going to wait for West Ham." They had only offered £500,000. Billy Bonds said to me, "The chairman wouldn't give me the money to get you."

'I waited as long as I could and then Curbs said, "Keegan has come in for you."

'I said, "Seriously, I'm not going to go, I'm not moving north. I didn't sign for Middlesbrough, I'll wait."

'Curbs said, "He wants to speak to you. He said Terry Mac's going to ring you in five minutes."

'Terry rang. I had pictures of Terry on the wall as well. He went, "Rob Lee? Kevin wants to speak to you." I said, "Terry, I admired you as a player, I admired Kevin as a player tremendously but I've decided I'm not going north." Terry went, "He just wants to speak to you. He'll ring you in five minutes."

'I said, "I'm genuinely not interested, really." I was sitting next to my wife and I'm playing it cool, and then Kevin rang up. I remember picking up the phone, and this voice goes, "Hi, Rob Lee? It's Kevin Keegan."

'I put my phone against my shoulder, I had a big grin on my face and I whispered to her, "It's Kevin Keegan!" I was like a kid. It was back to my school days. She knew who he was. She knew a little bit about football.

'He said, "I want you to play for me at Newcastle."

'It was Thursday and he said, "Look, I know your reservations, you're a London boy, but I really want you to play for us. You're the player I really want."

'I was honest, I said, "I'm not keen on the north."

'He said, "We've got a game on Saturday, Bristol City at home, I'll ring you at six o'clock on Sunday. Have a think about it but I really want you to come up."

'I said, "Right, OK, thanks."

'I watched the score coming through and they beat Bristol City five-nil and Franz Carr scored. I thought, no way is he ringing back, no way, he's not ringing. He rang at six on the dot. He said it again, "Just come and speak to me."

'"I'm not really . . ."

'"I've booked you on a flight."

'"Well, OK . . ."

'I went, OK, I've got to get on this flight. Derek Wright [the Newcastle physio] met me at the airport, he took me to the steps at St James' Park, Kevin came down and said hello to my wife and she went off.

'As I went up the steps he said, "I've booked a press conference for an hour." I was like, "What?" He said, "I can cancel it."

'We had a cup of tea with the secretary and I was with him in the ground for half an hour. I came out and met my wife and I said, "I've just signed for three-and-a-half years." She went, "Oh my God!"

'He just had this way.

'We had the negotiations and he said, "I'll pay you exactly what Middlesbrough were going to pay you, not a penny more."

'I said, "Fine, no problem, I'm not bothered." I actually went for less in the end! It was ridiculous.

'I remember I was owed five grand from Charlton for a loyalty bonus. Roger Alwen, the chairman, had said, "You can't have the loyalty bonus." Kevin asked me if everything was OK. I said, "I'm happy but I'm a bit pissed off with Charlton, I've been there eight years and they owe me five grand."

He said, "What's that for?" and I told him. He said, "Get Roger Alwen on the phone."

'Roger must have done exactly the same as me when Kevin phoned him. "It's Kevin Keegan!"

'He went, "Roger, I think you should give Rob that five thousand pounds, he's been at the club for eight years and he's been a great servant." Roger Alwen went, "Yeah, OK."

'He agreed to it straight away. Kevin was unbelievable. Roger will have been in awe of him like I was. He said, "Right, done."

'I never went to see Kevin about a contract again. After a year he said, "I want you to sign again." After another year, "I want you to sign again."

'I never went to see him and said, "I want a new contract." It was great, he rewarded you. I don't ever remember negotiating with him either. "Here it is." I just trusted him.'

That was understandable.

Lee assumed he would be meeting a member of staff at the club when he came up with his wife and eighteen-month-old son to go house-hunting for the first time.

'Kevin said, "We'll show you around the area," and I thought he would get someone from the club to do it. Kevin picked us up and went, "Put the car seat in the back," and drove us around Ponteland and Darras Hall, around all these places.

'It must have been three hours. It was surreal. I had Oliver strapped in his seat, I had my wife sat next to him in the back, I was sat in the passenger seat, and Kevin Keegan was driving us round eating midget gems, showing me the north-east.'

*

LEE'S FAMILY ARRIVED IN PETERBOROUGH ON 26 SEPTEMBER 1992 TO watch Lee play. They did not expect Tyneside to be waiting for them.

There is an eye to the past that Lee did not get told about by his mam, Joan, until he signed for Newcastle and was heading north. Her mother was called Mary

Jane Davey and she had been a Geordie.

Her husband, the granddad he had never known, had gone to London on the Jarrow March in 1936. When Lee flourished, his mum bought 35 T-shirts from the Newcastle fanzine, The Mag, that had her son's picture on the front and 'Bobby Lee for England' on the back. No one in the family ever wore them.

First there was Peterborough, when somewhere in the region of 8,000 Newcastle supporters turned London Road into a home game. It was Lee's first away game as a Newcastle player. He was astounded.

'On the coach going there, it was just a sea of black and white,' he says. 'I turned to Bez, and I went, "Are we at home here?" It was amazing.

'It was lunacy. It was everywhere. We were on a great run, I just thought, wow. It's strange what you're not used to. Because you're new, they're singing players' names. They're not singing your name because they don't know who you are and they don't know how well you'll do.

'That day the Newcastle support was massive. All you could hear was Geordies singing at Peterborough.

'The first game I'd played was Middlesbrough at home. I remember Liam O'Brien getting the ball in the first twenty seconds and he lashed it at me. I remember it flying towards me, and he hit it hard, and I remember thinking, just please control it.

'A lot hinges on that first touch, you've got to make a good first impression. I thought, fuck me, he's launched this! Luckily enough I stoned it dead and passed it on quick.

'Against Peterborough I put Kevin Sheedy through for the goal in front of where the Newcastle fans were.'

That was when those supporters realised how good Lee was.

'It was amazing,' he adds. 'You go to a new club and you want to make a good impression. Then they get to know you. When the Newcastle fans sing your name, it's the best feeling in the world. It's the best. You can't beat it.

'My parents couldn't believe it. They didn't say anything about the game when I saw them. They couldn't believe the fans. All they said was, "We can't believe what we've just seen. We're in awe of those supporters."

'At Charlton there were a couple of hundred for away games. They couldn't believe the amount and the noise the Newcastle fans made.'

Lee took to head tennis and Newcastle United and his new team-mates, but he was a long way from home and his family. Keegan fought as hard to keep him as he had done to sign him. Sir John Hall was onside as well.

'Kevin used to let me go home a lot,' adds Lee. 'The first year I used to drive more than people knew. I used to go home after games and if I was in training on Monday I used to leave at four a.m., get there and sometimes if I had Wednesday off I would drive back. Every away game I would drive home. He was brilliant.

'Bar the first six months I was never homesick at all. I was always made welcome. Kevin and his wife Jean met us for lunch. He made my wife feel really welcome, she was always really well looked after, which was important.

'Oliver was jumping all over Jean – he was all over the place – while she was having her dinner. I was like, oh God, but they were normal people, they had kids of their own and they made us feel at home.

'Sir John Hall was brilliant. I remember we had a big do at Wynyard Hall after promotion and I don't know how he found out, but we had a dog called Gemma, and it was rumoured the dog was homesick and he did this big speech and he brought this huge bone, about three feet long, and he said, "Rob, this is for your dog to make sure you don't go anywhere."

'There was nothing for me, just a huge bone that the dog couldn't possibly eat! I got all sorts of stick over it from the lads, but small things like that made you feel wanted.'

Keegan was extraordinarily good at details most would never dream about.

'Every now and again Kevin would ring up and I would hear him in the background talking to my wife. I would be like, ah, he must want to talk to me about something. And then she would put the phone down.

'I'd be like, "What did he want?" And she'd go, "He just rang to say your husband played brilliantly yesterday."

'He would just ring up out of the blue, which I thought was amazing. He made me feel special. You're away from home, you don't realise, stupid things like ringing you up every now and again and not even speaking to you. Brilliant.'

Keegan would later claim that the £700,000 he spent on Lee was probably his best bit of business. Lee was on board from early on with Keegan. He was challenged to get better.

'Kevin would say, "I will always buy better players, it's up to you to keep up with these better players I'm buying." I relished that. I loved that. I loved him bringing in better players.'

'When they bought players at Charlton, you would go, "He might take my place." When I got to Newcastle we signed Les Ferdinand and it felt different. I want to play with these players, they will make this team much better. It's up to me to get in the team.

'That's because of the confidence Kevin put in me, without a doubt. From when I was at Charlton sometimes I felt the players were better than I was. When I got to Newcastle I didn't care who he brought in: "He's not better than me." That was my philosophy.

'Kevin rang me up after the first season and he said, "I've got a great player you're going to love playing with. We've just signed Peter Beardsley." I was like, "Err, great, gaffer." Just ringing me up and telling me who he'd bought. That was brilliant.

'He said, "You'll love playing with him and he'll make you a much better player." He was right, he was spot on, I loved playing with Peter. He genuinely made half my goals when I started playing in midfield. How he found me sometimes I don't know. He used to drop deep and I would go, I'd run into the box, Peter used to pass it and I used to score.'

Lee relished the simplicity of what Keegan told his players. Nothing was complicated. It was football stripped bare.

'Kevin said, "I'll tell you a story about Johan Cruyff and Johan Neeskens. Cruyff was having a nightmare in a game and he turned to Neeskens and said, 'I'm not playing well today, but I'll run around and give you the ball because you are.'"

'Kevin said to me, "You can't play well every game, but you can run around, give it to the players who are playing well. Next week you'll be playing well and they'll be giving it to you."

'That was the best bit of advice I ever got. He was right. There are always one or two players who are outstanding. You think, actually, I'll get it and give it to him because he's on fire.

'I might be playing well and they'll give it me. The rest of the time, if it was someone else, I ran around and gave it to them. The way Keegan plays football is the way I would want to manage and coach.

'You can either speak to players or you can't. It's not one of them things you actually learn. The book might have said do this or do that, but actually, if you had charisma like Keegan did, you can talk to people, you can build them up. You learn what makes them tick, it's a natural thing. "Page thirty-seven: call player's wife and say husband did well. In bold, do not speak to player this time! Call back ten days later, if he does well!"

'The way we played, we never changed from how we played in the Championship to how we played in the Premiership. We attacked. Most of the time it was OK. We came unstuck a few times, but we were OK.

'We got promoted and Keegan said, "Man U, we're coming to get you. We're going for the title." As a player you think, fucking hell, we've just got promoted here, Kevin!

'But he was right, he didn't like the philosophy of saying this season is about survival. He wanted to push on. He never said consolidate. Why should we? Why shouldn't we aim for Man United? We've got good players.

'It rubbed off on all the players. He's done everything in the game, he must know.'

Newcastle played Oldham in their first season in the Premiership on a Monday night, on 8 November 1993, in front of the Sky cameras. They were 1–0 down at half-time. In the second half Andy Cole scored twice and Peter Beardsley scored with a fierce drive. There were 4,500 away fans behind the goal. The cameras caught the mood of those supporters. It looked pretty good.

'I remember when the tag started,' adds Lee. 'I think it was Richard Keys on the Monday Night Football with Andy Gray. Most of the games we were televised in were high-scoring games.

'We beat Sheff Wed four-two, Alex Mathie scored an unbelievable goal. We were losing there as well! They always saw good games. I think that's why they dubbed us The Entertainers. We loved it. It was a great feeling. It's entertainment. Keegan used to drum it into us, "Entertain the crowd."

'It was like the gladiator feeling, entertain them. He used to say, "It's a big arena, get them on your side." In the first ten to fifteen minutes we used to fly at teams. Sometimes we'd be two or three-nil up and it would be all over, it would be finished, you could relax and enjoy the rest of the game. Every game, he used to say, "Fly at them." That's what we used to do.'

When Leeds United arrived at St James' Park on 25 November 1995, Newcastle had played seventeen games in all competitions. They had won fourteen, drawn two and lost one. They had conceded eleven goals and were three points above Manchester United. They had also scored 43 times.

They trailed Leeds, who were seventh at the time, from the 31st minute, when Brian Deane headed in a left-wing cross from Tony Dorigo. Then, with twenty minutes remaining, Peter Beardsley dummied a Steve Howey pass and Rob Lee was on his way, running at two defenders, beating Dorigo and firing a low shot past John Lukic from the edge of the penalty area. Within a minute Lukic could not hold a David Ginola cross and Beardsley scored from close range.

'Robert Lee was a corporal in the army when he came here, but he's a general now,' Kevin Keegan said after the victory. 'Rob's the best player in the country at the moment.'

'It's a great feeling when your manager thinks you're the best player in the country,' says Lee.

'We were getting beat one-nil. We were playing well and then I scored. How did Peter Beardsley see me there? I have no idea. That started the comeback really.

'We always knew with Peter and Ginola and Les that we could score goals. Even if we went a goal down or two down we knew we could score. There were not many games we didn't score in. I don't remember playing in many nil-nils. We always let goals in or we scored goals.'

Newcastle ended the day six points clear of Manchester United, who did not play until the following Monday, when they drew 1–1 with Nottingham Forest.

'We knew we could win it,' adds Lee. 'We knew we had the team capable of winning the Premiership. I personally think we were a better team than Manchester United. They had some great youngsters coming through but at that time we had players who were better than them.'

More than anything, Lee fell in love with the north-east.

'I had this perception that Geordies didn't like Cockneys much,' he adds. 'When I first came I thought, I have to start well here or they won't like me. From the word go I got on with them unbelievably and we had a great relationship.

'People from the north are friendlier than people from the south.

'Even if I wasn't playing well I always tried my bollocks off. I tried as hard as I possibly could. You might be having a nightmare but there's nothing to stop you running around and kicking people.

'That's what I tried to do. I always gave one hundred per cent. I played better in most of my games. It helps when you're playing well and I did in most of the games. I took to the area. After a year I loved it up here.'

Ten days before Newcastle beat Leeds, Lee had picked up his fifth England cap.

'At that time, Kevin believed in me more than I did,' says Lee. 'Even when I had great belief in myself, he believed in me more. He always believed I could be a great player. I probably wish I'd met him earlier.

'Would I have achieved what I did in the game without him? No. Definitely not. One hundred per cent.

'You need a manager that likes you and takes to you. I was lucky enough to get that with Kevin. If you're a good player, you'll become a great player.'

29 NOVEMBER 1995

STEVE WATSON – MERSEY PARADISE

KEVIN KEEGAN TURNED TO THE THREE SUBSTITUTES BEHIND HIM. 'Watto, get warmed up,' he said. 'Shaka's injured.' Keegan wasn't smiling.

*

STEVE WATSON HAD BEEN HURTLING DOWN THE RUNWAY FOR THE triple jump at the Lightfoot Centre in Walker when he caught the eye of the man stood on the grass. It was Peter Kirkley. He wasn't smiling either.

'I saw him at the bottom of the sandpit,' says Watson. 'He was shaking his head.'

Watson was a county-level athlete. He played basketball to a decent standard and he was heavily into his gymnastics.

At fourteen, the juggling of sports was worrying Newcastle United. They were making their choices and he wasn't in. Kirkley told him there would have to be a narrowing of sports. Steve Watson was too versatile.

'I thought I'd missed the boat,' he adds. 'It got to fourteen and they'd all signed schoolboy forms. That was the year I had to step out of it and it killed me. I had one trial at Huddersfield and they offered me schoolboy terms but I went back and started playing at Wallsend Boys Club again.'

Watson had been at Burnside School. His dad, John, worked at the shipyards, as did his brother, also called John. He had never seen his dad show emotion in his life. His whole family, including his mam and his granddad, Fred, were Newcastle fans.

He went back to junior football and starting scoring a lot of goals.

'Something just clicked,' he says. 'I was playing striker. It was stupid figures. We were beating teams 32–0. You were scoring nine goals. That was the season it came together for me.'

Watson had played a game for Wallsend Boys Club in the morning and was back there in the afternoon, on the Astroturf, having a kick-around with his friends when Kirkley, who worked at the club in addition to his role at Newcastle, came over.

'Peter came to the pitch and he must have been to my house,' adds Watson. 'He came to the sports centre. He said, "Can I have a word with you and your mum and dad?"

'We went home and he said, "What we hoped would happen has happened, you've clicked. You've got your head screwed on at football now." I'm not sure I had!

'That was probably April. I was the last one to sign. Some people do things at a different time. I must have got the momentum. I left school in July and I made my debut for Newcastle in November.'

Steve Watson was 16 years and 223 days old on 10 November 1990. He was about to become the youngest player to pull on a Newcastle United shirt in the club's history at Molineux. Mark McGhee, in his second spell at the club, grabbed him as he came on the pitch. 'Come on, son,' said McGhee. 'We need you now.'

'I'd just wandered on,' says Watson. 'I think it was the kitman, Chris Guthrie, who told me to go on, not Jim Smith, who was manager. We lost two-one and it was a blur, but I remember Mark speaking to me, that meant a lot.'

John Watson waited for the Newcastle team bus to arrive back at St James' Park so he could give his son a lift home.

'I got in the car and he went, "What was it like?" He hadn't seen it. I went, "It wasn't very good, we got beat."

'He said, "Do you realise what you've done?" I said, "Well, kind of, yeah."'
Except he hadn't.

That would come on 5 January 1991 at St James' Park, when Newcastle played Derby County in the FA Cup. It was Steve Watson's home debut.

'You went through the whole experience of driving into St James',' he adds. 'My dad used to park his car at the Haymarket and walk up to the ground. All of a sudden he's got a car park pass and he's driving through loads of punters.

'Typical of my dad, he's going, "Get out of the way, man!" He turned to me and went. "What are they walking in front of the car for?"

'It was the Cup and Derby had Mark Wright, who was playing for England, and Dean Saunders. We won two-nil. I crossed the ball for Mark Stimson to score and I walked out with all the man of the match awards. I was like: What's going on?

'My dad gave me a lift home after the Derby game. I hadn't seen any real emotion out of my dad in his life. He was a rock-hard fella who worked down the yards, a man's man.

'When he got back home and seen my mum, he was still on a bit of a high. When she asked him how it was, I think it just hit him. He broke down. It was the most emotional I think I've ever seen. He won't thank me for saying it.'

His son became pretty near to being a regular. Watson was trusted by Jim Smith before his dismissal. He pointed to the possibility of something other than struggle, and when Ossie Ardiles filled the team with kids, Watson was right at the front.

He was also still a natural athlete.

'We used to get the bus down to Tynemouth beach and play heads and volleys,' he recalls. 'I had the ball in my hand and I was just messing about and I went to collect it from the ground and I tried to do a handspring with the ball, which looked like a somersault. It went miles up in the air but it really flew, I thought if I could get the timing right I could really launch it.

'We had to practise it on the beach because the ball wouldn't slip, it would stick in the sand, and luckily I got away with it. If you did it in the wet and slipped you could fall flat on your head. I was always trying to do it in the summer.

'Colin Suggett used to encourage it in the juniors because he saw how far it would go. We'd load it up so everybody went to the front post and Steve Howey would loop round to the back. Then I would do my throw. The amount of times it worked. Nobody is expecting me to be able to launch the ball to the back post.'

He had done it at Ayresome Park in a 3–0 defeat, when Smith was still in charge.

'The one at Middlesbrough was rubbish,' says Watson. 'I had to go up a step. The throw didn't go very far and I got loads of abuse off their fans. I don't know why I did it – well, I do know why I did it, I was a fucking idiot.

'Ossie stopped me from doing it. I did it once in a pre-season game in Scandinavia and I ran from the running track. He came in after the game and said, "Steve, what the fucking hell was that?" I said, "It's just this throw-in I do, Ossie." He said, "Don't ever do that again."'

Watson didn't do it again in a competitive game.

He remained one of Ardiles' favourites, however. Watson was more or less a seventeen-year-old regular. Then came the defeat against Charlton in January 1992, where he had cleared off his own goal-line with a diving header, only to see Pardew stab in the rebound, followed by an FA Cup exit at the hands of Bournemouth. The next match would be at Oxford United.

'Ossie pulled me and Lee Makel over at the same time in the hotel in Oxford and said, "Look, you won't be involved again for the rest of the season. I'm going to have to go with as many seniors as we can."

'I thought my season was over. Saturday came and went. I sat in the stands. My head had gone. I didn't even know the score. My season was finished.'

By the time of the next game, Newcastle and Watson had a different manager. Ardiles was gone and Watson was back in. He set up one of David Kelly's goals. 'I didn't realise things change that quickly in football,' he says.

'Just watching Kevin Keegan, just to meet him, was brilliant. We'd have settled just for shaking his hand, never mind him being manager.

'What Kevin's huge strength was that he could motivate you, especially young Geordies like us. We felt a million dollars when he was telling us how good we were. He said, 'You can do so much better if you have a bit of belief in yourself.' He made you feel head and shoulders above everyone else.

'The adrenaline on the first day was enough, the crowd was buzzing. It wasn't about Kevin's experience or coaching, it was about the masterstroke of thinking what person can you bring to the club that will galvanise everybody, from the players to the staff to the kitmen to the masseurs, everything. It was a case of what man can do it and the choice was perfect.'

*

WHEN WATSON FIRST DROVE INTO BENWELL IN A SOFT-TOP SUZUKI Vitara with Lee Clark, Robbie Elliott and Alan Thompson, he was hammered by everyone. The Anthill Mob was born.

'It was a grey jeep, the wheels were massive and the trims came right out and it had three go-faster stripes on it,' he says.

'You could take the soft top off but it would take you about an hour. It took an hour to put it back on as well.

'I used to go down to the beach with the lads when it was sunny and take the top off and play football and go in the sea. You could guarantee ten minutes after you took it off it would start pissing down. It's not like it was something you could just put back up. The car got drenched. I'd love to see that jeep again.

'I was seventeen, I'd just passed my test and the club put me through it. At the time I did some daft photos. One of them I had to sit on the bonnet of the car and rip my learner plates right in front of the Gallowgate.

'Can you imagine the abuse I was getting? I was wearing a shell suit as well. It wasn't even a club one, it was a tennis shell suit.

'When I signed my first contract all the older players were telling me not to get an agent, they said you don't need one with it being your first contract, so my dad went in with me.

'I remember we went into the office to see Keegan and I was thinking, I'll be all right, because my dad's with me, and he was just in awe. You could have offered him anything and he would have took it. He was nudging me, going, "It's Kevin Keegan!"

'I'm not sure he negotiated my best deal but I would have taken anything. Driving lessons. That was the only thing my dad managed to negotiate on the deal, I got my driving lessons through the club.'

Before then it had been a double bus journey to get to training.

'I was in the first team and it was still two buses to get there, one from Wallsend to the Odeon and then one from the Odeon to Benwell,' he says.

'You were so excited because you were getting on the bus with a couple of mates in Wallsend. You're going up to Newcastle every day to be a footballer. You'd travel four times as far if it meant that.

'I still had my three older players' boots to clean and they weren't even in the first team. It was the norm for us. It taught us discipline. When I got my first contract on the odd day I was lucky enough to be able to afford a taxi.'

When Newcastle United took off and romped to the First Division title in 1992/93, Steve Watson wasn't playing. He started just two league games.

Terry McDermott took Watson to one side in the summer for a chat. Newcastle were getting ready for the Premiership. McDermott held his hand out in front of him and moved it from side to side.

'He said, "We're like that with you," and he waved his hand,' adds Watson. 'He went, "We don't know if you're going to get to where you should be. You came on so well as a kid but you've had a dip. This summer is going to be vital for you. I can't tell you how to live your life and how you spend your summer, but listen, this is make or break for you."

'It was a kick up the arse, basically. You can take it one of two ways: fuck you, I'll prove you wrong but not do anything about it; or do what I did.

'The mood around the club changed in Kevin's first full season and if I'm honest I wasn't partaking in much of it. That was my dip season. I remember Keegan put me back into the kids for a few games and I think it had all maybe got to me, not just the pressure, the easiness of going and seeing loads of people and getting loads of attention.

'I was never big-headed about it and my family have always been brilliant but I probably lost focus. He put me back and brought me back towards the end of the season. He was right, one hundred per cent. Then I was involved in all the promotion parties but I didn't get a medal. That really hit home in the summer and then came the chat with Terry.

'We did the open-bus parade, went to Ayia Napa with all the team and I didn't go on holiday after that.

'I came back – I'd just met my girlfriend/wife at the time so I was settling a little bit anyway – and then that was where Steve Black [a respected fitness coach] came into it.

'I spent all summer with Blackie and the Newcastle rugby lads and we got on great and Lee was training every day. Tommo had his accident by then [Alan Thompson broke his neck in a car accident but returned to play in the Premiership with Bolton], and Robbie was the other one. Virtually every day we'd be on Tynemouth beach or on Castle Farm with the whole of the rugby squad, who were phenomenal fellas and amazing trainers.

'We were in awe of the way they set about their training. Glenn McCrory [the former IBF cruiserweight world boxing champion] was with us quite a bit because he was in training.

'We had a little group of sports people and we were all pulling each other on. Glenn, being a boxer, would be doing sit-ups, and we'd go in for as many as we could, and he would keep going and we would rotate and then come back in on the third time and he'd still be going.

'The rugby boys had the power, we'd try to tackle bags with them. It was brilliant. I've never been fitter. I came in at the start of pre-season and I was flying, absolutely flying. People realised I'd turned the screw again.'

As Newcastle romped through the division and qualified for the UEFA Cup for the first time in sixteen years, Watson was in the middle of it, playing almost forty times, as a right-back, a right midfielder, a central midfielder and very rarely as a centre-forward, but never as a goalkeeper.

*

WATSON HAD BEEN SUCH AN ATHLETE AS A YOUNGSTER THAT HE played up front for Wallsend Boys Club Under-14s on a Saturday and in goal for Wallsend Boys Club Under-15s – as he did for the county – on a Sunday. That small fact was known inside Newcastle United. Watson was still useful with the gloves on when he was twenty-one. On a three-man substitutes' bench Watson would be covering every position.

'Sometimes if there was three subs Kevin used to put me on as sub keeper, he would take a chance – if the keeper went off, I would go on,' he explains.

'Kevin used to say to me every now and then at St James', "Listen, do your warm-up, as you would, but then go and take a couple of crosses as well," in front of a packed Gallowgate End. It was embarrassing.

'You know what John Burridge was like. Budgie couldn't just do it under the covers, he would be shouting and bawling at me, "Get your Vs [the angle of a goalkeepers' thumbs] right, Watto!" I'd be like, "Fuck off, I'm not getting my Vs right!" Half an hour with Budgie was hard, man.'

On 29 November, three-and-a-half weeks after he had played in centre midfield and scored the winning goal against Liverpool at St James' Park following a fumble by David James, Keegan turned and made his call.

'Shaka went down,' Watson recalls. 'Derek Wright looked across at the bench and he was going, "Give us two minutes." Usually he would say he's fine. When the thumbs didn't come up I went, "Fuck!"

'I sat there and I thought, I'm not going on in goal at Anfield at the Kop, surely. Then Kevin told me to warm up. I couldn't believe it. They were a long couple of minutes.'

Finally Hislop raised his thumbs.

Ten minutes had passed from Hislop's initial injury when Les Ferdinand took a whack on the head. Watson was back warming up, this time to go on as centre-forward. The score was 0–0. Newcastle were shooting towards the Anfield Road End, which was full with 6,000 Newcastle supporters.

In the 77th minute, Watson went off on a mazy run inside the Liverpool half. He could not be tackled, until finally, with no support and Liverpool shirts still all around him, he stopped and chipped the ball with his left foot from just outside the Liverpool penalty area.

You get shunted into all parts of a ground as an away fan. Sometimes you get lucky. Nothing beats chipped goals: the artistry, the cheek, the grace and, of course, the wait. Standing in a seat right behind that goal you could see James had no chance. The ball floated over the Liverpool goalkeeper and into the Liverpool goal. It took forever. It was a truly magical moment. You never forget times like that.

The away end erupted.

'It's the goal you dream of scoring for Newcastle when you're a kid,' adds Watson.

'I got to the stage in the run where I'd hit a brick wall. I'd travelled as far as I could and there was no one near me and there's four of them now around the ball. With it being my left foot I was never going to try and ping it from twenty yards so the chip was the only option.

'That was the best single feeling I had as a Newcastle player. It was some feeling, that. You know when you score a goal like that it's going to be your best. It was the perfect scenario.

'Lee comes to me and slaps me on the back of the head when I was celebrating.

'You do think, if it stays like this, what will it feel like? What will it be like if we win? But I also had two chances after that. David James made a good save and I put one wide from an angle I should have scored at.

'It was an incredible feeling when the game finished.

'Kevin tried not to praise me too much afterwards because he knew I was the type of player who needed a kick up the arse. He just shook his head and smiled, as if to say, "Christ, I don't believe that."

There was jubilation in the away end when that whistle went, complete and utter joy.

Top of the league. Through in the cup. We used to get battered here.

The mood was one of triumph. That it was against the odds made it sweeter. Newcastle didn't have a centre-forward and they were still scoring.

For the third time in four visits Newcastle left Anfield victorious. It had taken 32 games and 69 years to record the previous three victories at the famous old stadium.

Finally, Newcastle's hoodoo at Liverpool looked over.

PAVEL SRNICEK – SOME SAVES ARE BIGGER THAN OTHERS

THE THROUGH BALL FROM PETER BEARDSLEY HAD TRAVELLED 35 yards. Les Ferdinand did not have to break stride before cleverly steering a left-footed shot into the bottom corner of Neville Southall's goal. It was becoming familiar but it had not yet touched predictable. There was still a raw excitement to the power of the team.

It was not like Keegan's first side in the Premiership. Then it was more subtle. Now there was more muscle. Still the craft existed, it had to, with Beardsley and Ginola and Lee.

There were good players everywhere and when Ferdinand got on the end of Beardsley's pass after 17 minutes, to score his 21st goal of the season, it felt like another afternoon to embrace what had been created.

Then, in the 33rd minute, Andrei Kanchelskis broke through. Clear through. John Beresford was quick but he could not catch him and there was a lunge and a fall and in an instant the game changed. Beresford was sent off.

Everton, under Joe Royle, had picked up the mantle of the Dogs of War. St James' Park rolled up its collective sleeves and readied itself for a fight. It felt like the good old days.

Newcastle were the underdogs and Tyneside was quite used to that, thank you very much. The crowd that day took Beresford's shirt as he walked off the park, and the fit was pretty good.

It was the first time this new team had been rocked on the ropes. By the second half, Newcastle were struggling for air. In the 81st minute Anders Limpar, the Swedish winger, shot from the edge of the penalty area; it was heading towards the bottom-right corner of the Newcastle goal when it struck Steve Howey. The Newcastle goalkeeper moved with the original shot. Pavel Srnicek and his goalkeeping gloves were going left.

*

HE WAS SEVEN WHEN HE FIRST WENT IN GOAL, BECAUSE HE WAS the smallest there and no one else fancied it. Srnicek didn't have any gloves but he did well. 'I had no money,' he says. 'We were poor.'

Srnicek's parents, Bernadette and Pavel, worked on a smallholding they did not own in Bohumin, a village around ten miles from Ostrava and three hundred from Prague.

There were five children, three sisters and two brothers. Srnicek went home after that first game and took a pair of his father's old work gloves.

'I took the palm off an old table tennis bat and tried to glue that to the inside of the glove,' he says. 'They were huge. Anything like that to hold the ball better. I have to say, I had a hard time growing up. We lived in a small village and we had no money in the family.

'My parents worked hard. My mam looked after cows and my dad looked after pigs on a farm, but it wasn't a farm because it belonged to the government. Because we were poor I went to the farm with my mam and had a shower and then I'd go to school and then wait for my dad to come back from work, take his bike, because I had no money, and then go on his bike to the training session. This was my childhood.

'At that time I did not feel anything proud of it. I would say I was ashamed more than anything. I couldn't afford things. I had to wear the old jumpers of my sisters. It was a horrible feeling but we had the food and we had everything we needed.

'On the other hand I was lucky with my childhood. Outside my house there was a football pitch, then there was a tennis court and a gym, everything, right next to my house.

'We played away from home for the whole day, we swim, we play basketball, we play tennis, we play football, we play everything. Then all of a sudden people say play a different sport, you got no problem. You can play any sport you want.

'When I start to play football I thought there is only one thing I want to do with my life. I never thought I would do anything different. I said I wanted to be the best in this sport. I know I wasn't the best but I was good straight away, everybody say that. That's why nobody said they wanted me to leave the goal. They said stay there. I played for my first club, Viktorie Bohumin and I wasn't supposed to because I was too young.

'They said, "You're better than the older one, so we make black ink for you on your registration." When I was seven and eight years old, it was illegal to play until you were nine so I was playing early. It was good, everybody was taller, I never had a problem. We played in a lower division with a small village. Nobody made a fuss about it.'

He continued to stand out as a goalkeeper.

Bohumin was about farming, mining and a steelworks that employed thousands. Srnicek started a job there when he was fifteen.

'You gave me the little steel thing and I put it in the machine and I make everything from it, in a lathe,' he adds. 'I was learning to be a sheet-metal worker. Because I was a good football player I worked and I played for that company. I was also going to school there. I lived like a proper football player. I was seventeen when I signed a contract with the first team.'

He adds: 'Look, I know what a working life is because I watched my parents work. My mam go to work at three o'clock, I go with her. I knew what it was like. My childhood was like this; hard work and nothing else. If people ever said to me I don't know what it was like to do proper work, I would always say, I do, I really do.

'Everything has a different side of the coin. I never drink, I never smoked, I never went to the disco because I was training all day. I work, I go to school and I train, nothing else was in my life at that time. People would say to me, "You're crazy."

'Maybe I was crazy. People can think what they like. It was about dedication and sacrifice. That is the key. I know what is the working-class people and I know what is the rich people because I had seen both sides. I had a bad life and then I had a good life.'

The good life was still some way off.

Banik Ostrava had been keen to sign Srnicek for years. He resisted. 'It's good when a top club wants you but they were full of prima donnas,' he adds. 'I remember when the people came to my house. My mam never goes to school, my dad never goes to school. My mam cannot even write properly. My dad can't read. He doesn't write.

'My parents didn't have a degree or anything. Then people from Banik Ostrava came and I wasn't at home. My parents didn't understand what they wanted. My mam said to me, "Some people come from a football club but I don't know what they want.'

'I was fifteen then. I said, "Don't worry, I know, it's not a problem." My dad doesn't like football. Then a coach and this one other guy came and they said, "We want your boy, we want to give him school, this, this and this." My mam said, "I don't know, leave it to him, if he wants to go, go."

'We didn't have money. We didn't have a car. We didn't have anything and my parents didn't have a clue. I was fifteen and I was from a small village. If I travel to big town I had a bad feeling, the people were snobs. The football players are prima donnas, they could buy whatever they want to buy. I didn't have a thing. I'm thinking, I go to part-time work instead, and I built a crematorium with five friends.'

There is always a reason to work.

'I took that job to make my first money to buy a pair of jeans, yes jeans!' he says. 'When I get the first money of the month I went to the shop and I bought my first jeans, Wildcat jeans. I had my first jeans and that meant I could go to Banik! That was the thing. I had nothing. When Banik come back again after a year I said I will go to Banik.'

The jeans were a better fit.

'I didn't feel good again because they take the mick out of me because I was from a village. I didn't know how to live in a town. I was so wide-eyed and naive. They lived that life for so many years. They were different to how I was.

'They did not take to me straight away. The sad thing was after six months I came back to Bohumin. I wasn't homesick, I just didn't like it. I didn't like the people, I didn't like the attitude of the players. They were too snobby for me. There was no honesty. After six months I wanted to go home.'

Srnicek went back to Bohumin once more. He returned again to Banik, older and wiser. 'I was nineteen and I wanted to get married. Banik gave me the money because they thought I was a good player. I said I want five thousand koruna, a lot of money, and they gave it to me. I went shopping with my mam and I showed her the money. She was crying. She said, "Where did you get this money?" I told her I got it from Banik and I was going to get married. I had a flat, I got the mortgage and I was getting married. At that time I had everything I dream of. I didn't know whether I should feel guilty or I deserve this.'

National service followed. He got married on 4 April 1988 and joined the army on 6 April. He spent three years there and played for Dukla Prague, an army team in the domestic second division.

'What did I do in the army? Play football!

'The thing was, when I was a third-year it was like a normal soldier, out at six o'clock, on the field, come back, have a shower, have the food, do a couple of hours' work, how to walk, how to do the work, how to take the gun.

'In the evening, we secured the premises for an hour then we changed again every two hours. Then we went shooting. We did everything. Then two o'clock in the morning there was an alarm, you had to be ready in two minutes with a gun and everything outside. All of this was only in the third year. In Dukla Prague it was not like this. No alarm, we just played football. That's all we did.'

Srnicek's life changed on the smallest of decisions. His mother had been born in France and left when she was a small child. It gave her son the chance to take a French passport. 'She said to me when I was fifteen, "I have no money but if you take the French passport maybe it will be an advantage for you because you will have two passports and can travel to France and have no problem."'

Bernadette Srnicek had no idea she had opened the gateway to England. Ludek Miklosko had been waiting for three months to get a work permit. He was 29 and had been capped 70 times. Srnicek had played three times for the Czech Under-21s. He got his permit in two days. 'I was like, "Thanks, Ma!"'

In January 1991 he flew into Newcastle, where he met the then manager Jim Smith and the club secretary Russell Cushing.

'I said to the club, "I need a car." They gave me a white Nissan Bluebird and there was snow. In England, of course, they don't change the tyres, like we did in Czech Republic.

'I didn't know that! I came in the car, I drove slowly because I didn't really know how to drive. I had three-month licence and no car. I went to the car park at the Civic Centre. There was a lot of snow. I drive in that car park, there was the entrance and beside the entrance was a small column, I thought it was snow. I went round the column and I hit it. I get out of the car and had a look at it, what the hell! In the door was a huge bash. I looked at my wife, I was going, "Look at this, who did this?" I was thinking, is this me?

'I came back to St James' and the guy was there who looked after the ground. I went up to him and I said, "Look, look." He said, "What have you done? It's the first day!"

'Then I stay in a hotel for a few months. I had too much bill for the phone. I was on it all the time. I had a little baby. The good thing about it was I had the bill for about £700 in the hotel and I didn't even have that much money.

'But the guy who was the owner of the hotel in Osborne Road was a Newcastle fan. He said to me, "Pav, if you sign for Newcastle I will let you out of the bill, you don't have to pay. If you don't sign, you pay."

'He said, "It's something from me to you." I signed! I have to stay in Newcastle because there is a bill!'

Srnicek moved to a new home. He was bought by the club for £300,000. Within three months Jim Smith was sacked and Ardiles arrived. 'I liked Ossie. He was a good lad. He said, "Pav, blah, blah, blah." His English wasn't good, my English wasn't good, so I understood him better than anyone else!' Srnicek's wife learned English first. The pair were looked after by Bjorn Kristensen and Kevin Scott. Ardiles did not last long. Then Keegan arrived.

'In the Czech Republic because [until 1989] we were a communist country we didn't get too much information about sport or football or anything,' he says. 'I knew who he was but not much more.

'I had an interpreter and he said to me, "He's an ex-Newcastle player, one of the best, he's a former European Footballer of the Year, he did everything. He told me people loved this man in the north-east.

'I felt the excitement in the city. It wasn't like you went in the shop and people didn't know. They did and they were talking about it. The pictures of Kevin, this Kevin, that Kevin, everywhere Kevin.

'When I find out the things I still think there is nobody bigger than the club.'

It is a telling statement from Srnicek.

First came survival and then lift-off as Newcastle won the First Division title. Tyneside had taken the son of Bohumin to its heart. His innocence had charmed the region. He was loved. As the Newcastle dressing room prepared to empty on 9 May 1993, Lee Clark handed Srnicek a T-shirt. 'It's off my brother,' Clark said. 'Put it on at the end.'

'When I came back to the dressing room after the game I put my hands on it and I'm looking at it: "Pavel is a Geordie". I just went, "Clarky, that's great!"' adds Srnicek.

'I walked back on the field in that shirt and I was so proud. I felt fantastic. You know what happened, we were celebrating, everybody stayed in the town.

'I drove my car past the ground, did a left and went past the bank on my left. You go on that main road and on your right is the round car park, opposite is the pub, the Three Bulls. There was traffic lights and I stopped. I was a happy man.

'Then somebody came out of the bar and spotted me, he goes, "Hoy, it's Pav!" Forty people came running out of the pub and they surrounded my car and started bouncing it, shouting, "Pavel is a Geordie, Pavel is a Geordie, la la la la". They kept singing and pushing the car.

'I opened the window and I went, "Boys, boys!" And then they started leaning in the window, going, "Pav, man, do you want a beer?"

'Then they started singing my name and bouncing the car again. Listen, the lights went green, nothing happened. The lights went red, nothing happened. The lights went green, nothing happened. I went, "Boys, please let me go!" After the third or fourth time of green and red the people let me go. If they hadn't I would still be there today. I came home and I was covered in beer!'

The fight to get into Keegan's heart was one Srnicek could not win. Keegan used Tommy Wright 20 times that season. In the first year in the Premiership he signed Mike Hooper, who would make 24 starts. Then in the summer of 1995, Newcastle paid Reading £1.5 million for Shaka Hislop.

'The big thing is, Kevin didn't buy me,' he adds. 'Every time anything happened in the club, Kevin wanted to say, "This is my team," and I wasn't part of it. He didn't buy me.

'I never feel he treated me like a player. He treated me like a person but not like a player. He would bring in a new goalkeeper every year. He would challenge me always and I would always have to prove myself. He would put me back. After two years I got fed up. Mike Hooper, Shaka, Tommy Wright. All of them, we could talk about everybody.

'I had the feeling that Kevin never treated me like other players. The one thing was I knew that [it was a] battle when in a story in the papers people said they wanted me in the goal. Kevin went in the papers and said nobody will tell him what to do.

'Then he walked on the pitch after this and the fans shout my name. I knew I had won the battle against the manager. It wasn't a battle I wanted to fight or win but I felt so good because I knew I would be given a chance.

'Maybe if he brought me to St James' I would be the golden boy but because of that I wasn't. I was a fighter all my life and I would never give up.'

Srnicek had sat on the sidelines as Newcastle soared. He played for the second team in training games. By December, Hislop was injured. Pav was back, going through the old routine.

'Each game I had my ritual, I run on the pitch, I clap my hands, I run across the pitch and to the eighteen-yard box to one side, clap my hands, run back, clap the hands and then go to the goal and then say hello to everybody who was behind the goal.

'Same people, week in, week out. There was the disabled people behind the goal. They were very close to the game, they could feel it with the team. I would go, "Hello, John, hi, Tom, how are you?" They would go, "Hello, Pav," and that was fantastic.

'I would go to the other side in the second half and it would be the same thing.

We had this special relationship, like you feel they are your family. Like I said, every time you walk on that pitch, we felt we had something different. Once Keegan said, "The badge is what you're playing for. You're playing for these people." In that case he was spot on.'

*

IT WAS BACKS TO THE WALL STUFF AND THEN LIMPAR SHOT AND Srnicek went with it, but it was the wrong way. In midair he turned and followed the new trajectory of the ball following the deflection. It looked for all the world a goal. Then came a hand and a breathtaking save. People were on their feet. It felt like a goal had been scored.

'I was going in the other direction and I came back and forward with my hand and pushed it away,' he says. 'Everything had to be there, the agility, the ability.

'Gordon Banks was there. After the game he said that save was in the ten best saves in the history of English football. People were talking about it a lot.

'You don't think about it at the time, it just happens. You go, and then you go back and it's only because you think you have a chance. I tried to get back and I managed to get to it and I tipped it away.

'The whole ground stood up. You feel you can't go over the top because the game continues and you don't want to cock it up. Don't spoil it. Carry on. Keep going.

'The whole stadium was shouting. I'm thinking, should I clap my hands? Do you know what I mean? What are you going to do? If you do too much something could happen. You have to go back to the game. You cannot go over the top.

'I was lucky all my family were there. There was my wife and a lot of my friends from England. I didn't really feel nervous because I have these feelings before; in out, in out, in out, here I am again.

'That feeling when the whole stadium stand up and clapped and shouted my name, I don't know if too many players experience that.

'This one was special, so special. People say they cried. I was nearly crying. I saw the people around and I thought, I came from Bohumin, a little village, and here I am now and they are standing up and singing my name.

'It's something people will never have. They will win trophies and money and everything they dream of but they will never have this.'

Newcastle won 1–0. Srnicek left the field to a standing ovation. An unforgettable one.

KEITH GILLESPIE – NO LOVE LOST

'GOD, THOSE FANS ARE GOOD, AREN'T THEY?'

*

KEITH GILLESPIE WAS THIRTEEN THE FIRST TIME HE WENT TO OLD Trafford. There had been a trial at Rangers two weeks earlier but Gillespie, who grew up in Belfast, had pictures of Bryan Robson, Norman Whiteside and Mark Hughes on his wall. His dad Harry, a prison officer in the Maze, supported Manchester United and so did all his family.

He played against eleven-year-olds when he was eight at Rathmore Primary School. No one could catch him and people began to realise he was a bit special. He flourished and competed for the area in the 100 metres, the 200 metres and the long jump. By the time he was thirteen Gillespie was playing for a team called St Andrews. Manchester United were rather keen on Gillespie. He went on trial, and, in his own words, did OK.

'I must have,' he says. 'They wanted me to sign straight away.'

He went back over with his mum and dad.

'It was massive,' he adds. 'I'd never been to Old Trafford before to watch a game. They beat Middlesbrough one-nil and Bryan Robson scored and he was my hero. It was a big thing; down in the changing room before the game, meeting the players. I didn't say too much. I went about and got some autographs.

'The night before we'd gone out with Alex Ferguson and his wife for a meal and he slipped the waitress a twenty-pound tip. You're talking 1988 and it was like,

"Twenty quid!"

'When he had a player, he knew everything, your mum's name, your dad's name, even your sisters' names. He knew everything. With that sort of little personal touch it means a lot. My mam and dad were happy it was the right club for me.'

Keith Gillespie moved to Manchester and England from Northern Ireland in 1991, when he was sixteen.

'July the ninth was the day I went over and it was four days after we had buried my granny. It was an emotional time. I remember flying over and it was daunting. You're sixteen, leaving home and going to a new country, whereas you look at the youth team, and you had Gary Neville, Ben Thornley, Scholesy and Nicky Butt who were local lads. It was no different for them. They were still living at home.

'We had to adjust. You had to deal with homesickness because it was tough at first. You did miss home but you just think, this is what I want to do so I have to be focused. I went home every six weeks for long weekends and you looked forward to that. In between, you focused on playing.

'I was in digs with Robbie Savage. Me and Sav got on really well. We were with each other at training, we'd get home, we were in the same room, we got close. In digs life you have to have a laugh because it can get tedious and boring. You're not earning much money, forty-six pounds a week doesn't go an awful long way.

'There were good times but it was still quite tough. At sixteen years of age most people are still at home living with their family. I was in a different country.'

There was a lot of attention. Ferguson had been eager to develop from within, to raise young players within the Cliff, the club's training ground. He wanted players who had cared for the club from a young age. It would follow the lead set by Sir Matt Busby forty years earlier.

'We got a lot of press coverage about this great youth team,' adds Gillespie. 'You had people like Bryan Robson and Steve Bruce referring to us as the dream team. We didn't get above our station. At Man United you're not allowed to.'

It would become a celebrated youth side but Gillespie, whose form had dipped, was left out of the first leg of the FA Youth Cup final in 1992 against Crystal Palace. He returned as a sub in the victorious second leg.

His first-team debut for Manchester United came in January 1993, at Old Trafford against Bury. Then he went on loan to Wigan.

'The surreal thing was a year and a half earlier, I was still at school,' he says. 'Then I'm making my debut for Man United, the club I support. I set up the first goal after eight or nine minutes then I scored the second. You can't ask for a better day.

'I didn't play exceptionally well but scoring and setting one up, it's what dreams are made of. Oh God, it was incredible walking off the pitch. Straight home and straight on to the payphone in the digs, and the whole family is going mad. It was an incredible feeling.'

The following week he was back in the youth team.

Gillespie played six more times that season.

By the start of the following campaign, he was still around the first team. On 21 August 1993 he was sat next to Ben Thornley for Manchester United's second home game of the season.

'We were still apprentices,' he adds. 'I was sat beside Ben and I said to him, "God, those fans are good aren't they?" It had a big effect on me. I don't think I would have said that about anyone else.'

Midway throughout the second half, the visitors' centre-forward, Andy Cole, scored his first goal in the Premiership, at the Stretford End. Newcastle equalised, and 'those fans' went wild.

Nobody could have predicted the seeds that had been sown.

By the time Gillespie had another meaningful conversation with Thornley on a substitutes' bench, in January 1995, he was on his way to play for those supporters.

'It was a mental night,' he says. 'You're going to Bramall Lane for a cup tie and I'm actually thinking, I've got a really good chance of playing.

'I'd been in and around the first-team squad. I knew I had Andrei Kanchelskis in front of me but you're always going to have someone in front of you. There was a bug going about and he wasn't fit. I thought I had a chance of playing and then the team was announced and I wasn't in.

'After the team was named Alex Ferguson pulled me aside and mentioned to me what was happening. "Manchester United have had an offer accepted by Newcastle for Andy Cole," he said. "But it is conditional that you go in the other direction. Have a think about it and I'll speak to you after the game."

'I sat on the bench and I didn't tell Ben, but I was picking his brains. My head was spinning.

'When the whole deal was put to me by Alex Ferguson, the fact it was Newcastle and what I thought about them after seeing them and after I'd played at St James' in the League Cup [helped]. The atmosphere then was great as well.

'I was actually quite surprised how easy it was for me to make that decision and say, "Yeah, I'm going to go." This from a diehard Man United fan.

'The decision was pretty easy for me and I never thought it would be. It was a chance for me to become a regular, which I wasn't at United. I was biding my time and having games here and there but you're nineteen years of age and you want to be a regular. I was able to do that by going to Newcastle.

'In the changing room I spoke to Steve Bruce. Brucey, being a Geordie, went, "You've got to do it. It's a great opportunity." I'd already made my mind up but it was nice getting a senior pro's take on it.'

Gillespie and Ferguson met Keegan, Freddie Fletcher and Freddy Shepherd in a Yorkshire hotel. Ferguson phoned Keith's mam, Beatrice. 'He said, "Don't worry, I'll make sure I get him a great deal."'

He was true to his word.

'My head was still spinning and I had Alex Ferguson acting as my agent,' he adds. 'I was on £250 a week and he sort of bluffed a bit and told them I got £600 a week. I was like, what's going on here?

'Kevin didn't have to sell the club to me. I think everybody who knows Kevin knows he can sell Newcastle to you in a couple of seconds, like that. I'm sure Les said it.

'Anyway, the Manchester United bus had gone. I was in a car with Alex Ferguson. He drove back and dropped me off at home. He was on and off the phone. This was obviously massive, seven million pounds, a new British record, so he was speaking to people on the phone, trying to get things sorted, a press conference the next day, stuff like that.

'There were things said. He said he would not have let me go other than the fact I was Irish, and because of the whole foreigner rule and how it was affecting Man United in Europe.' (At the time, players from Scotland, Wales and Northern Ireland were counted as 'foreign' by UEFA and subject to limits in European competitions.)

By an incredible twist, Newcastle played Manchester United the following weekend. Neither Gillespie nor Cole was allowed to play. The match was a 1–1 draw.

'When Paul Kitson scored I was off the bench, cheering,' says Gillespie. 'If you'd told me five days previous I'd be jumping off the bench cheering a Newcastle goal against Man United I'd have been, "No way."

'It was a crazy four or five days. I had trained on the Thursday and the Friday. I trained Saturday morning and then in the game on the Sunday I can't play.

'I remember Saturday night I hit the Quayside for the first time and I was like, bloody hell! I was just in complete shock at what was going on. I thought, I've made the right move here! It was incredible.

'I had no problem whatsoever settling. The first start for me was Wimbledon. I remember getting the ball after a minute and a half and I totally skinned the fullback and put a cross in and I think maybe a lot of the fans didn't know an awful lot about me but I just hit the ground running.

'It's so important to do that when you change clubs, get the fans on your side, and I felt I did that straight away. As for settling in, not a problem whatsoever.

'We lost in the quarter-final of the FA Cup to Everton and that was disappointing. We had had good results. I think Ruel Fox had a good chance late on and he should have scored. It was a scrappy goal that Dave Watson got for them. There wasn't much in it.

'We were two steps from Wembley and it was disappointing. We finished the season sixth. Kevin had it in his head the long-term players he wanted to get for the next season.'

One of them, from France, became Gillespie's new room-mate.

'David came in and he was a little bit unknown. During the first game of the season, you went, bloody hell, he's a good player isn't he? £2.5 million! What a player.

'Just those few players that finished the jigsaw. The likes of my position, winger, David, winger, that's the sort of player that gets people off their seats.

'He was great, smoking away in the room. I got on great with him. The first time we got to the room, by four in the afternoon for an evening game, straight away I've gone, "I'm ordering a toasted sandwich, I'm going for ham and cheese. Do you want one?"

'He said, "Yeah I'll have that." He was raging because the cheese wasn't hot enough for him. It was always ham and cheese and the next time, he would stand there beside me on the phone and go, "Make sure you say it's hot, Keith, hot, hot!" I'm like, "Can you make sure it's hot, please, it's a cheese and ham toastie for David Ginola!"

'He wasn't really a big drinker, it would often be a case of, "Everybody back to mine," being as I was the young single lad.

'I just remember looking out, and it must have been about five in the morning and he's lying in the front garden, paralytic, so he is, with a can of Carlsberg next to him. I think he had a cigarette as well. You're talking about this really cool French guy, in your garden.

'It was a great city for a night out. I thought I'd struck gold signing for Newcastle.'

Ferguson was so concerned during the summer about what Keegan was building that he tried to sign Gillespie back.

'I remember the answer machine clicking on and hearing the Scottish accent,' he explains. 'I grabbed the phone and he wanted to buy me, he was going to speak to Kevin Keegan. Nothing was said to me.

'He went through Kevin. Gary Neville was in the England squad and he had spoken to Peter Beardsley, who was obviously close to Kevin, and he said they had offered four million pounds. That was never put to me. I had no problem with that. I was happy at Newcastle.

'The season started and we were flying. We played really well in the first game against Coventry. You go to Bolton in your second game, difficult place to go, Rob got the second and Les got the third, and I remember looking across and thinking: We're not bad. We've got the makings of a good side.

'You win the next game, at Sheffield Wednesday, Ginola's first goal. That Middlesbrough game, David just turned Neil Cox inside out, inside out, and the first four games we've won. We didn't play well at Southampton and then we just went on winning games, so we did.

'Ginola left, me right, and put the ball into the middle and Les will do the rest. He was a dream to play with. I've heard him give myself and David a lot of credit but for us he was such a great target man.

'The beauty was in the simplicity of it all. Kevin was just an incredible motivator, the best man-manager I've ever had. He could make you feel like the best player in the world, just by one sentence. The time when we were flying, the team talks were two minutes. It was more or less, "Same again". We had a very settled team. You weren't changing players all the time. He was superb.

'As I said about team talks, there was no complications. We knew we had the players going forward. People were banging on about should we have shut the door at times and ground out results, but that wasn't our style and it wasn't in our make-up. We had players who were match-winners. If you score three, we'll score four. We had players who liked to express themselves. That was the whole attitude. We didn't go on about defensive things. We had five-a-sides. It was the most enjoyable training I've ever had. Because it was simple, we knew what we were doing, as soon as we went in.

'It was just a great time. There was so much bounce about the whole place. Three or four games in you could feel the place rocking.

'Ah, it was incredible being in the city at the time. The place is like a goldfish bowl anyway. The fans are so passionate and I love that. They'll get behind you and we had a lot of nights out as a group of players in the town because we had a good bond. You're out and you're totally mobbed. Everyone wants a piece of you and that's no bad thing!

'It was just a great time to be a player at this club. That sort of period, the fact we were such an entertaining team. We did become everyone's second team.'

Manchester United had always been Gillespie's first team. By the time he returned, two days after Christmas, his new team were ten points clear of his old team. It was only halfway through the season but Manchester United could not afford to lose.

'You want to do well going back to your old club,' he adds. 'My whole family supported Man United, it was a big build-up for me. I was a United fan and I was going back and we were leading United.

'I hadn't imagined leaving the club when I did. It was a big thing for me. You want to go there and prove a point. Yeah, I was sort of more nervous before the game. I had left mainly because of the foreigner rule. They needed English players. I was judged as a foreigner.

'It was a real chance for us to go there and make a mark. They were our closest challengers.'

In the fifteenth minute, Phil Neville clattered into Gillespie. It was an unforgiving challenge. Gillespie was absolutely wiped out. His evening was finished, as was Newcastle's.

'I was completely open, my other leg was going the other way,' he says. 'He took me out. He didn't get the ball, no, I can't remember if we even got a free kick. I was on the ground and I was carried off on a stretcher.

'It was early on in my first game back at Old Trafford. To be carried off after fifteen minutes on a stretcher, for the game to be over for me, I was totally gutted. I knew straight away that it was serious. Injuries are the worst thing in the world for a footballer because there is nothing you can do about it.

'It was a nightmare. It drives you mad. I knew I was going to be missing at an important time in the season, having played quite a big role previous to that. It was a big disappointment to me.

'Of course, you don't envisage leaving on a stretcher. You have positive images in your head beforehand. You think you'll score, or you'll win. You don't foresee being carried off.

'I was straight to the dressing room, and then I was on crutches. It was a real bad injury and I hadn't had many bad injuries. It was a freak one. Derek Wright hadn't seen it before.

'Phil didn't speak to me about it afterwards. Anybody can make a rash challenge. I didn't say, "You were out to get me." I'll never put any blame on him.

'It's what happens in football. Players get hurt. It's not a grudge. I don't think I was targeted. Look at the players we had, so many good players. Obviously they knew me inside out because I'd grown up there since I was thirteen but, of course, it was really disappointing.

'It was an injury that even the physio had never seen before. I had a bruise all the way down from my hip to my knee. Derek actually sent me so they could do research on me. It was one of those where I was told I would be out for eight weeks and I think I was out for five.'

Peter Schmeichel twice saved well from Les Ferdinand but Newcastle, with the right half of their armoury taken out in that challenge, were second best. For Cole, the other half of the swap, it was a night to remember for a far better reason. He scored after just six minutes and so, after 53 minutes, did Roy Keane.

Gillespie sat in the away dressing room, underneath the stand in which he had spent his formative years as an apprentice, listening to the roars of the Manchester United support.

'Even though we lost it wasn't the worst thing because we were so far ahead at the time,' he adds. 'We didn't do ourselves justice.

'I went back on the bus after the game. No, I don't think it was flat. We were still in an unbelievable position. You're not going to win every game.

'We just didn't turn up. That was the whole thing about it. That was the disappointing thing. We were sort of seven points clear. We would have taken that at the start of the season. Going into the New Year and you're seven points clear at the top of the Premiership. Yeah, we were still pretty happy with life!'

LES FERDINAND – WONDERFUL CHRISTMAS TIME

THERE WAS A COMMOTION IN THE CENTRE OF NEWCASTLE. A BIG group of men were playing keepy-ups.

'It was right in the centre of town,' says Les Ferdinand. 'It was the old Eldon Square.

'Shaka Hislop was a throwback from the 1960s. He had big platforms and a big Afro. John Beresford was a sergeant major. Steve Watson was Fred Flintstone and Lee Clark was Barney Rubble.

'Someone had a football. Freddie Flintstone and Barney Rubble were arguing, someone did a slide tackle and it went on from there. We were all doing keepy-ups, some people had big clown shoes on and platforms and it was one-touch and if you missed you had to stand on the side against the wall. It was Eldon Square!

'Punters were standing there laughing, going, "What's going on, that's Newcastle United!"

'It was our Christmas party. Everyone was there, in fancy dress.

'My face was quite visible but Freddie and Barney had their hats on. Shaka was going for headers with his big Afro. It was Christmas. We were top of the league. I was laughing my head off.'

STEPHEN MILLER – THANK YOU FOR THE GOOD TIMES

'HAVE I GOT ANY ADVICE FOR YOU? YEAH, THROW IT AS FAR AS you can!'

*

STEPHEN MILLER WAS THREE THE FIRST TIME HE MET KEVIN KEEGAN, at Newcastle's Benwell training ground.

Keegan went into the clubhouse and returned with the only strip he could find, John Anderson's number two. He stood and chatted with Stephen and had his photo taken.

'It was lovely to see him with Kevin,' says Ros, Stephen's mam. 'There was nothing about his disability. Kevin treated him the same as everyone else. It was just lovely for us to see that kind of thing. He chatted for quite a long time, we met Peter Beardsley and Terry McDermott as well. Kevin said, "Keep in touch."'

Stephen Miller was born in 1980 at the Princess Mary Maternity Hospital. He was born in the breech position and starved of oxygen. It meant he had athetoid cerebral palsy, a condition that makes balance and coordination more difficult than usual.

It never stopped him.

In 1983 he met Keegan and in 1984 he went to his first game, Keegan's testimonial against Liverpool. 'I thought every game ended with someone leaving in a helicopter,' he says. 'The next few games I went to after that I kept looking for one in the sky!'

Stephen kept in touch with Keegan. He took his old Johnny Anderson shirt to the training ground after Newcastle had won promotion at Grimsby. The whole squad signed it with a silver pen.

When his first wheelchair needed replacing, it was Keegan who helped with fundraising. When the chair arrived he was invited to Maiden Castle to meet the Newcastle squad.

'Kevin and Arthur Cox presented it and the team were on the photo,' he adds. 'I knew nothing about it. I was fourteen. It was brand new. The first one I had was from a care home. I needed a new one because I'd gone to high school. I could walk around at middle school, but high school was a lot bigger so I needed it to get around. I remember Ruel Fox was lying in front of us and I was like, "God, that's Ruel Fox!"'

When Newcastle played away at Arsenal, Stephen was mascot. There was talk of using the wheelchair, but Stephen wanted to walk to the centre circle at Highbury.

Ros remembers: 'When they had to get him off, Kevin came over and said, "Ros, we're going to have to get him off the pitch, quick." Will he mind if Steve Howey runs on and carries him off?'

He didn't.

'Steve ran on and chucked me over his shoulder!' adds Stephen. He had been a Junior Magpie for four years. His family had season tickets.

'It was perfect with Sir John Hall taking over, getting money into the club, it all came together at the right time,' he says.

'It's probably the best season I've ever seen. I remember every game you went expecting to win. You didn't think about getting beat, you thought about how many goals you were going to score.

'I would rather play exciting attacking football. Kevin knew that's what the fans wanted and that's what he gave them. That's why it was a great season. You looked forward to every game. Everyone was together, the club, the fans, the players and the media. Everyone was happy.'

Stephen had first met Peter Beardsley when he was three. Gudni Bergsson had cancelled out Paul Kitson's early goal for Bolton when Beardsley struck his 100th league goal in a black and white shirt. It was enough for a 2–1 victory, but the margin should have been greater. The gap at the top of the table had stretched to twelve points. Manchester United were now third.

The region felt inspired.

Stephen had been fourteen when his own talent in athletics had begun to emerge. He made the England team and at fifteen qualified for the Paralympics in Atlanta, where he would throw in the F32 club class.

'Kevin said, "Come back and see me before Atlanta." About a week before I was due to go out, I went to see him and I said, "Have you got any advice," and he went, "Throw it as far as you can!"'

Stephen, then sixteen, flew to Atlanta on his own. His parents, John and Ros, went the following day. The Atlanta Braves' stadium was full to its 80,000 capacity for the opening ceremony.

The Four Tops sang, Jerry Lee Lewis did too, Christopher Reeve introduced the countries and when Aretha Franklin sang 'Climb Every Mountain' there was not a dry eye in the house.

'I was in bits,' says Ros. 'That was our first experience. We were trying to see our son in the middle of it all. It was unbelievable.'

'Walking out there was one of the most amazing moments of my life,' adds Stephen.

He did not compete until late on the final day, because of a hurricane. There were 20,000 in the stadium.

'I'd had a good year. I'd thrown really well but nobody knew how I would cope. I remember my first throw I got a red flag.'

You throw in sets of three. The next two went a bit better. By the end of the first round, Stephen Miller from Cramlington was in the lead.

'I thought, I can win this,' he says. 'I had a lot more in the tank. I started getting a bit cocky and I was on the big screen. We were the only competition still going.'

His next set of three was even better. He upped his best throw by two metres. No one could throw it as far as Stephen.

'It takes a while when you win a big competition to sink in that you've actually won it,' he says. 'It was twelve o'clock at night. You dream about winning it. Is this really happening? I've won the Paralympics.'

Then came the medal ceremony. 'It was amazing, singing the national anthem, with a gold medal.'

'We just had so much pride in what he'd achieved,' adds Ros. 'We didn't stop him from doing anything from when he was little. We couldn't see the point of him not living his life. You're so proud, watching the ceremony.'

'Kevin was part of the inspiration to become a sportsman,' insists Stephen. 'He was one of my idols. The next time I saw him he said, "I see you took my advice!"'

Kevin Keegan takes his seat at the press conference to announce he has signed for Newcastle in 1982. *(Newcastle United)*

Keegan is picked up by a supporter before his debut at a packed St James' Park. *(Mark Leech/ Offside)*

Keegan scores on his debut and runs towards the Gallowgate End in sheer delight. *(Mark Leech/ Offside)*

Kevin Keegan is mobbed on the pitch and struggles to make his way back to the centre circle after his goal against Queens Park Rangers. *(Mark Leech/Offside)*

Sir John Hall is flanked by Freddy Shepherd as he introduces Kevin Keegan as the new manager of Newcastle United. *(Newcastle United)*

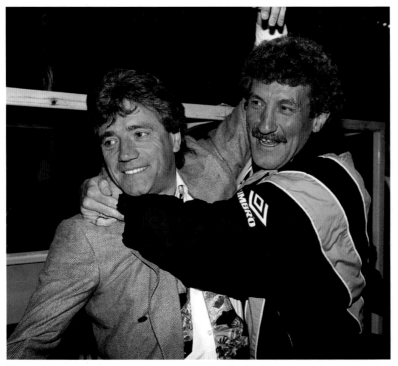

Terry McDermott grabs Kevin Keegan as Newcastle clinch promotion to the Premiership, and the Championship crown, at Grimsby, in May, 1993. *(Action Images)*

Keegan is given a crown and mobbed by fans after Newcastle win the Championship at Grimsby. *(Newcastle United)*

Kevin Keegan holds the Championship trophy aloft with the full first team squad after beating Leicester 7-1 on the final day of the 1992/93 season. *(Getty)*

The Gallowgate End is demolished as part of the redevelopment of St James' Park. *(Newcastle United)*

Peter Beardsley, flanked by Sir John Hall and Kevin Keegan, signs for Newcastle for the second time in 1993 as the redevelopment of St James' Park takes place in the background. *(Newcastle United)*

Rob Lee scores the fist goal of the 1995/96 season and is mobbed by Les Ferdinand and Lee Clark. *(Newcastle United)*

Kevin Keegan and Alex Ferguson share a joke pitch side at the 1993 Ibrox Tournament. *(Newcastle United)*

David Ginola leaves the field at Hillsborough, followed by a cameraman, after scoring his first goal in English football. *(Newcastle United)*

Lee Clark scores Newcastle's fourth goal against Wimbledon and team-mates Steve Howey, Peter Beardsley and John Beresford join the celebrations. *(Newcastle United)*

Peter Beardsley and Les Ferdinand race off in celebration after Beardsley's goal put Newcastle two-one ahead against Leeds. *(Newcastle United)*

Kevin Keegan salutes his midfield general Rob Lee. *(Newcastle United)*

Les Ferdinand carries Peter Beardsley and is hugged by David Ginola after scoring against Arsenal. *(Action Images)*

With 13 minutes remaining of Newcastle's League Cup tie at Anfield, the substitute Steve Watson shoots for goal. *(Newcastle United)*

Les Ferdinand attempts a header as Newcastle face title-chasing rivals Manchester United at St James' Park in March, 1996. *(Newcastle United)*

Newcastle's training session at Maiden Castle proves a huge draw for the club's supporters. *(Newcastle United)*

John Beresford and Kevin Keegan continue their row after the defender is substituted just 25 minutes into Newcastle's Premiership game with Aston Villa. *(Getty)*

Bench shot of Kevin Keegan and Terry McDermott McDermott and Keegan, side by side in the Newcastle dugout *(Newcastle United)*

Relief and delight are everywhere as Les Ferdinand celebrates his winning goal against Aston Villa. *(Newcastle United)*

Faustino Asprilla curls the ball around David James and into the Liverpool goal to put Newcastle 3-2 ahead at Anfield in a game still regarded as the best the Premier League has ever seen. *(Action Images)*

Asprilla is surrounded by delighted team-mates after putting Newcastle ahead at Anfield. *(Newcastle United)*

Kevin Keegan is mobbed as he gets off the Newcastle team bus at Elland Road, with just three games of the season remaining. *(Newcastle United)*

Terry McDermott and Kevin Keegan show the pain as Graham Fenton scores to put Blackburn Rovers 2-1 ahead at Ewood Park. *(Getty)*

Keith Gillespie is congratulated by a delighted Les Ferdinand after putting Newcastle one-nil ahead at Leeds. *(Newcastle United)*

The entire Newcastle bench show their despair at Nottingham Forest as Ian Woan equalises for the home side *(Newcastle United)*

Kevin Keegan and Howard WIlkinson walk off together at Leeds after Newcastle had secured a one-nil victory that put them within three points of Manchester United with a game in hand. *(Newcastle United)*

Kevin Keegan puts his head into his hands during the final game of the season, against Tottenham. *(Action Images)*

Geordies Lee Clark and Peter Beardsley shake hands with Nottingham Forest's players after the one-one draw that took the title out of Newcastle's hands for the first time in the entire season. *(Newcastle United)*

David Ginola applauds a still packed East Stand at St James' Park as Newcastle walk around the pitch after the final game of the season. *(Newcastle United)*

Ginola raises a black and white flag as he prepares to walk down the tunnel at St James' Park. *(Newcastle United)*

Keegan salutes the Leazes End, which is still full, as slowly embarks on a lap of honour after the final home game against Tottenham. *(Newcastle United)*

FAUSTINO ASPRILLA – HOW SOON IS NOW?

'WOULD YOU LIKE A GLASS OF WINE, TINO?'

Faustino Asprilla was having his lunch in the team hotel on Saturday, 10 February. He was in the north-east and it was deep winter. He looked at those around him. The consensus was he would be OK. Kevin Keegan had already told him he would not be playing that afternoon, four days after he arrived in England.

'Si,' he replied.

Asprilla saw his glass filled up with red and took a mouthful.

'When I arrived Kevin Keegan told me I wasn't playing so I could have a drink if I wanted one,' says Asprilla. 'I went with the directors for a meal and I ordered some wine. It was only one glass and I wasn't playing.

'I had been in Parma on Thursday waiting for the papers so I could play in England. Keegan called me to say he'd send a private jet so I could come over and watch the game.

'Then on Friday I got the papers, but I was still just going to watch. On Saturday they took me to lunch in the club hotel and I ordered wine because in Italy that's what we had. I wasn't allowed to drink Coke in Italy, you would be fined. I drank the wine, but I never liked wine so I mixed it with water.'

Two hours later, he was sat in the visiting dressing room in the Riverside Stadium. 'You'll be OK to sub, Tino, won't you?' Keegan had asked. 'Don't worry, you'll not be coming on.'

Sixty-seven minutes had been played at Middlesbrough's brand-new stadium. The home side were twelfth in the Premiership and had lost only four times at home since moving from Ayresome Park. They were leading 1–0 through an own-goal from John Beresford. Newcastle were not playing well.

Kevin Keegan turned to Asprilla and asked him in Spanish if he would be okay to come on for 20 minutes.

Asprilla took off the layers that were not keeping him warm. Five days previously, on Monday, he was not even moving to England.

The directors from Parma and Newcastle had met in Milan. Newcastle had argued there was a problem with Asprilla's knee following a medical in England and wanted the fee reduced. The Parma chairman, Giorgio Pedraneschi, was furious. He said he was ready to seek arbitration from FIFA.

'If we do that,' he said, 'it will be above all to protect ourselves and so that everyone knows that the contract is valid and that the player is healthy.'

Asprilla had scored 25 goals in 84 games for Parma but he had not played for nearly a month, when he had come on as a substitute against Cagliari. There had only been four appearances all season. Despite the protracted move, and the claims over his knee, Newcastle and Keegan remained keen.

Asprilla had been one of seven children, brought up in rural Tulua, in Colombia. 'We grew up in a big house,' he says. 'I had four sisters and two brothers. My father worked in sugar cane, my mum ran the house – she had seven children to look after.'

By the time he was seventeen, he had signed with Deportivo Cucuta. Then he moved to the Nacional of Medellin. He was handed his debut with the full Colombian team. Four years after his debut with Deportivo, he was the Colombian Footballer of the Year.

He went to Italy when he was 22. By the time he reached 23 he had won the European Cup Winners' Cup.

'I felt the love of people,' he says. 'Of course there were some difficult times too. Life in Europe was very different from Colombia. Everything was very organised. It was tranquil. Punctuality was very important to Italian football, I discovered that.

'It wasn't like Colombia, everything was precise. I'd turn up late. I got fined a lot. I lived with Mum, my sister and my wife at the time, she was pregnant. My mother, Marcelina, died when I was at my peak in Parma.

'My mother was special. She was the most affectionate person I've ever seen. I owe her a lot. The first six months in Italy were hard for me, I was close to going back to Colombia but she helped me. She stressed that I would succeed, that once I showed them what I could do, then I could come back home.'

He would prove his worth. He would lift the European Super Cup and the UEFA Cup in 1995. Parma would finish in the top five for three successive seasons. It was a golden period for the club. But by the start of the new season, he was not in manager Nevio Scala's plans. Nor was he in those of Fabio Capello, who had been lined up to take over.

Keegan wanted a fresh spark to give his team something different. 'I came because of the love Keegan showed me when they came to Parma looking for me,' adds Asprilla. 'He was such a great person that persuaded me to join.

'He said I was the best player at the moment and he thought that from when he first saw me. That was what convinced me to play at Newcastle.'

The two sides would finally agree a £7.5 million transfer, the highest in Newcastle's history. Asprilla landed at Newcastle International Airport and stepped out of his plane into snow. He had a huge coat and he looked pensive. Tyneside is a lot of things, but it is not Colombia.

That was Thursday. By Saturday, when his new team-mates were preparing to go to the Riverside Stadium, Asprilla was having a glass of wine.

Newcastle had taken twelve points from a possible fifteen when they kicked off against Middlesbrough. They were still nine points clear at the top of the table but Keegan wanted a fresh attacking outlet.

'It is very hard to leave a new country when you have set up your life there,' adds Asprilla. 'You get used to a new city and you make friends. I had been voted one of the top three players in the world at the time but Keegan talked to me with such passion, the love he had for the club and the city was amazing.

'He was transferring that love into me. I knew I'd be loved. Keegan was right, I was. The only complaint I could have about Newcastle was the weather.

'My exit from Parma was controversial. The only reason I left was because Fabio Capello was going to be their new manager and he said he didn't want me. That was a condition of his pre-contract [Capello instead went to Real Madrid].

'I'd heard of Newcastle but I hadn't seen them play. When I came here for the medical and there were so many people chanting my name I thought, where the hell am I?

'The first difference I noticed was that, when I looked in the mirror, I didn't have on my Parma shirt and I couldn't believe it. I had so many great friends in Parma.'

Making new ones in Newcastle would not take long.

*

'KEEGAN TURNED TO ME AND SAID, "WARM UP." THEN HE WENT, "You're on!" I wasn't nervous but I wasn't even prepared. I never drank before games!'

Faustino Asprilla had been on the field for five minutes when he drew his first foul in English football.

By the sixth he had created Newcastle's equaliser, and mesmerised a stadium – as well as Middlesbrough's defenders – in the process. Asprilla teased and tormented Steve Vickers on the far side of the Middlesbrough penalty area, beating him twice before crossing into the six-yard area, where Steve Watson powered in a close-range header.

It said everything that Watson had to run across to join the celebrations around Asprilla. Four minutes later, from a Peter Beardsley pass, Les Ferdinand struck a shot that sneaked under the body of Gary Walsh. With ten minutes remaining, Asprilla almost glanced a Beardsley cross past Walsh. He dragged the ball backwards through the legs of Chris Morris near the game's finish. Nobody could touch him.

'I couldn't see until I put Tino – or Faustino Asprilla – on, where the spark would come from,' Keegan told Match of the Day after the game. 'When he came on, it could have been four-one to us.'

'When you come to a different country and you don't know the language and the culture it is difficult,' adds Asprilla. 'But when you play football it is a universal language. It doesn't matter if it's hard to understand people. I did what I could when I was asked to play.

'I signed for Newcastle because of the passion and how much Keegan wanted me to come here. I knew nothing of Newcastle before I joined. I'd only been to London before, and to Leeds, because they tried to sign me.

'My first impression on arriving at Newcastle was how cold it was. At the beginning I didn't even understand what the people in Newcastle said.

'I never liked English food, my stomach couldn't cope with all the seasoning. I always went out to Italian and Spanish restaurants.'

His debut, and the wobbly-legged skills of Asprilla, made an impact that day in Middlesbrough. Nobody was quite sure what it meant, but Newcastle, with a £7.5 million signing, had yet more artillery.

'The Newcastle fans were impressive,' he adds. 'I have never had such a strong reception anywhere else.

'I realised very quickly that Kevin, despite being the manager, was best friends to all the players. He was always supporting the players, he was always helping the players.

'I could not have imagined coming on like I did against Middlesbrough. English football was very different to Serie A but I had made an impact.'

WEST HAM UNITED V. NEWCASTLE UNITED

21 FEBRUARY 1996

DARREN PEACOCK – NOWHERE FAST

DARREN PEACOCK HAD NEVER BEEN TO THE NORTH-EAST OF ENG-land for anything other than football, prior to his signing.

'The first time I drove up to Newcastle the road just went on and on,' he says.

It is getting on for 300 miles from Maiden Castle, where Newcastle trained, to London. The club went on a bus.

'We would have an eight-hour-plus round trip for a game in London,' he adds. 'We flew to Southampton and Norwich. That was it. QPR, Arsenal, West Ham, Wimbledon, Spurs, Chelsea, all on a bus.

'We would get on the bus at Maiden Castle and you'd drive down there. You've got four or five hours on the bus.

'It's a tight area to be in for eight hours. It was at least four or five hours to the centre of London, before you played football. You got sick of the A1 and the roundabouts.

'You play cards, get the videos on. There's a lounge at the back. I used to sit there with Steve Howey and Tino. Sometimes people would play cards and listen to music. You're just fighting the boredom really. It's five hours in one direction, basically.

'West Ham was a Wednesday. We went down on the Tuesday.'

By the time Newcastle rolled into Upton Park, they had played six games in the capital, four of them in the Premiership. Only one had been won, at Queens Park Rangers. There had been two draws, at Tottenham and Wimbledon, and then a defeat at Chelsea. Five points from a possible twelve.

Newcastle had drawn at Chelsea in the FA Cup through a last-minute Les Ferdinand goal (losing the replay on penalties). They had lost 2–0 at Arsenal in the quarter-final of the League Cup on a bad-tempered night when Ginola took exception to his treatment from Lee Dixon and Nigel Winterburn and was sent off.

In the opening moments at West Ham, Peacock headed against the crossbar. By the seventh minute Danny Williamson had fired past Srnicek. In the second half Asprilla beat Ludek Miklosko but his shot cannoned back off a post. With eight minutes remaining, an unmarked Tony Cottee hooked in the game-defining second.

Newcastle's lead was down to six points, albeit with a game in hand.

'On the way back I was minging,' adds Peacock. 'I shouldn't have played but I wanted to. I was coming down with something.

'The travel on the way back after a bad result felt even longer. On the way back we'd usually have a couple of beers. I didn't have any that night.

'We left Upton Park at half-eleven. We had at least four hours on the bus, straight home. You'd be on the bus forever and reach Scotch Corner and there was another forty miles to go. By Saturday we were back down in Manchester to play Man City.

'The logistics of it were draining.

'You're stuck in the middle of nowhere. That's what I thought when I first drove up. I was driving and I was thinking, when am I going to get there?'

PHILIPPE ALBERT – LUCKY MAN

TWO MEN STOOD UP IN THE EAST STAND SEATS AT FILBERT STREET.
They looked tentative before voicing what sounded like the theme tune to 'Rupert
the Bear'. There were confused glances; maybe it was a bet.

It was 1994. The ground was quiet, a huge contrast to the chaos of the final day
of the season just over two years earlier. Leicester were in the Premiership and they
looked a lot less angry about being there.

The two Newcastle fans, Micky Edmondson and his friend Paul O'Donnell,
sang it again. By now, people near to them were joining in. Then came a third airing
and it was becoming clearer that it was 'Rupert the Bear' all right, but that the words
had been subtly changed.

Within a minute, the away following at Filbert Street, around 2,500 strong, was
on its feet and singing: 'Philippe, Philippe Albert, everyone knows his name.'

*

PHILIPPE ALBERT'S DAD, GUY ALBERT, WAS FOURTEEN WHEN HE
started working in a factory in the south of Belgium, in Bouillon. He would work
there for 36 years. He married Francette and they had four boys. Philippe was the
eldest, and also the tallest by some distance, a legacy, the family thinks, of Guy's
uncle, the only other six-foot-plus Albert.

Philippe was eight when he started playing football and he was a central midfielder. He joined local club Bouillon. He was there for a decade and played for two
years under a coach called Francis Adam. Adam told Albert to play centre-half.

'I had played in midfield so technically I was able to play,' he says. 'When I went to central defence I still wanted to play football. I've never been a defender who only wanted to defend. I like playing football and I like going forward. That was the case at that time as well.'

He was still in Bouillon when he was eighteen.

'When you are in that part of Belgium at that time there were no scouts to go there and watch a young player,' he adds. 'I was a little bit disappointed but my mum always said to me, "If you have qualities, somebody one day will come and you can play at a higher level because you have the ability to do it."'

Her belief was well founded. In 1985, Charleroi came calling and paid £10,000 for Philippe. His dad, who had also played for Bouillon in the Belgian fifth division, told him there would be twelve months to make it or he would follow his father into the factory.

'He said, "You go to Charleroi and if it's OK you can have a professional career, but if it doesn't work you come back to us and live with us but you have to work." My dad wanted me to join him in the factory and I would have done it without a problem.'

Still, the desire to be a footballer went to a new level in Charleroi, who were in the second tier of the Belgian game.

'You had to work very hard, you know,' he adds. 'Physically I became a different player. When you train twice a week and you are amateur it is difficult to progress. Arriving in Charleroi, it was difficult for a few months but after it went perfect for me.

'There was never a spell when I thought I would not make it. I did not want to fail my parents by going back. When I first went to Charleroi, I gave two hundred per cent every day for four years. I worked very hard and a club came in for me and I moved again in 1989.'

His new club was KV Mechelen, who had won the European Cup Winners' Cup in 1988. Albert's lot was rising, and so was the fee. He was now worth £500,000. Mechelen were the champions of Belgium when Albert arrived. By then he was also a full Belgian international.

'My debut was unbelievable,' he says. 'It was away against the Republic of Ireland. My mum was very happy. My brothers told me that my mam and dad were crying before the match when they heard the national anthem.

'It was on 29 April 1987. My mam and dad are born on the same day – not the same year – 29 April. It was the best present that I could have given to them.

'Frank Stapleton gave me an elbow five minutes from time and I had to go off. I had six stitches around my eye. We drew nil-nil. It was my first cap; we kept a clean sheet. I was very glad, even with stitches.

'When I joined Mechelen I had to move from Charleroi to live there. Charleroi is a French part of Belgium, Mechelen is Flemish. I was twenty-two and I went there and after three months I spoke Flemish perfectly.

'It was a good experience for me, not only football but human as well because I learned the language and that was very important for me. When you move you have to adapt to the city or the area you go to. It is not the people who are already there who have to adapt to yourself.

'My three years in Mechelen were fantastic. We lost two times in the Belgian Cup final and two times we came runners-up in the league but it was still great memories because the people in the area were tremendous.

'I left a positive image of myself in every club where I played. I am very proud of it.'

That would become a theme.

In 1992, two years before the World Cup finals in America, Belgium's biggest club made their move; he would cost them £1 million.

'I was making people money and I got a better contract as well,' he adds. 'I played two years in Anderlecht. It is very professional and you know you always win something. In two years I won everything that was possible.

'We finished twice champions and we did the double in the second season before the World Cup. I won the professional football award in Belgium and best player. One is given by the footballers and managers and the other by the skippers and the journalists.

'I had signed a five-year deal at Anderlecht but the thing that made me change my mind was the World Cup.'

Those World Cup finals in the USA would alter the course of Albert's life. In 1989 he had turned down Juventus and a £350,000 signing-on fee because of the two central defenders already there, the Brazilian Julio Cesar and the German Jurgen Kohler. Before the World Cup, Fiorentina were interested but a move was blocked by Anderlecht when the Italian team failed to match their asking price.

He was still an Anderlecht player when Belgium played their long-term rivals Holland on 25 June 1994 in a Group F qualifying game. Albert, by now an elegant, ball-playing central defender, immediately caught the eye. He scored. Belgium won 1–0. It was an historic day for his country.

In the second round, Belgium were losing 3–1 to Germany when Albert got the ball inside the centre circle. He did a couple of one-twos with team-mates, ghosted past two German defenders on the edge of the penalty area and curled a shot with the outside of his right foot past Bodo Illgner. It was a stunning goal.

One ITV summariser took in both games and could not quite believe what he was seeing. Kevin Keegan had found his dream centre-half.

'I was very lucky he was there,' adds Albert. 'I have always been lucky in my life. Kevin Keegan was working for the television in the World Cup and he watched two of my games, against Holland and Germany. As you can see, I have been lucky!

'For a defender that goal was not bad. It was one of my best goals with the national team. Technically it is one of my best.

'When I was a kid and Kevin played for Liverpool I was a fan. Germany, Hamburg, twice Footballer of the Year. When I talk about him I still have the goose bumps on my arm. When I was a kid he was my idol. I had posters of him on my wall.

'I go home after the World Cup and go on holiday with my wife and I start training in July with Anderlecht for three weeks. [Former Gateshead player] Peter Harrison used to play with me in Charleroi. He called and he said to me, "Newcastle are interested."

'The next day I took the plane. We went to Leeds and had a meeting. Kevin was there. I was very impressed with him. I was a little bit nervous. We talked about football for an hour and then we talked about money for two minutes. Money wasn't important to me.

'The fact was that Keegan, the manager of Newcastle United, who had finished third in the league the season before with Andy Cole and Peter Beardsley, wanted to sign me. When a club like this comes, if you say no, you are crazy.

'Yeah, I had watched them the season before. The Premiership was on telly in Belgium as well, not much, but a few games. At that time going from Division One and finishing third was big news and people were talking in the papers about Keegan and Newcastle as well.'

After meeting Keegan in Leeds and agreeing to move in principle, he consulted his family.

'For two days I came back to talk to my wife and my parents and I·went to Newcastle on 10 August, which is my birthday, and I signed the contract that day. Another wonderful thing for me again. I signed a four-year deal. A few days later the Premier League started.'

Albert did not realise the song he heard that day at Leicester was aimed at him until several days later.

'I had only arrived a few days before the game,' he adds. 'I didn't think most of the Newcastle fans knew my name as well. A player told me what song it was. It gives you great confidence.

'When you arrive and you play in fantastic games and you have a moment like that, as I did, you feel adopted. You feel straight away at home, even if I was in England. It was like I was in Belgium. The club at the time was a family club. The atmosphere between the players and Kevin was great, you know, always friendly.'

Newcastle won their first four games. Albert was elegant and skilful. He had his own song. No one in England had a centre-half like Philippe Albert. Everyone knew his name.

Then he went to the Quayside.

'I've never seen something like this in my life,' he says. 'The first week we had three games so we didn't go out. It was a couple of weeks before we organised a night together.

'When we did, people were everywhere, queuing to go in pubs, queuing to go in nightclubs and everyone was very polite. In Belgium, you don't see anything like this. I was very impressed and I felt at home, after a few weeks.

'The fans wanted to shake your hand, they were buying you a drink, talking about football, that's what I like anyway. It doesn't bother me if I have to shake hands with two hundred people, if I have to sign an autograph for five hundred kids I will do it.

'Peter Harrison and Kevin Pugh, who I had played with at Charleroi and was from Newcastle, told me I was going to live something special, and I did. I felt it straight away.

'There were 2,500 [Newcastle] fans at Leicester. With Anderlecht you have 700. It was something completely different. The passion is different as well. It was more passionate.

'It meant something that the support was working class and I was from a working-class family in Belgium, of course.

'I've always considered myself as a working-class person. When I went out in Newcastle and people didn't recognise me, I didn't say, "I'm Philippe Albert, I'm not queuing to get in here." I never did it and I will never do it because that is the way I was educated by my parents.

'The fact the fans were working very hard during the week and then coming to the game with season tickets is not cheap. You want to give something back to these persons. That's what we did. Even away from home people used to like us. Even when we went to Liverpool, people liked the way Newcastle were playing.

'At home, people were very happy, very glad and after the game, they had seen goals and a good match. Of course you go home happy and you have a good weekend. That is the most important for those people.'

The bond between Albert and his new manager became particularly strong.

'Keegan was like a father,' he says. 'He was always in contact with you, always nice, I mean he used to train with us as well. We had respect for a manager like this. He was forty-four and he used to train every day, Terry Mac as well, unbelievable. In Belgium the trainer would stand in the middle of the pitch and give you advice. That was something special.

'He was very caring for every player. Honestly, it is the best manager I've worked with by far. As a human person as well. Keegan in the north-east is like a god.

'It is not very often you see a guy being adored and loved by so much people. For the first few months I stayed in the Gosforth Park Hotel because I was alone. My wife was still in Belgium with Julie [the couple's daughter], who was three at the time.

'She came with me in October or November. We had an apartment in the hotel. It was good. We stayed in the apartment for a few months then we moved to Jesmond, ten minutes from the city centre, a nice place, very good neighbours, no problem with anybody. It was a great time, not just footballistically, when you talk football, even normal life, you know, I was training every morning, we had a social life as well, which was very important for us.

'Katty, my wife, had no problems settling. We needed no help from Kevin with this. All the club was with us. Freddy [Shepherd] was very important. We went to one of his houses. His wife was very important for my wife as well. The players' wives as well; before the game and then after the game with the kids and everything. Honestly, my wife settled straight away, as I did.'

Just as they had settled, it was time to go home. Newcastle had a European campaign for the first time in sixteen years. The first game they played in the 1994/95 UEFA Cup was in Belgium, against Antwerp.

'It was unbelievable,' he adds. 'I think 10,000 people went from Newcastle. It was the first time the club had been in Europe for a long time. We were away from home and even the supporters and the players of Antwerp did not believe it as well.

'What a game! We should have scored ten. I remember one Antwerp player in the Belgian press saying, "You don't need to look any further, Newcastle will win the UEFA Cup this season."

'The reaction of the media was good. Kevin was very friendly with everybody. The day before the game we trained on the pitch of Antwerp and he let some supporters of Antwerp in to watch the session. I was booed because I played for

Anderlecht and Mechelen and in Antwerp they don't like anybody apart from them.

'It gave me a lot of confidence. The next day I wanted to play a very good game and beat them. After forty minutes it was three-nil.

'To see so many Newcastle fans there when you walked out gave you motivation. It gave you something else. You know, you had to be prepared for a European game but when you come to the pitch and you see 10,000 Newcastle supporters, they had travelled from Newcastle to Antwerp and they went home happy. We gave a lesson to Antwerp, not only for ninety minutes but in the game at home as well.

'When you see that support you have to do something special. If you've got a huge support, even if you win one-nil, it's OK, but with 10,000 travelling, you have to give something special and that's what we did. Rob Lee scored a hat-trick with three fantastic goals.'

It finished 5–0.

'You sat in the dressing room after and went, "What happened there?" It was something special for us as well.

'My parents, my brothers and my friends had travelled from the south of Belgium to watch the game. I was very happy and I met them afterwards. Kevin gave me half an hour to stay with them. They said, "You left a very good team but you have signed for a sensational team."

'Their eyes were wide open. My dad said to me, "I've never seen a team like this, I've never seen a team playing this kind of football, it was incredible."

'Of course, they spoke about the support. I said, "When you come in a few months you will see what a real atmosphere of football is."

'They came a few weeks later and my dad was like a kid, you know. They came in November. They would come, probably, for two weeks, so a long time. They would spend some time with Julie and Katty. My parents said, "What a nice town it is. The people are very friendly." My dad is not a difficult person, he knows where he comes from, he talks positively all the time about Newcastle.'

Newcastle were 3–0 up in the next round of the UEFA Cup against Athletic Bilbao. Even European football looked easy. The crowd at St James' Park did a Mexican wave but by the time the game finished the lead was just one. Keegan said afterwards that he had never liked the waves. In the second leg, on an unforgettable trip to northern Spain, Newcastle fell to a late Jose Angel Ziganda goal. Ziganda had scored in the first leg as well. Bilbao had opened its arms to the people of Newcastle. It was a thrilling snapshot of the life of a big club.

Those Newcastle fans would never forget the welcome they were afforded.

Europe, however, was finished and then Albert injured his knee on the training fields of Durham. He was still in a lot of pain on New Year's Eve while at the Gosforth Park Hotel.

'I couldn't move,' he says. 'Somebody knocked on the door and it was Kevin, on New Year's Eve, to send me his best wishes. Which coach would do something like this to an injured player? I don't think there is many. That is another example. He was always like a father for us.

'It was a long layoff, and despite rejoining the squad in the summer, by the time Albert was back to full fitness, Newcastle were top of the league and flying.

'I was back in the squad in July. Most of the time I was on the bench. The team was doing very well.'

Even if you are called Philippe Albert or Rob Lee, if you are not in the team for a few months and you come back and the team is doing well, you will not play.

'Kevin was very honest with everybody. I wasn't so lonely. I used to work with Derek Wright and Paul Ferris [another physio]. I had a very good relationship with them. Thanks to them two I came back to my best level.

'When I came back I thought, this team could win the title. I watched the start of the season. The team was flying.

'I think Kevin knew we wanted to play for the league. You know your level, you see Man U and Arsenal and we are probably maybe better than those teams.'

Albert had regained his place by the start of the year. When Newcastle rolled up at Manchester City on 24 February, Keegan was experimenting with a back three of Albert, Darren Peacock and Steve Howey. It would be another roller-coaster afternoon.

Ginola struck a post early on and in the sixteenth minute, Georgi Kinkladze broke down the left; he was forced inside, where Nigel Clough's shot from twenty yards deflected in off Niall Quinn. On the stroke of half-time Albert got the ball in the centre circle in his own half. He kept going and took an exquisite return pass from Asprilla that he volleyed with his left foot into the roof of the City net.

On the hour Kinkladze crossed to the far post and Quinn's header deflected into the Newcastle goal off Srnicek's midriff. Again Newcastle responded. Ginola found Albert on the edge of the City penalty area, his shot was parried by Eike Immel and Asprilla tucked in the rebound.

It was 2–2 but City weren't finished. Steve Lomas shot, it missed everyone and at the far post Uwe Rosler tucked in a third scruffy goal. It was three days after the punishing 2–0 defeat at West Ham. Newcastle had to find something.

Perhaps the spirit of the team Keegan built was an element that was not praised enough. They came again, at the death.

There was a minute remaining when Albert finally earned Newcastle their point. Taking a pass on the edge of the City penalty area from Lee Clark, he let the ball go through his legs, received a lay-off from Ferdinand and then drilled a left-footed shot into the bottom corner of the City goal.

'It was a tremendous game,' he says. 'I could have had a hat-trick! It will still be in my mind for the rest of my life. When you are a central defender and you score two goals.

'If you take the other side of the story, we conceded three goals as well so we didn't defend well. We scored three. That was why football is life. It is games like this. City were tough. We played attacking football as usual. For the fans it was a fantastic game.

'When you see the finale of the game Kevin was happy with the point. When you are losing three-two at the end of the game and you take a point, it could be a crucial point. He was still happy with the result and the performance.

'Defensively we needed to work a little bit more. He wanted to play that kind of football. He always said at the time, "I don't care if my team concedes two goals and we score three, it's not a problem." That's the way he wanted us to play football. That's the way the fans wanted us to play football. That's what we did.

'Oh yeah, I was happy playing that way. That was the football I liked. When you can go forward sometimes and be dangerous for the other team, it gives problems to them, and they didn't know what to do.

'I thought we could be champions. We were still on top. We knew we had a difficult end to the season and we had a lot of respect for every team but we were not afraid. No fear. When you've got players like Tino, Beardsley, Ferdinand, Ginola, Rob Lee, you don't have to be scared. You play your football and it's up to the opposition to try and find the key to stop that kind of football.'

Against Asprilla at Maine Road, Keith Curle tried everything. Asprilla responded to the treatment. During the game he elbowed Curle and at the final whistle butted the Manchester City captain. He was charged by the FA but escaped a ban.

It meant he was available for Newcastle's next match. The thoughts of the club's supporters had been on the visit of Manchester United for months. Now it was on the horizon, in ten days' time.

'We didn't think about Man United after the game,' adds Albert. 'That wasn't a problem. Everybody was relaxed. We had the time to recover. We were ready for that game. We were prepared for it.

'We did not feel pressure going into the game. Even if we lost against Man United we would still be top of the league. The pressure was on Man United. They had to win at St James' to have a chance to be champions.'

4 MARCH 1996

STEVE BRUCE AND PETER SCHMEICHEL – SHOOT YOU DOWN

'THIRTY-SIX THOUSAND? IT SOUNDED LIKE NINETY-SIX THOUSAND.'

*

THERE WAS 59,000 THERE THE FIRST TIME STEVE BRUCE SET FOOT inside St James' Park. He was eight years old.

Bruce's parents lived in the east side of Newcastle, on the edge of Daisy Hill. He had been born in Corbridge, about fifteen miles outside Newcastle, in Northumberland. He was born late and because of that had to go to a maternity hospital. Newcastle could not accommodate Steve Bruce. That was to become a theme.

By the time he was eight it was 1969 and Newcastle were playing in the second leg of the semi-final of the Fairs Cup against Rangers. Newcastle had to win to reach their first major final since 1955. Bruce went with his dad. 'I have a vivid memory of the game,' he says. 'It was the first time I had been. Iam McFaul had saved a penalty in the first leg.

'In the second leg, my first game, the Rangers fans came on the pitch. I'll not forget that. I went to the final with my dad as well. After that we went in the Gallowgate End and eventually we ended up going back into the Popular Side, opposite the main stand. For years I followed them.

'I lived in an area called Daisy Hill which is just on the suburbs of Wallsend. I used to go to Wallsend all the time on my Chopper bike. I used to watch the ships being built. I remember seeing the SS Northumbria. We went to the boys club at Wallsend to play football. It has produced player after player.

'I had trials at Newcastle and I was turned down. We used to train in a car park. It was ridiculous. That was the way the juniors would train. It was a crying shame, that was why there were so many Geordies who made it elsewhere. Newcastle weren't really paying any attention to the youth at all.'

Instead, like several promising youngsters, Bruce ended up at Burnley.

'I'd been there for three years when Newcastle played Burnley in the semi-final of the FA Cup at Hillsborough. Burnley sent me tickets and I was all excited at getting these tickets and going with my mate. I get the tickets and I'm in the fucking Burnley end! Supermac scored two and I'm jumping up like an idiot with my pal! They were my finest memories, Terry Hibbitt, Supermac, Tony Green, Irving Nattrass.

'All my family and my wife's family too are Newcastle fans. Everybody supports Newcastle; my mam and dad still live in Walkergate. Janet's mam and dad live at Four Lane Ends, me brother lives over the road from me mam and dad in Walkergate. We are all born and bred in the suburbs of Newcastle.'

After failing to convince at Turf Moor Bruce left Burnley and after a brief period working at the Swan Hunter shipyard was eventually handed a trial at Gillingham because of Peter Kirkley's links with manager Gerry Summers. He signed and flourished. In 1984 he moved to Norwich City. In three years at Carrow Road he caught the eye of Alex Ferguson (and Arthur Cox) and signed for Manchester United in 1987.

On 4 March 1996, Steve Bruce was the Geordie captain of Manchester United. He had already picked up the Premiership trophy twice, ending their own 26-year wait for the domestic crown.

As Newcastle pushed for the title, Joe Bruce watched his son lead out the team that was doing its damnedest to stop them.

'I would like to think my family wanted me personally to win,' he adds. 'I don't know what Janet's dad thought. Listen, if it hadn't been Man United I would have loved Newcastle to win it.

'I think the whole of the country, probably the whole of the world, wanted Newcastle to win. They had a flamboyance and a style that was definitely Kevin. You have to take your hat off to him. It was a spectacular rise from the Championship.

'He did fantastically well. It gets lost as to how good a job he did. It was also the rebirth of Newcastle. All of a sudden it awoke the city. It was incredible. It was Kevin. He deserves a big pat on the back. He got himself together a really, really good side. Howay, Ginola, Beardsley, Ferdinand, Rob Lee, Batty, Gillespie, Albert, Beresford, he got really good players. The front three in particular were pretty spectacular. They started off like a house on fire.'

In 1992 Manchester United had led the race for the last ever Division One title by seven points from Leeds. Alex Ferguson at that point had not won the English title, nor had his football club since 1967. History weighed heavy.

'We were flying, we came up to February time and, as they say in Geordieland, we took the watter in,' he says.

'No matter how you try to stop the water coming in, it doesn't. It becomes more and more difficult. Newcastle started so well. We had experience and we had great players to handle the big occasions. We enjoyed the chase and we had a superstar up front.'

When Newcastle faced Manchester United at St James' Park, the lead between the two teams was down to four points. It was the biggest occasion at St James' Park since Bruce had stood on the Popular Side as a supporter.

Tyneside came to a standstill.

There was no other topic of conversation for days. There was no space in bars as kick-off approached. The air around St James' Park was electric; fear and hope. It could be won tonight, not technically, but there was a chance to quell the Manchester United resistance.

It could effectively be won, in March, and everyone knew that fact, including those from Old Trafford. You cannot quantify the build-up of emotion in not being champions of England for 69 years, but you could hear it, inside the stadium.

Bruce, bred on the banks of the Tyne, walked out as the region opened its lungs.

'Thirty-six thousand? It sounded like ninety-six thousand, I have to tell you,' he adds. 'It was a phenomenal atmosphere, it was absolutely crackling. It was brilliant to play in. That night at Newcastle was right up there with the likes of Galatasaray. It was deafening. It certainly was.'

"It was in the lion's den," said Ferguson. "The support was magnificent. It was an incredible atmosphere. The Newcastle fans were absolutely out of this world. They were fabulous. It was the most important game for years, possibly."

The first half was a massacre.

'They absolutely battered us,' added Ferguson.

'We were struggling,' added Schmeichel.

Newcastle charged down the hill, down the slope, towards the Gallowgate End, where people used to be executed for real. Manchester United, too, were slaughtered.

An early Asprilla flick-on saw Ferdinand through but Schmeichel was out quickly at his feet.

Then Ferdinand went through, out-muscled Bruce and his left-foot shot was saved by Schmeichel's left wrist. It looped into the air and the Manchester United goalkeeper, worriedly, picked the ball out of the air. He did not know where it was going.

Beardsley struck a left-foot drive and Schmeichel went down low to his left, fumbled and took it at the second attempt. The same player shot from twenty yards and Schmeichel took it high to his left.

Asprilla did a one-two with Ferdinand and shot low to Schmeichel's right. Then Albert struck a superb free-kick from thirty yards. It bore the swerve of a left-footer and for once the Manchester United goalkeeper was beaten. Then the ball cannoned back off the crossbar.

'The first half, he was unbelievable,' added Ferguson. 'There was chance upon chance they were getting. Peter Schmeichel defied them. He just kept defying them. He was magnificent.'

'You don't go on to the pitch thinking, oh, tonight I have got to be better than everyone,' said Schmeichel. 'You go on to the pitch thinking, tonight I have to do my job, and you deal with whatever situation you're presented with.

'If you start to think otherwise you get ahead of yourself, you lose focus, you lose concentration, and if you start thinking you need to prove something, you need to show something, then it will all blow up in your head.'

Manchester United's players sat in the visiting dressing room at St James' Park and looked defeated. Ferguson let rip.

Keegan, meanwhile, understandably, asked for nothing more of his players, other than the same.

'We were superb,' he said. 'If you've ever seen a team get hammered nil-nil at half-time that was it.'

'Kevin said to us, "That was fantastic,"' remembers Warren Barton. 'We didn't come in and say, "Don't get beat". We said, "Let's go and beat them".'

'We absolutely battered them,' agrees Rob Lee. 'Ask their players, we annihilated them, Schmeichel was unbelievable. We could have been five-nil up. He was the best goalie in the world.'

'To be fair, they gave us a doing in the first half,' says Bruce. 'Pally [Gary Pallister] did his back getting off the bus going and he was bad all night so he couldn't play. Gary Neville played at centre-back alongside myself and to be fair Peter Schmeichel was terrific, he was absolutely fantastic. He single-handedly kept us in it.'

Neville would later talk of the significance of kicking down the hill in the second half. Manchester United, with their Geordie captain who used to stand on the Popular Side, had won the toss. The knowledge would prove crucial, at least in Neville's opinion.

Momentum turned. Ruud Gullit sat in the television studio at St James' Park and said Newcastle could not maintain the dominance and pressure.

Schmeichel thought similar. 'I knew that in every game we played in that period, there was a storm we needed to ride,' he said. 'If we could get past a certain point in the game, then we would start getting chances. The frustration from the other team sets in.'

Six minutes into the second half, Andy Cole took a pass from Ryan Giggs on the edge of the Newcastle penalty area, at the Gallowgate End of the ground. He slipped away from Albert, passed to his left and Phil Neville hoisted a left-foot cross to the far post that the despairing John Beresford could not intercept. Eric Cantona watched the ball and volleyed it into the ground; the bounce took it away from Pavel Srnicek and into the far side of the Newcastle goal.

St James' Park had been rebuilt for a night like this. It was a stadium and it was an all-covered bowl and the atmosphere had swirled around the heads of the players in red for 45 minutes. They were intoxicated by the football and the noise. Newcastle had done everything right, bar score. Just a goal. That was all Newcastle wanted, but this time it had not come, and when Cantona shot, it was a painful body-blow that took the wind from the sails of anyone in black and white.

'We got done with a sucker punch,' adds Barton. 'It gave them a lot of momentum; it gave us doubt. It was a real kick in the teeth. Schmeichel was phenomenal. We dominated them. Unfortunately we kept going forward and got caught with a counterattacking goal.'

The gap was down to one point.

'Well, it's a race now,' said Ferguson. 'It closes the whole thing up. It's going to be one incredible finish.'

16 MARCH 1996

ERIC CANTONA – HERE IT COMES

SEVEN MINUTES OF INJURY-TIME HAD BEEN PLAYED AT LOFTUS ROAD when Steve Bruce forced his way, through sheer desire, to the QPR by-line. He held off Alan McDonald and played the ball back to Ryan Giggs. Manchester United were trailing and Newcastle were still top of the Premiership. They would have two games in hand as well. When the ball reached Giggs, the cries for the whistle held by Robbie Hart, a referee from Darlington, to be blown, were at their highest.

Giggs crossed to the far post. He was looking for Eric Cantona.

*

SIR ALEX FERGUSON WAS SAT IN BED AT HOME WITH HIS WIFE CATHY when he decided to go looking for Cantona.

Cantona had grown up in Marseille, in southern France. His father's family were from Sardinia in Italy, his mother's from Spain.

The family home was converted from a cave in the hills of the Caillols district. His grandmother had discovered it. Cantona had two older brothers. He loved football and art (his father Albert used to draw in a workshop at the family home). 'I am a son of rich people,' he said in his autobiography. 'In truth there is no finer childhood than that which is balanced between sport and the imaginary.

'You know you have a passion for the game when you can't stop playing it, in the streets and the playground. Football in the streets gave us a tremendous need for freedom.'

As a child he would be Johan Cruyff. His brother Joel would be Kevin Keegan.

Eric Cantona signed for Caillols. The club president, Yves Cicculo, said he was 'hot-headed, but a genius'. His mother said: 'I always taught him what was right. My son never liked injustice.'

He was offered a place at Roux but instead travelled 400 miles to Auxerre to begin the formative years of his career. Three years later he was back in Marseille, and playing for Marseille. He threw his shirt down in a game. He was sent to Bordeaux on loan. He then went to Montpellier, threw a pair of boots in a team-mate's face and had a fight in his own dressing room. He was suspended but still played for France under Michelle Platini. He still won the French Cup, and he scored the winning goal.

Cantona went back to Marseille, under the ownership of Bernard Tapie, when Franz Beckenbauer was in charge. He was overlooked and moved to Nimes.

It did not go well and he threw the ball at a referee during a game. He was banned by a commission for a month; he went up to each member of the commission and said 'idiot' to their face. His ban was doubled. At 25, Eric Cantona retired from football.

Then Gerard Houllier, the France number two, suggested to Platini that he should tell Cantona to move to England. Cantona agreed and believed he was about to sign for Sheffield Wednesday, under Trevor Francis. It was only a trial. He did not want to stay and Wednesday did not pursue the £1 million transfer. He was ready to go back to France.

Howard Wilkinson, then manager of Leeds, had seen Cantona in an Under-21 tournament. He spoke to Houllier and was encouraged to sign the player. Leeds were pushing for the title and Lee Chapman, their first-choice centre-forward, had broken his wrist. Wilkinson met Cantona and agreed to move to Elland Road on a loan deal with a view to a permanent signing. He was peripheral, starting just six games, Leeds' style far too direct for him (a hallmark of Wilkinson), but they still won the title. The transfer was made permanent. Nimes received £1 million.

He didn't start the next season well, fell out with Wilkinson, had a row about his jacket, and Houllier, concerned about the implications for France, called Sir Alex Ferguson because he knew he wanted a centre-forward. Manchester United had bid for both David Hirst at Sheffield Wednesday and Alan Shearer at Southampton (as had Newcastle) but Hirst stayed put while Shearer moved to Blackburn.

Cantona put in a transfer request and later that week Bill Fotherby, the Leeds managing director, called Martin Edwards at Manchester United and asked about the availability of Denis Irwin. He was knocked back. Ferguson was in the room. He told Edwards to ask about Cantona.

Leeds said yes. For £1.1 million, Ferguson bought Eric Cantona and transformed the history of Manchester United.

In his first season at Old Trafford, Manchester United won the first Premiership by ten points, their first title in 26 years. In the 1993/94 season they did the double and lost in the final of the League Cup.

They were top of the Premiership when, on 25 January 1995, Eric Cantona launched a flying assault on Crystal Palace fan Matthew Simmons at Selhurst Park, during a night game. The fan had racially abused the Manchester United forward following his sending-off for kicking out at Palace centre-half Richard Shaw.

When the fan came at Cantona again the French forward delivered a right-hand to Simmons, who had charged to the front of the stand to shout at the player.

Ned Kelly was Manchester United's head of security. He sat with Cantona in the visiting dressing room.

'He was sitting on the bench next to his stuff, very quiet, shirt off, thinking about what had gone on,' he told Radio 5 Live in 2015, looking back after twenty years. 'It was dead silent, you could have cut the atmosphere with a knife. Sometimes you step back and realise you don't say anything.'

Ferguson did not truly realise the enormity of what had happened until he was back home and his son, wide-eyed, told him it was a kung-fu kick that his player had dealt the supporter.

Ferguson watched re-runs of the video after getting up at four o'clock in the morning. 'It was pretty appalling,' he said.

Manchester United came out strongly and banned Cantona for the remaining four months of the season. He was also fined £20,000.

The Football Association fined Cantona a further £10,000 and extended the ban to nine months.

'There were all kinds of suggestions that the club should terminate his contract and all the rest of it,' recalled Maurice Watkins, a Manchester United director and a solicitor. 'But the club felt they had to stand by the player. We were disappointed when the FA decided to heap on a greater punishment.'

Cantona was charged with assault and had to appear in a magistrates' court. He was sentenced to two weeks' imprisonment. 'You could have heard a pin drop when the sentence was imposed,' added Watkins.

Cantona was taken to the cells for three-and-a-half hours. 'Eric was in a bit of shock,' added Kelly. 'He said, "I can't be bothered with this, I might be better if I just serve this fourteen days."'

Manchester United instead appealed for bail at the Crown Court and were successful. Cantona was eventually sentenced to 120 hours of community service at Croydon Crown Court.

Cantona would later appear at a press conference to utter his famously enigmatic line: 'When the seagulls follow the trawler, it's because they think sardines will be thrown into the sea.'

In order to keep Cantona fit, Manchester United arranged behind-closed-doors games with Oldham, Rochdale and Bury. After news of the first game broke, the FA censured the club for playing Cantona in what they deemed friendlies.

Cantona was 26, a complex character who could not play football competitively. He was being verbally abused by opposition supporters when he went out. Cantona informed Manchester United he was moving back to France. He would leave English football. When Ferguson went to see him in his hotel in Worsley, he had just finished his dinner, alone, in his room. 'I don't get any peace in the restaurant,' Cantona told him. 'I prefer staying in my room.'

Ferguson agreed with his decision, until he was sat in bed later that night, with his wife Cathy.

'It's not like you to give up so easily, especially against the establishment,' she said to him. Ferguson relates what happened next in his autobiography.

> The next morning I contacted Eric's adviser, Jean Jacques Bertrand, and told him I was ready to fly to Paris.
>
> I said it was imperative that he met me and listened to some points I had to make. Cathy had kick-started my determination and there was no longer any thought of tamely accepting Eric's plan to leave us.
>
> Fleet Street had the hounds out at Heathrow and on the plane, with reinforcements waiting for me when I landed in Paris. I made a dash past the reporters and off into the city.
>
> I was contacted by Cantona's lawyer, Jean Jacques. He said he would be collecting me at 7.30pm and the porter would come to my room for me.
>
> 'Follow, Monsieur Ferguson.' I trailed after him along corridors, down stairways and out through the kitchen to the backdoor of the hotel, where Jean Jacques stood holding two helmets.
>
> He handed me one of them. 'Quick, put this on.' Off we went on a Harley-Davidson through side streets to our destination. It was a restaurant in which Eric was waiting for us with Jean

Jacques Bertrand and a secretary. There was no one else in the place and the owner had put the 'ferme' sign on the door.

Eric was delighted to see me and hear what I had to say. We had a wonderful time. I told him of my conversation with my wife and how it had galvanised me and brought me to Paris to make sure that he wasn't going to give into the pressures assailing him. We would find a way of easing his troubles.

I believed he wanted me to put an arm around him and convince him that everything would be all right, and in a sense that was what I was doing.

The other point I made was that he had to get out of that hotel and into a house. He agreed such a change was essential.

The pair talked for hours about old, classic games.

Cantona was coming back to Old Trafford. Newcastle's rivals would have their talisman.

By the time Manchester United's game at Loftus Road had entered its 97th minute, Cantona's tally for the season stood at seven goals (his season starting on 1 October where, in his comeback game against Liverpool, he bagged a penalty).

When the cross came from the left, it was Cantona who pounced at the far post to score a headed goal. There was uproar. Cantona raced with the ball to help Rangers restart the game.

There was no time. Robert Hart, the north-east official, blew his whistle. As soon as he did the cacophony of jeers filled one of English football's most intimate stadiums. There were chants of 'Cheat'. Manchester United had gone to the top of the Premiership for the first time in the entire season.

Back in Tyneside, hearts sank.

ARSENAL V. NEWCASTLE UNITED

23 MARCH 1996

SIR JOHN HALL – GET
THE MESSAGE

THERE WAS A RACE TO CATCH THE TRAIN NORTH, BACK TO NEW-
castle. First class was in the end carriage. It was where Sir John Hall and his son
Douglas were sat. It meant their carriage filled at the death, with Newcastle fans who
were not supposed to be there.

'First class was at the back of the train, not at the front,' says Hall. 'I was sitting
down and Douglas smoked and there was a section for smoking. All the lads were
late so they were jumping on the train.

'I heard them: "Oh, the chairman's here in the first-class bit." They moved everyone out of the first-class carriage. They went, "Do you mind, wor chairman's here,
will you go through to the next carriage?" They went through to the next carriage.

'The carriage we were in ended up full of supporters, they were lying on the
racks. It turned into a question-and-answer session. "What's he say, ask him this
question, chairman, what about this?"

'That was the rapport we had. It was a wonderful time. I'm glad we'd been able
to put it together. It was a team effort and we did have a team.

'I was the driver and the visionary but Freddy Shepherd and Douglas and Freddie Fletcher were the ones who dealt with it every day.'

Hall had opened the lines of communication to the supporters early. Along
with the Magpie Group he held talk-ins all over the north-east before he took over.
Nights like the one at the High Pit Social Club in Cramlington were packed and
they were raucous.

'The power of the club was tremendous,' he adds. 'We gave talk after talk. The
one thing we did, when we wanted to take over the club, we had meetings all around

the area.

'We went to the supporters and explained what we were going to do and we said, "We need your support."

'We always had this dialogue. The dialogue is essential. You have to tell them what you are trying to do – you can't tell them everything – and you have to keep them in the picture of what you are going to do.

'The way it went and the one thing I learned in all of this is a lot of people live their lives for the football club. It becomes part of their life. We have businesses and jobs, they probably work for someone. Some might have mundane jobs.

'They might want to get away from it and need something and here was the football club.

'When we travelled we couldn't get enough tickets. We had five thousand every match going away. It is a people's club.'

Hall had spoken to fans lying in racks when Newcastle had won at Highbury. It was 1994.

By the time the train pulled out of King's Cross on Saturday, 23 March 1996, Keegan had already laid into his players following a 2–0 defeat.

'We can't be disappointed in the result,' he said after the match. 'We didn't deserve to win. You can afford to carry one or two players but not five or six. I can give you a list of those who didn't play well. There was Les Ferdinand, Faustino Asprilla, Rob Lee, David Ginola and Peter Beardsley.'

Newcastle would not play in the capital again that season. They had picked up just five points there from six matches – thirteen points had been dropped in London alone.

'We wanted to bring a centre-half in,' adds Hall. 'We had started to think of signing a new centre-half when we were twelve points in the lead and when we had started to let goals in.

'We started to leak goals and we wanted to bring someone in. We told Kevin. He wouldn't. He said, "I'll do it my way."'

Manchester United played at home to Tottenham the following day.

'Their goal came from a goal kick when Tottenham should have had a corner,' says Keith Gillespie. 'Andy Sinton crossed and it should have been a corner and it went for a goal-kick. They went on and scored from it.

'When Cantona scored I thought, maybe this isn't going to be our year.'

Four days earlier Manchester United had beaten Arsenal 1–0. They had picked up ten points from four games and had scored just four goals in all of those matches.

Eric Cantona had got every one of them.

TERRY MCDERMOTT – THE LONG AND WINDING ROAD

'HOW CAN YOU HAVE A GO AT THE PLAYERS AFTER THAT? THEY were brilliant.'

*

TERRY MCDERMOTT WAS TEN THE FIRST TIME HE WENT TO ANFIELD. It was round the corner from where he had lived when he was first born, on Scotland Road. His family moved to Kirkby, a new town on the edge of the city, because of the overcrowding.

He used to go to the Kop at one o'clock on a Saturday with his dad, his uncles and his brother. 'You go there dreaming to be one of them one day, not believing for one minute you will ever actually play for Liverpool,' he says. 'We used to get to the Kop early, you wouldn't get in if you didn't. I don't think there was too many season tickets. People didn't have the money.

'There were 28,000 fanatical Scousers in the Kop and in a little corner, as you look from the pitch, it was to your right, the boys' pen, and it had big fencing and wire on the top, I used to go in there.

'I can still remember the team now. They were my idols. Where we lived at Kirkby, we didn't have a lot of money, but we always found money to go to the match.'

Sacrifices came elsewhere.

'There would be a big hole in my shoe and they put the cornflake packet inside the shoe to make it look like something was there,' he adds. 'If you didn't put that in, your feet would be touching the ground. I had cornflake packets in my shoes because we couldn't afford new shoes. My mam and dad did everything to get you them but there was no money.

'We used to go to Southport for our holiday, fifteen miles away. Or go across the Mersey on the ferry to Wallasey or New Brighton, that was like going to America.

'We used to take bottles of water and a jam butty or, if you were lucky, we would take a banana butty, or a sugar butty. That's what we had. Or brown-sauce butties. Honestly, we couldn't afford anything else.

'When I was playing for Kirkby Boys, to try and get some money we would go potato-picking or pea-picking. We would be up at half-six and go to Kirkby station and the farmer would come up in the tractor with a trailer and he'd take the first twenty on.

'If you weren't one of the twenty you would be hoping another fella came from another farm. When you realised how it worked you had to fight to get on and you made sure you did. I don't know how much we got but it was a pittance. I was fourteen.'

Kirkby Boys was where it started to happen for McDermott, not that anyone realised, not then anyway. They were the pick of the area teams at the time, despite the greater numbers Manchester or Liverpool Boys could choose from. 'We had three schools and we used to beat everyone.'

That ensured the entire squad was signed to schoolboy forms with professional clubs. Everyone, that is, except two players: Terry McDermott and Dennis Mortimer.

'At the end of school, in June, I hadn't been offered an apprenticeship. My mam said to me, "You need to get a job."

'I had about six jobs in three weeks. I worked in a wood factory, lifting wood, big long strips of wood, about twenty foot long, and moved them from here to there, about six bloody feet away, I was thinking, what a fucking business this is.

'I done that. I was spray-painting for a bit and I still don't know what that was. I was putting paint on something, walls? I didn't fucking know. I was stood there going, "What am I doing?" It was the same with all the flaming bits of wood. Just stood there going, "What in God's name is all this about?"'

One night he went to Anfield to see Liverpool play. And that night, his life changed.

'I remember we went to watch Liverpool against Burnley and Dennis had been there as well,' adds McDermott. 'When I came back, me mam said, "There's been a scout from Bury here for you."

'I said, "Bury, where's that?" She said, "I don't know, I think it's Manchester way." I said, "What did they say?" She said, "They've left you forms."

'Colin McDonald was the chief scout and he'd left a contract. My mam said, "He's been to see Dennis as well. I told him you were at the game."

'Straight away I said, "I'll sign, no one else wants me." I filled in the forms and I sent them back. I went to see Dennis, I said, "What are you doing?" He said, "I'll wait and see." I think he went to Coventry.

'I went to the worst one, in the old Third Division. I went anywhere they would have me. All of a sudden I was on schoolboy forms with Bury.

'My dad used to take me on the train, we couldn't afford a car, from Kirkby to Bolton, get off at Bolton for a train to Bury, play there at eleven in the morning, for their under-seventeens.'

He got an apprenticeship and moved into digs, opposite Bury's ground.

'You would train in the car park,' he adds. 'It was shale and concrete and no grass if the weather was bad. It probably manned me up. You weren't getting pampered. I used to be frightened because the older players would be screaming blue murder at you if you didn't pass to them or if it was a bad pass. It helped me because I never really got nervous before games after that.

'When I broke into the team there was a fella called Billy Urmston. He told a few white lies because I was in the reserves learning my trade and he was the manager. One player got injured and they needed someone to play for the first team in the next game. The manager spoke to Bill and asked who did well in the last game and he said, "Definitely Terry Mac, he was different class, brilliant, worked like a Trojan."

'I'd played in that reserve game and I was shite. The first team was playing Tranmere. I had to play because of what Bill had said. We won eight-nil against them at Gigg Lane. The following week I wasn't playing.'

An impression, however, had been made.

'I started getting in the team and doing all right. We played Man City and we beat them in a League Cup game. We played Chelsea at Gigg Lane and we should have beat them as well. That set me on the road to my career really. Then you start hearing stories Liverpool are interested in you, but you think it's bollocks.

'I played at Bury for two years and then Joe Harvey came down with Newcastle's chief scout, Len Richley, to watch me play. There was no motorways then and we were playing Reading.

'I was told they were coming. It was foggy and they had to call the game off an hour before it was supposed to start. Joe was there waiting to watch me. A week later I got a call saying Newcastle want to sign you.

'What was my first feeling? I didn't want to go. It was too far. I loved being in Bury. I've always been like that. Where I've been I wanted to stay. I had a lot of good friends there. We had great drinking sessions every Sunday.

'I get the call from Newcastle to go and I didn't want to. I asked the chairman of Bury if I could have a few quid. I said, "I didn't cost you anything, I've worked hard for you."'

The fee was set at £22,000.

'The Bury chairman said, "We'll give you a thousand pounds," or something like that. He said, "We can't pay you all at once, you'll have to come back to Bury Social Club," and he'd be in there and he'd give me an envelope and there might be two hundred quid in it.'

So Terry McDermott went to Newcastle.

'I had never been to Newcastle in my life,' he says. 'I was twenty-one when I went to Newcastle in October 1972.

'We drove up from Bury to Newcastle and the manager drove me. We had a puncture on the way up on the A1. We got there and they offered me something like fifty-five pounds a week. At Bury I was on about twenty pounds. It was like, Christ, what's going on here? I signed and I found out Joe had never seen me play.

'The first time he saw me play in the reserves at St James' Park he turned round to Len and went, "Fucking hell, what have I bought here?"

'Len turned and went, "Don't worry, he'll be all right."'

✱

THEY STILL TALK ABOUT TONY GREEN, AND HE HASN'T PLAYED A game for Newcastle United since 1972. He only played 33 times. That should tell you everything.

Joe Harvey once said of Green, 'After they made Tony Green, they threw away the mould. I couldn't hope to buy a similar player, not even for twice the amount.'

McDermott saw him play. 'I remember watching Tony Green from the stands and I thought, what a player this fella is.

'He got injured. It was only because of Tony getting injured. It would have taken a lot longer if he hadn't. I was a midfield player. Joe threw me in and I never looked back.'

He remembers playing at St James' Park for the first time.

'It was electric,' he says. 'It was nothing of a ground but the atmosphere, Christ, don't forget I'm going from 15,000 to 45,000. Playing in front of them was daunting. I will never forget the atmosphere.'

Harvey, who won the Inter-Cities Fairs Cup as manager in 1969, had put together a strong side.

'I think I coped all right,' says McDermott. 'I was a regular from then on. I played every week. Joe Harvey, he would be your dream manager, he couldn't give a fuck. He used to smoke all the time and he would go, "What's the matter now?"

'We were on the training ground one day and we were playing five-a-side and Keith Burkinshaw sent me off for swearing. Something happened, I said, "Aahh, fuck off." He goes, "What? Fucking get in now."

'I went across the pitch to the changing room and I was taking my stuff off. The next minute Joe came in and he goes to me, "What are you fucking doing in here?" I've gone, "That long streak of shit has kicked me off." He's gone, "What for?" I goes, "He said I swore." Joe's gone, "Fuck him! Get fucking back out there!" I had to put my stuff back on and go back out!

'He was brilliant. He was just an ordinary bloke, a really, really good guy. We had so many good players: Terry Hibbitt, Supermac, John Tudor, 'Jinky' Jimmy Smith, what a player he was, he should really have been a George Best. He could have been but he had other things on his mind other than football.

'We had a great team. Stewart Barrowclough was a great player, John T. ran his bollocks off, Tommy Gibb was a great midfielder. We had Bobby Moncur, Pat Howard and David Craig, another great player, a great fella. We had a really good squad.'

Newcastle had won the Anglo-Italian Cup before embarking on an extraordinary run to the 1974 FA Cup final (they would also win the Texaco Cup in April of that year).

'It was unbelievable when you think about it. We were held at home by Hendon, we drew one-one. We played the replay at Watford. We beat them four-nil. We beat West Brom three-nil away from home. Every game up to the final we won away from home.

'We had the Forest game when we were losing three-one and the fans came on the pitch. That was incredible. We came back to win four-three but they made us play it again, so we had two replays at Goodison Park. All my family were there.

'Then we had the semi-final at Hillsborough. You'll never forget it because of Malcolm Macdonald. Colin Waldron was chasing him and trying to pull him back and Supermac virtually carried Colin before he scored.

'I always remember coming home on the A1, back from the game, and it was a sea of black and white. I remember that. Cars stopped because of the volume of traffic. There were twenty-odd thousand going home. We were driving on the side and in the middle of the road people were jumping out of the cars and onto their car roofs.'

The final was painful. Newcastle lost 3–0 to Liverpool. They did not turn up. McDermott was voted Newcastle's man of the match.

'That was the first time I put a Liverpool strip on,' he adds. 'It was Phil Thompson's strip. We went up before Liverpool. It was the first time anyone had went up the steps with the opposing team's shirt on. Phil Thompson came up with mine on. He was a mate.'

There was still an open-top bus parade through the streets of Newcastle. Thousands turned up. St James' Park was filled. Bob Moncur held up an imitation FA Cup. He looked embarrassed.

'Look at the amount that turned up,' adds McDermott. 'And we had been beaten. You never forget it.'

Terry McDermott had moved in with Alan Kennedy and his mam in Penshaw when he transferred to Newcastle United from Bury. It was a short-term thing, for a month, until he found digs. The best part of two years after signing, he still wasn't looking very hard.

'His mam was lovely,' adds McDermott. 'She worked in a chippy. I used to get them every night. My protein was a pint of lager!

'When I was at digs at Alan's, I would play against Man United at St James' Park and at twelve o'clock I would have roast beef, Yorkshire pudding, gravy, three veg and roast potatoes.

'It was a full Sunday lunch and then apple pie and custard! That was me for the game. I didn't feel any different. That's what I had as a pre-match meal and I was renowned for my running!

'You're fit, it's a gene. It's in your genes, whether you're quick or not, whether you've got stamina. You've either got it or you haven't. I could run all day.

'I'd been out on the drink after the game. Alan came in and I was still in bed at about one o'clock! He said, "Joe Harvey wants to see you, you've got to go to the ground." I said, "What for?" He said, "I don't know," I went, "Shit." I didn't know what I'd done.

'I went to St James' and Joe said, "Liverpool have come in for you. What do you want to do?" I said, "I don't know."

'I didn't want to leave Newcastle. I didn't want to go. If it had been any other club I wouldn't have gone. I loved Newcastle. I just loved being around the people.

'Joe said, "It's up to you but we've accepted the bid." I said, "If you've accepted it you want me to go. I came here for £22,000 twenty months ago and you're getting a lot more so surely you'll give me something for going." He said, "We don't want you to go, so we won't give you anything." I said, "If you've accepted it, I'll go."

'He said, "Go down yourself." It wasn't chauffeur-driven then, no private planes. It was get yourself down there tonight. I got nothing and said thanks Joe and off I went.

'The letter was on the passenger seat and I was desperate to see what was in it and I opened it. It was the figure and the fee and everything: £166,000. I went straight to my mam and dad's. I got in my car, took my dad to Anfield and the chairman was waiting for me with Bob Paisley and Peter Robinson. Within fifteen minutes it was sorted. I had a small medical and then I signed and that was it done.'

After signing in November 1974 it did not happen quickly for McDermott at Liverpool. It was two years before he was a regular. Some things are worth the wait. By the summer of 1977, Liverpool had reached the European Cup final in Rome's Olympic Stadium, against Borussia Monchengladbach.

'We had won the league and we played the FA Cup on the Saturday and the European final on the Wednesday,' he recalls.

'My mother was dying of cancer. That was in May. She died in June. She was on her last legs then. I knew when I was playing in an FA Cup final and a European Cup final and she didn't know anything about it. She was full of morphine or whatever it was. I would have loved her to have been there in Rome to see that. She was in a bloody cancer unit.

'It's only when you look back and think: How did I get through that, playing in those games knowing my mam was dying? It was a hard time. I would have loved her to be there. She couldn't. She was a month away from dying.'

Instead, there was a Liverpool game, and Terry McDermott, his dad, his brother and his uncles all went, just as they had in 1961 when he was ten and was put in the boys' pen.

This time he was playing.

In the 29th minute, Terry McDermott set off on a trademark run from deep and ghosted behind two German defenders on the edge of the Borussia penalty area. It was spotted by Steve Heighway, who slipped in a neat pass, and he clipped his shot into the bottom corner of the Monchengladbach goal. It never looked like being saved.

Barry Davies, commentating, said: 'That's nice, that's McDermott and that's a goal! Beautiful build-up, McDermott finding a lovely position, he sees things early, he takes up good positions in the box, just look at him running, he's in space, the

German defender has to come across, leaving Keegan, and McDermott tucks away superbly into the corner. Lovely stuff and a fine goal.'

'How did I feel as a Liverpool lad scoring the first goal in the European Cup final against Borussia Monchengladbach? Fucking hell, man! That's how I felt!

'Fucking hell, I can't believe it, I'm playing for my home-town team, in a European Cup final, and I've just scored.'

Liverpool won 3–1. Terry McDermott, the Kirkby lad with cornflake packets in his shoes, lifted the European Cup.

He did it again the following season, at Wembley, and then again in 1981 in Paris. (His pal Dennis Mortimer lifted it as Aston Villa's captain in 1982.)

He won the First Division five times, the League Cup twice, the UEFA Cup, the Super Cup and four Charity Shields (once shared).

It was a breathtaking haul of honours.

In three seasons at the very top level of club football, McDermott scored 58 goals from midfield.

'I never thought I was any different to anyone else,' he says. 'Players were special in them days because you were winning trophies. You were adored by half of Liverpool.

'It was such a vibrant city. You had had the Beatles, all them pop groups, Cilla Black, Jimmy Tarbuck and Ken Dodd. It doesn't get any better. To play for Liverpool was something I never thought would happen.

'We were winning and the people loved you. It was a purple patch for Liverpool in the 1970s and 80s. Everyone wanted to buy you a drink and I loved that, but I was just an ordinary guy and I've always been that.'

In 1980 he became the first footballer to win both the PFA and the Football Writers' Association Player of the Year awards.

The first award was on a Sunday night at the Grosvenor Hotel in London.

'That's my night out, Sunday, in Kirkby, in a working men's club with my dad and my friends and my family. My brother was a singer there. What did I want to go all the way down there to London for? They said they'd send a private plane. Myself, Kenny Dalglish and Roy Evans flew down.

'I did all the speeches and that and then I was going, "Come on, get going." I came off the stage and I was off. I phoned up my club, it was about half-ten and in them days there was a curfew of when you could drink. I said, "I'm on my way, get some beers in!"

'I swear I got there at quarter to twelve and it was heaving. It had been on television. I didn't realise they were waiting for me to come in. They all started cheering when I arrived. It was a lovely touch, then the pints started arriving, we were there till about four o'clock!'

Then came the FWA award. Norman Winn, the chairman of the FWA, telephoned McDermott.

'I said, "Hi, Norman," he said, "You've won the player of the year." I said, "You're joking." He said, "I'm telling you, you've won it." I went, "How can a rag-bag player like me win a trophy like this?"

'I was quoted and he put it in the paper a few days later. I was the first to win both.

'I told my dad, he said, "Bloody hell, fantastic." But we weren't one of those who start hugging each other. It was like, "Well done, get us a pint."'

His train was delayed on the way to the awards. McDermott went to Chester races instead.

'Bob Paisley was doing the presentation,' he adds. 'I didn't know that. Bob said, "If he's done another blind-side run, it'll be the last one he ever does."

'I got battered off the press. Apparently, I'm the only one who didn't turn up. I regret not going now. What were you doing, you plonker? It was a great honour and I was very proud.'

McDermott played 25 times for England.

Yet by 1982 he was losing his regular starting role at Anfield.

McDermott more than most had followed events closely at St James' Park that summer. He had become good friends with Keegan from their time with Liverpool and England. 'We were decent mates at Liverpool,' he says. 'I got on well with him.'

Perhaps more than most, he understood what would happen.

'I knew as soon as he's gone there that there was going to be an explosion,' he adds. 'I knew. I fucking knew. I remember watching it. I know what he's like, what a fella he is.

'I'd known him with England and Liverpool and we were decent mates and then he went to Hamburg. I just knew. I remember when Newcastle played QPR and they won one-nil. He scored and the crowd were hysterical, I thought, fucking hell.

'It was an explosion. I knew. I remember watching it and the hairs on the back of my neck went up, you had the goose bumps just watching. I knew what the fans were like. You knew there were 35,000 there from twelve o'clock. I knew the place would erupt and take off when he went there. I knew the people there would love him.'

The opportunity quickly came to follow Keegan to the explosion at St James' Park. McDermott took it.

'I came to Newcastle because of Kevin,' he adds. 'I could have stayed at Liverpool. I had two years left, which would have taken me to my testimonial. I'd lost my place in the team, I was more out than in.

'I knew they were interested in me going. I arranged to meet Arthur Cox and Joe Harvey halfway up the A1. They said, "We want you, do you want to sign?" I said, "Yeah." I agreed to it like that.

'I went back to Liverpool and told them I was going and I think I played against Dundalk in a European Cup game, my last ever game for Liverpool. We won. I knew and not many others did that I was driving up to Newcastle to sign for them. If it hadn't have been for Kevin I probably wouldn't have gone. I moved to Newcastle because Kevin was there.'

McDermott made his second debut for Newcastle against Rotherham on 2 October 1982. There were 12,436 in Millmoor that day, and 5,000 were from the north-east.

Keegan had been left out of the England squad named by Bobby Robson, the new England manager, without a phone call. Newcastle won 5–1; Keegan scored four. McDermott set up the first goal for Keegan, within fifteen minutes of his first appearance in a Newcastle shirt for eight years. Then he won a penalty. The away support, who had jumped around to the Dexys Midnight Runners' song 'Jackie Wilson Said', were similarly vocal in asking whether the England manager was watching on the box.

In that first season Newcastle came fifth in Division Two.

'It was fantastic, I loved every minute of it,' adds McDermott.

He scored twelve times in his two years back in the north-east.

'People ask who's the best manager you've had and I would have to say Joe Harvey, Bob Paisley and Ron Greenwood, and I would put Arthur Cox alongside them,' he says. 'He understood players. We make mistakes and do things we shouldn't have done.

'He confronted you and he told you in no uncertain terms what you'd done wrong but he wouldn't hold a grudge.'

Cox, Keegan and McDermott helped lead Newcastle to the First Division. McDermott was given the captain's armband for the penultimate fixture of the season at Huddersfield when Keegan was injured. There was a lap of honour in the final game against Brighton, and then a final friendly against his old club, Liverpool.

'We bowed to the fans at the end and we meant it. They deserved a trophy. There were some great games that season and we played football the right way.'

Keegan left in his helicopter but there was to be no such spectacular departure for McDermott.

'Kevin was leaving and then Arthur Cox fucking left! I was devastated,' he says. 'Then Jack Charlton came in. My contract had finished but in them days if they held your registration you couldn't go anywhere.

'I went to Ascot races with Alan Hansen and Alan Kennedy and I got a phone call off Joe Harvey. "Jack wants to see you," he said. "Joe, I'm in Ascot." "Terry, you need to get up." I said, "I'm getting married next week." He said, "I think you should and come and see him."

'I drove up to Newcastle to his office and I was supposed to meet him at eleven and he was late. He came in, "Sorry about that." I said, "Don't worry, Jack, nice to meet you."

'He said, "Your contract's up, as you know, here's what we're going to offer you."'

'I said, "Jack, it's the same as last year. We've just gone up to a new division and I took a drop to come from Liverpool to Newcastle. We've been successful and you're offering me the same." He said, "I think it's a good contract." I said, "I don't."

'He said, "What are you going to do?" I said, "I'll leave then." He said, "Go on."

'I got up. As I'm walking towards the door, he says, "You'll be back." I opened the door as I was going and I said, "I won't, you fucking watch."'

McDermott never played for Newcastle again.

'He was battering me in the Evening Chronicle, saying I was being greedy. I was battering him, saying I wasn't and that I had taken a drop to come back.'

The stand-off lasted months.

'Jack lived near me. I used to go to a mobile chippy that got around. I was in the queue one night and the next minute he was in the queue! Straight away I've gone, "Are you all right, Jack?" He goes, "Err, err, yeah, I'm very good."'

McDermott briefly went to Cork before moving to Cyprus for two seasons, where with Apoel he won the domestic title. In 1987 he retired.

For a short period he put money into a catering company.

'Say if you went to Old Trafford or to the Great Yorkshire Show or to Aintree they would do a lot of the hot food there, hot dogs and burgers, that kind of thing. I used to go there. I enjoyed the craic.

'It's not right that I worked on them. I used to go. It was a bit of colour in the stories. Imagine me serving fucking hot dogs! I was like a silent partner.'

Still, McDermott ended his foray into catering. For four years he was not involved in football. By 1992, he was close with Micky Quinn, who had fitted seamlessly into the Newcastle number nine shirt, albeit a touch more snugly than his predecessors.

'I used to ring Micky every day at the training ground at Benwell, talking about horses,' adds McDermott. 'He loved horses too, we'd pass on tips. Kevin had only got the job the day before. I phoned up Micky and Derek Wright [the Newcastle physio] answered it. "Hi, Del Boy, you all right, mate?" "Yeah, great." "Where's Micky?" "Hang on, Terry, someone wants to speak to you."

'Kevin came on. He goes, "You all right, mate?"

'I've gone, "Yeah, well done, I didn't know you were going, what happened there?"

'He's gone, "I know, it came out of the blue. I'd like to have a chat with you. I'm a bit busy at the minute, I'll come back to you tomorrow night.'

'Then Micky Quinn came on and we got chatting about horse racing.

'The next day Kevin didn't ring when he said he was going to.

'I used to go training at Liverpool at Melwood with Dave Johnson, to keep in trim. We went there before they all came in. We didn't want to be seen to be getting in the way.

'We were a bit late leaving and they were coming in. Graeme Souness was the manager and as we were walking out he said, "Where you going? Come and have a little jog around."

'All the lads like Ronnie Moran and Roy Evans were going, "You'll be up to Newcastle shortly, won't you?" I said, "What for?" They said, "Well, Kevin, surely he's rang you. He rang you, didn't he?" I said, "He was supposed to ring last night."

'They went, "It's obvious what he's going to ring you for. He'll want you to go up there." I said, "You what? Nah, I can't see that happening." They went, "No danger."

'Anyway, I went for a light jog with Graeme and he said, "Listen, I think Ronnie Moran is packing in at the end of the season. I'll probably move things around and you can take the reserves."

'I said, "I've not got any badges." He said, "Fuck it, just pick the team. But until he goes I'll try to get you in."

'I told him what had happened. He said, "Well, you know what he's ringing for. He'll want you to go up there and help him run it.'"

That night he rang.

'Kevin went, "Sorry, mate, I was snowed under last night. I'm only here till the end of May to try and keep them up. Do you fancy coming?" I said, "Doing what?" He said, "You'll be helping me."

'I went, "But I've got no badges, I never had any intentions of being involved in coaching."

'He went, "Terry, I've known you long enough, I want people around I can trust."

'I said, "When do you want me?" He went, "Tomorrow morning." I said, "I'll be there."

'I got there and that was it. He'd had Benwell fumigated. He said, "I'll give you x amount." I said, "No." He said, "That's what you're getting and that's it done."

'I think he paid me out of his own pocket, out of his own wages.'

Keegan and McDermott were back together. They moved into adjacent rooms at the same Gosforth Park Hotel that Keegan had been spotted in, ten years earlier.

'Every night we'd sit in there and look at the league table,' he says. 'I'd go, "How the fucking hell are we going to get out of this?"'

The crowds returned but the sailing was never plain.

Two wins in three games set up a home game with Swindon. The day before it, Keegan grabbed McDermott.

'He said, "Come on, we're going." I went, "Where?" He goes, "I'm not bothered, we're going." I said, "Where do you want to go?" He said, "We'll go to the Lake District."

'I knew there was a problem. Of course, I'd known there had been a row.

'We got in the car and he said, "It's not what they said it was going to be. They were going to do this and that and they've never done it."

'He was getting angry. The one thing about Kevin, if he's said it, at the end of it all, it's true. When other people don't do it and they say they are going to do it, he gets peeved.

'People say it's spitting the dummy out, it's not. It's what is right and what is wrong. If they say they're going to do it, they should do it. It happened a few times where they didn't. I think it was money for players that didn't come.

'He just went, "I'm not putting up with this any more." I was thinking, what are we doing?

'I said to Kevin, "Whoever's upset you, Freddie Fletcher or John Hall, it's Newcastle we're trying to save, it's the club. Why don't you go and win the game and then you can walk away from it?"

'He went, "Yeah, you're right."

'We were at Haydon Bridge by then, I don't know where the fuck we were going to go. We had no clothes or anything!

'I think he wanted me to persuade him. Normally his word is his bond. On this occasion he didn't want to walk away from it. I said, "Let's go and win the game and you go back to Southampton and I'll go back to Liverpool."

'He said, "Yeah, you're right. We'll go and win."

'We went back and we won and then he left. He wouldn't go back. He phoned me and he said, "After what they've done, that's it."'

Over the weekend, Keegan and Hall spoke. Keegan phoned McDermott again. 'He said, "We're going back."

'What did I think? Brilliant! Fucking brilliant. I loved it. I loved being around the players and having a laugh with them, winding them up, trying to give them what you went through as a player. Because of what you've won they respect you.'

McDermott became Keegan's buffer. It sells McDermott short, but it was a title with a history.

'Kevin mentioned it. That was what we used to call Bob Paisley to Bill Shankly. Kevin said, "He will be my buffer." I used to say, "If it's good enough for Bob Paisley to be a buffer, it's good enough for me."

'You're a buffer between the manager and the players. They would ask, "What should I do?" Then you tell them, "I'd do this if I was you."

'They would sooner go to the assistant. The assistant is the go-between. I would say, "I'll have a word with the gaffer if you want, but only if you want. I promise I won't if you don't want me to." They would say, "Don't say anything."

'I can get in trouble as well because I can know stuff the manager doesn't. You have to get respect from the players. If they trust you they will open up to you; it's no good being an assistant if they hate you or can't trust you.

'I like to think I got on with them. They knew I wouldn't snitch on them. I realised what I needed to do. I used to talk to them.'

More than that, McDermott found a calling he had not expected, on the training field.

'People say coaching is telling them to run here and there and do your weights. Is that coaching? What is coaching?

'There is coaching, putting on a session like Derek Fazackerley. He would say, "What do you want to do this morning, Kevin?" Kevin would go, "Five-a-side, quick work." And Derek would do a session for that.

'Then you get other people who are coaches, like me, who don't put on sessions but you go and talk to them. I used to do it all the time. Explain. I'd say, "You've got to get on the ball a bit more, you're not in the game enough." They'd go, "It's difficult." I'd say, "You need to want it more. Don't be mute. Scream at them, 'Give me the ball!'"

'People would say, "You don't put sessions on." I don't need to put sessions on. I like to think I'm very good at talking to the players and seeing things and adding that to their game.

'After a training session, I would take a player off to work with them, maybe some shooting, for two hours. Spend a bit of time with them. "Listen, we'll do this every day, you come to me, I'll put on a couple of things to work on, we'll get your passing to be better, or your movement, or dropping your shoulder, if you want me to help you, you can get better."

'I would take them to the far corner and we'd do long passing, short passing, shots from outside the box, balls whipped in, movement in the box. That's coaching. Not because you're putting sessions on.

'I could show them, knocking balls in, passing or shooting. You talk to them more. They respect you. They go, "He's won three European Cups." They listen. They give you their respect. If you have respect you have half a chance. If you shout about what you've won, the players won't listen.

'With Kevin being who he was, he got the respect straight away, and from being an England captain as well. All the players loved him. He would upset the ones he didn't play or the ones he gave a bollocking to. He could be ruthless, but he could also be the nicest man in the world, and he was.'

They were long nights in the Gosforth Park Hotel.

'I remember Micky Quinn was due to get a new contract, before we took over. I rang him to talk about horses. He said, "My contract's up, they've offered me a new one." I said, "Ask them for more. You're the main man, you're the goalscorer."

'He said, "You're right." I said, "Say you want x amount. Even if they lower you down you get more than they offered you."

'He got an unbelievable contract. He phoned me and he goes, "Well done, lad, great, thanks mate."

'Weeks later, Kevin gets the job. He needed to see all the players' wages and what they were on. That's part and parcel of it.

'Kevin goes, "Bloody hell, have you seen Micky Quinn's contract?" I goes, "It's a lot, ain't it?" He said, "Who gave him that?" I said, "Me!"

*

NEWCASTLE LOST FIVE SUCCESSIVE GAMES AFTER KELLY'S GOAL AT home to Sunderland.

'We could have been sacked after that run,' adds McDermott.

They weren't. After Kelly's goal against Portsmouth came victory at Leicester.

'I remember I was on such a high, we knew we were staying up. I was going back to Liverpool. Kevin went back to Newcastle.

'I remember getting home and going out celebrating. It was a big thing for me. I'd never been involved in that side of football before. I enjoyed it that much, I was going to people that night, "I hope he goes back." But I wasn't sure.'

It was touch and go. Keegan was proving in those weeks to be the manager that Newcastle United had needed for generations. Newcastle, the club emerging under Hall, had to prove that they were ready for him. Keegan was not bluffing. He was ready to go if there was not the desire to cast off years of mediocrity.

'We'd finished, and I knew he was still in negotiations with them,' adds McDermott. 'He rang me up and I was hoping to go back. He said, "Terry, we're not going back, it's not going to happen, mate," I said, "No problem, all right, Kevin, I understand, keep in touch."

'A day later, Keegan called again, he went, "We're going back." I said, "You're joking," he said, "No, get your bag packed, Terry, we're going."

'Was I pleased? The best five years outside of playing I've ever had were about to happen.

'We'd just had a baby, Greg, and we signed a three-year contract. I thought, well, why don't we move up there? I love it up here. My wife is from Liverpool. She said, "Let's go up there." I said, "Fine, let's do it."

'Greg was only six months and it was big wrench. We rented and then we had a house built and we moved into it. I loved it.'

Something changed at Newcastle that summer. Keegan poured his positivity into a football club and a region. It was easier and more effective as a manager than even as a player. A football club changed. A region opened its eyes like a newborn baby and looked around in awe as it realised how beautiful football could be.

'I loved going into training,' McDermott adds. 'It felt different. We used to watch the training session every day and I used to drool over it. It was like watching us again at Liverpool. We started the season and we won eleven on the trot. That was amazing. I actually said to Kevin after we'd won the tenth game, "If we beat Sunderland we'll go through the season unbeaten."

They did, and they didn't, but anything seemed possible, and plausible.

People were watching their dreams. Newcastle, dormant for so long, were becoming a force.

They played Oxford at St James' Park, three days after winning the title at Grimsby.

'We were drawing nil-nil and Kevin comes in at half-time and says, "You're a disgrace, we've got 30,000 fans out there and you're playing like this. You better get out there and prove to them that you want to win games." Then he went. He fucked off. He left me in charge.

'He was on his way home. We won two-one and they were all saying, "Where's Kevin?" I said, "His wife has got the flu."'

Payback came against Leicester.

'We were unbelievable that day,' he adds. 'The best football I've seen at that level. The best performance since we were there. The football was beyond belief. It was a lovely sunny afternoon, it was like a carnival. It was brilliant.'

Newcastle had momentum. A force was on the move.

'I remember saying to Kevin on numerous occasions, "I love coming in every morning and watching these play,"' says McDermott.

'Training was unbelievable. The football we used to play in training was something else. Then Kevin wanted the crowds to be part of it at Maiden Castle. Eventually there was a hot-dog van there during the training session. That was unheard of.

'Me and Kevin used to stand there at the side of the hot-dog van eating a bacon butty or a sausage sarnie watching the training. We were blown away by the football. It was an absolute pleasure to watch. It was going to get better because we started getting better players and the internationals in.

'Everything he touched turned to gold.

'It was all about simplicity. Kevin wasn't one who filled their heads with shit or technicalities, going, "I want you to do that." You're like a robot in the end if that happens. He said, "Go out and do what you're good at, play football, pass the ball quickly, find space, put the ball in the net." He would give them confidence that way.

'Keep it simple. That was the message. He gave the players trust. We trusted the players. We had players who could sort it out. We had leaders. Paul Bracewell, Brian Kilcline; Killer was massive for us. Then we started getting internationals like Philippe Albert and David Ginola. It was getting better every year.

'We had a great season after promotion and then it got better and better. We've gone from being a very good entertaining team to an excellent entertaining team. Better. Better players. They were brilliant, the ones before that. Then the new ones came in and it was a different ball game. Players renowned all over the world.

'Kevin was just so good the way he talked to them. He treated them like men. He didn't treat them like kids going, "You don't do this and you don't do that." He let them get on with it.

'He was great at picking players. They trusted Kevin, they loved him. He might upset them a bit by saying things but he was just being honest and telling them the truth.

'He would tell them what was expected of them. "Just go out there and show what a good player you are," he would say to them. He would come in and bollock them if they weren't playing well. He wanted to win every game.

'He would always say to them in the dressing room, "It's for the fans. Do it for the fans."

*

IT WAS A WEDNESDAY NIGHT WHEN THE NEWCASTLE TEAM BUS rolled through the very streets where a young Terry McDermott had grown up 35 years earlier.

Despite their lead being devoured by Manchester United in the space of five weeks, Newcastle were just three points behind, in second place, with two games in hand and a goal difference two inferior. Liverpool were effectively gone in the title race, having being sat on its cusp for much of the season, a further five points further back.

Newcastle had been back to Anfield twice in the Premiership with Keegan and McDermott in charge, most emotionally on 16 April in their first season back, when, after a two-nil victory through goals from Cole and Lee, to mark the fifth anniversary of the Hillsborough tragedy, a father and his son emerged from the away support and carried a bouquet of flowers to the penalty spot at the Anfield Road end of the ground. Men cried that day.

This time, on 3 April, the duo were taking a Newcastle team to Anfield that was fighting for the title.

'I felt pride as the bus pulled into Anfield,' says McDermott. 'We knew we had a good team on that bus.'

It would go down as the greatest game in the history of the Premiership. McDermott and Keegan, back at Anfield. It had everything.

Newcastle's players were told to keep it tight early on, to find a foothold in the game. In the second minute, Stan Collymore got past Steve Watson deep on the Newcastle right and crossed, Srnicek came and went back, and Robbie Fowler headed downward and into the visiting goal.

The game had begun; the pace never stopped.

Barely eight more minutes had passed when Watson took a throw-in down the Liverpool right. There was a fine first touch from Peter Beardsley, sliding a pass inside the home penalty area to Faustino Asprilla.

Asprilla put the ball through the legs of Neil Ruddock, then he cut it back to

Ferdinand. The Newcastle forward touched the ball to the side of Mark Wright and smashed his shot past David James, in front of the Kop.

The game of all games was on.

Three minutes went by, just three minutes to clear the senses in the away end, before Ferdinand took a long clearance and killed it; then, with the outside of his right foot, he sprayed a pass thirty yards to his right, to where David Ginola was galloping at full pace, like a thoroughbred in the final straight. 'Go on, son!' They were the same throaty roars you hear from a racing crowd.

Jason McAteer made an effort to catch him but the French winger stepped across the defender's line as he bore down on goal. A tackle was impossible. The finish was sublime, left-footed, stroked with power and precision into the corner of James' goal.

After fourteen minutes, Newcastle led 2–1. Ferdinand and Ginola had scored. Newcastle were level at the top of the Premier League table with Manchester United, behind only on goal difference, but with a game in hand, at home, against Queens Park Rangers.

But it did not stop then. The game that had everything kept giving, and the supporters in black and white took more than you are supposed to.

In the second half it would become, at times, unbearable in its intensity.

In the 55th minute, Liverpool equalised: McManaman ran at Albert, crossed low to the edge of the penalty area and Fowler charged in to strike a low shot into the Newcastle goal. He dived into the net in an attempt to head his own goal in celebration.

It was just about tolerable then, in the Anfield Road end, but there was so long to go.

Two minutes later Beardsley slipped a fine pass through to Rob Lee, and the midfielder waited before dissecting two Liverpool defenders. Thirty yards from the Liverpool goal, Asprilla took the ball; James had come to the edge of his penalty area but there were red-shirted defenders around him. No one saw what would come next.

Asprilla, without breaking stride, stroked the ball around the Liverpool goal-keeper with the outside of his right foot and it took a bounce laden with spin into the Liverpool goal. It was right in front of us. You couldn't will that one in because it had too much spin, but you could watch it and admire it and thank God you were there to see it nestle in the bottom of the Liverpool goal.

'It's in! Jesus, it's in!'

You travel a lifetime in football, emotionally and physically, for one of them. It made sense again. Everything made sense. Except it was the 57th minute. There was too long to go. Too long to recover from the celebrating, for reality to kick in. There was too much time, too big a period to think and worry and feel the anxiety creep through your coat and your top and into your soul.

Another ten minutes had passed when McAteer curled a cross from miles out and it span across the face of the Newcastle six-yard area and no one got to it except Stan Collymore.

Three-three.

We have another 25 minutes of this? Christ.

The men in black and white fought for their lives, they gave everything. The desire and effort was staggering. With just over 10 minutes to go Philippe Albert clipped a long ball down the left, to Ferdinand. His strength saw him turn Steve Harkness and stride to his left and suddenly, eight yards from goal, he was through. He shot for goal and James blocked it. He didn't look like he knew if it was his arm or his body, but he blocked it.

You couldn't comprehend how big a save it was, and what would come next.

The clock would show it was the 92nd minute when it happened, but you were too numb to feel time at that point. Then only the fight to stave off the pain mattered, not time. You knew how it felt and where it hurt, and that was agonising and everywhere. You didn't see Barnes and Rush get the ball stuck under their own feet in the Newcastle penalty area. You didn't see the exact detail of Barnes squaring it to Collymore, who then crashed a shot past Srnicek, the seventh and final goal of an historic game.

But you knew instinctively that something very bad had happened.

It was not a noise of anything good, not for Newcastle

'Horrible, horrible,' says McDermott. 'You can't believe it, fucking sickening. In all my time in football that's the worst I've felt, ever.

'Les took the first goal well. It was a good finish and fucking hell, what a goal from Ginola. What a finish. And then Tino's goal, it had side-spin on it. That put us three-two up and then we lose. You can't believe it. It's sickening.

'When the final whistle went I was sick, absolutely sick. The players deserved to win it. We had heard stories before the game that Liverpool would let us win, there were rumours, they will let you win because if we don't win, Man United will win the league. You hoped but it would never have happened.

'You saw them when they scored the fourth goal. They went ballistic. Fucking hell, it was horrible.

'I can't believe it happened. It was a great game but that's the most sickened I've

t. It scarred Kevin. I'm convinced of that. It scarred him.

w can you have a go at the players after that? They were brilliant. Liverpool
good team: Steve McManaman, Robbie Fowler, Collymore, Jamie Redknapp,
had a lot of good players. You go to Anfield and score three and you get beat.
It means nothing how good the game was.

'I sat and thought, if we win this game we'll win the league. We went three-two
p and then it was three-three after sixty-eight minutes.

'It's the most sickening game ever from a Geordie point of view. If you come
away with a draw it's a great result. We were thirty seconds from a great result.

'There were so many emotions. My family was in the crowd. My brothers were
there and my uncles. They were Liverpudlians but they wanted us to win. Liverpool
weren't going to win the league so they wanted us to.

'I remember walking around the dressing room and the lads were obviously
gutted but I was going up to every one of them, shaking their hands or tapping them
on the head, "You were brilliant today, son, well done."

'I knew we still had a chance. If it had been the defining game it would have
been a lot worse but it wasn't. We still had seven games. I remember saying, "We've
got seven games left, we can still do it. We're still in a great position."'

Everywhere you looked, however, people seemed exhausted, drained. I don't
recall a game lasting so long. Keegan had slumped over the advertising hoardings
in front of the visiting dugout when the fourth goal went in. Once more, his mood
mirrored those following the club. Deflated. It was impossible not to be.

The hoarse screams of delight at Collymore's goal from the home stands cut
through the skin of those from Tyneside. Forty thousand Scousers scraping their
fingers on a blackboard at the same time, that's how it felt. Does beating us mean
that much?

Some supporters were caught in tears on camera. It looked like indulgence. The
real hurt filtered its way through the back of that stand, into cars and buses, and
took an infestation of negativity and pain back to Tyneside. How could it not?

The players climbed on the bus to leave Anfield.

'Everyone was brilliant on the way home,' adds McDermott. 'We were gutted
we got beat but we were positive. There were seven games to go. We thought, we
can still win it.'

PETER BEARDSLEY – COME HOME

'YOU'RE LISTENING TO RADIO CFUN,' SAID THE NEWSREADER. 'AND now for the sport.'

The newsreader was Canadian.

'The England captain Kevin Keegan has today signed for Newcastle United.'

In a two-bedroom apartment in Vancouver, Peter Beardsley turned to his wife. 'Bloody hell, Sandra, did you hear that?'

*

THE YOUNG AND CUNNINGHAM VALVE FACTORY IN KILLING-worth was less than a mile from where Peter Beardsley grew up in West Moor, North Tyneside. Each day began the same for the sixteen-year-old from Longbenton.

'I'd be there for eight o'clock,' says Beardsley. 'At nine o'clock I used to take the orders. It was a five-hundred-yard walk from where our factory was to the shops. Some would want cigarettes, some would want sandwiches. Between nine and ten I used to take my ball and go and get the shopping. I'd come back at ten. They would have a break, so would I. At half-ten I would take the fish order. They had fish and chips every day. I'd take my ball to the chippy. I took it everywhere I went.

'I'd take it to work with me. George [his brother] would go, 'Will you piss off with that ball.' The only time I would pick it up was at the flyover. I'd go past the Post Office and go down to the left, you can get to the Flying Scotsman pub over the railway line but there's a set of stairs. That was the only time I picked it up, to go over the stairs. I would kick it all the way. I would drive people mad.'

ball was a Mitre caser, given by his brother Ronnie. George worked at the
next door. 'He was a skilled worker,' adds Beardsley. 'I wasn't. I got twenty-
pounds a week and that was a fortune. I used to give my mam and dad a fiver
se I lived at home. That left with me twenty quid. I don't remember paying

'I had twenty pounds spending money every week. I felt like I was rich. I spent
all on chocolate. My brother used to work on the same site. We used to walk
up every morning, me and George. He used to work at Godfrey Syrett, he was a
furniture upholster. He was skilled. Ronnie and George were very skilled. I was just
a labourer.

'The factory made big valves for ships. My job was to clean the machines. They
would almost step aside so I could clean around them. Then they would put a fresh
valve on and start again.

'If they left the cuttings on the machine I had a massive bin, I could just brush
it into it. If it was on the floor, because the texture of the floor was rubber, it was
harder to get off, it was a nightmare.

'A lot of them would put all their cuttings on the floor deliberately. They would
treat you like a piece of shit.

'Maybe that was my own fault. I wasn't badly educated, I loved school, I went
every day but I didn't bother with the homework. I was just playing football every
night. To be fair to my mam and dad, they didn't push me. They always knew I
would get on, be it labouring or whatever, because I had a good attitude.'

Peter Beardsley was born in Longbenton. He lived in a high-storey flat near the
Rocket pub, went to Somervyl Middle School, a couple of good goal kicks away, and
then moved next to Benton Cemetery. He played for his school team on a Saturday
morning and for Longbenton Boys Club on a Saturday afternoon.

He went to Forest Hall Juniors, then to Cramlington Juniors and then to
Wallsend Boys Club. 'These boys clubs had so many players I wasn't good enough,'
he says. 'That was why I moved. I was too small.'

Instead Beardsley, when he was fifteen, started playing Sunday morning football
for the Fusilier pub, along with his two brothers. 'It was two hundred yards from
where we lived. It wasn't scary. They put me on the wing. I was out of the way. It
was good for my education.

'Without being cruel, people were so obvious when they were coming to smash
you. You could get out of the way, you knew when to. It taught me well. Sometimes
you get kicked.'

Most of the kickings came off the pitch.

His first trial was at Gillingham. Beardsley had never left Newcastle when he climbed the steps on the National Express coach at the old Gallowgate bus station, in the shadow of St James' Park. 'I went all the way down to Victoria,' he says. 'I'd never been to London before. I had to get a bus to Gillingham.

'I was there at the same time as Micky Adams and they kept him and they got rid of me. Brucey [Steve Bruce] was already signed. I went for a week and unfortunately I just wasn't good enough.

'Obviously I was disappointed. My dad used to call me golden feet. He would say, "You'll get sorted, maybe not today or tomorrow, but you'll get sorted." The amazing thing is, he never went to watch me. He was a long-distance lorry driver but he used to always keep out of the way when I was playing. The only time he watched me was when the three of us played in the same team. He used to say, "I'm not watching you, I'm watching them."

'Gerry Summers [Gillingham's manager] was really good. It's not easy telling people bad news. He said, "You might come back to prove me wrong. Good luck."

'I came back and went to the factory. As soon as I got there I heard the same. "We told you, you're not good enough."

'It didn't bother me. A chap called Dave Newberry worked in the factory. He was like a charge hand. He used to stick up for me. He would see people sweep their stuff on the floor and he would go, "Is there any need for that?"

'The way he was talking was as if he knew I would be a player. He said to me, "One day you'll come back and laugh at these." He was different class.'

Next up was Cambridge. After three days of a week-long trial he was told by the manager John Doherty that he was not good enough following a friendly against Newmarket. 'Peter Graham was a coach and I stopped with him and his wife. A family relative of his had died and he was going up to Doncaster.

'John said, "You might as well go back with Peter." That was my trial finished. I was expecting to be there for a week. I couldn't even tell my mam and dad because we didn't have a phone. I got back to Central Station and I walked from there to home in Longbenton [about four miles]. The first thing my mam and dad said was, "What are you doing here?" They thought I'd done something wrong.'

From Cambridge came Oxford. 'They said I wasn't good enough, I accept that.'

Pushing Beardsley through this was Peter Kirkley, who had taken a shine to him.

Next was Burnley, where Harry Potts was the manager. He also said no to Peter Beardsley.

'Peter kept telling me I would be a player. He said, "You'll get fixed up. You mustn't get fed up, keep going." Then he said, "I'm going to send you to Carlisle.

They've got a pre-season friendly against Blue Star at Woolsington."

'Bob Moncur was player-manager at Carlisle. He played and we beat Blue Star three-two. It was a brilliant game. Woolsington was a beautiful pitch. Bob Moncur was playing at the back. I was running here, there and everywhere. I was chasing lost causes and I set up a couple of goals.

'I went into the Diamond pub in Ponteland. They put on a buffet for us. That was 1979. This was the Thursday night and we went into the pub and Bob said, "I want to sign you." I thought it was a wind-up. He said, "We play Darlington tomorrow night. I want you to come to the game, we'll get you picked up and I want you to sign there, in Darlington." I said, "I'll be there."'

By then Newcastle had finally shown interest. Jimmy Nelson, then a youth team coach, had given him a trial in a friendly.

'To be fair to Newcastle I had basically played one game at Marden for them,' he adds. 'I think we drew two-two and Jimmy said he'd be in touch.

'What happened was, when I was going to play this game for Carlisle, Geoff Allen [a Newcastle scout] came to my door on the morning of the game to go training. I pretended I wasn't in. I wanted a rest for the Carlisle game. I didn't want to train, it was just a trial. Carlisle was a game. I didn't feel I could do both. I probably could have but I didn't want to spoil one. My mam said I wasn't in.

'He wanted me to go on trial for a few days but they couldn't do anything until Bill McGarry [the then manager] came back. McGarry was down in Torquay and Plymouth with the team.

'I had the chance to play for Carlisle and Bob Moncur wanted to sign me. I'd had trials that hadn't worked. I couldn't take the gamble. I thought I had to go for it. Billy Elliott was the manager of Darlington and I remember signing the contract in his office. It was amazing. I signed a two-year contract for thirty pounds a week.

'I went into the factory the next day. They hadn't heard, nobody had a clue. I told Dave Newberry. He was ecstatic. He was more excited than I was. He said, "Fantastic, I knew you could do it. Now you can go and tell these old bastards to fuck off."

'There was an old man called Sid who worked in the factory and he was really nice. He'd been there for fifty years. He said, "We've given you a lot of stick, son. That's the way it is in this world. It wasn't meant nasty, it really wasn't, and I wish you all the best. It's your dream and I hope it works out for you."

'He never showed that personal side when I was working there but it was nice he said it. They'd hardened me up. They all said I'd be back in a year, I could well have been. They said, "We'll keep your job open."

'How did it feel when I walked out of the factory for the final time? It felt weird. It had always been my dream to be a footballer. I had my ball. I did one-twos off the wall, all the way home.'

*

IN 1969, BOB MONCUR, A CENTRAL DEFENDER, SCORED THREE TIMES in the two-legged final of the Inter-Cities Fairs Cup (later the UEFA Cup). They were the only goals he scored for the club in the near 300 games he played. Newcastle beat Ujpest Dozsa 6–2 on aggregate. Moncur had been the last Newcastle captain to lift a major trophy for the club. In 1979, Peter Beardsley moved into Moncur's family home in Wreay, three miles from Carlisle. He stopped Beardsley from doing the usual menial tasks of apprentices.

After life in the factory, that was a start.

Beardsley's first appearance for the reserves was on a Saturday against Wrexham. Camille, Moncur's wife, cooked him steak and chips for his pre-match meal. All the first-team staff had a club jumper with the badge on, the fox and 'CUFC'. 'I thought the jumpers were amazing,' says Beardsley. Alan Ross, who had played 600 times for Carlisle, was the commercial manager. 'He told me I could have one if I scored a hat-trick.' Carlisle won 5–2. Beardsley scored three times.

He was allowed to go back to Newcastle and told to return on Tuesday. On Sunday a telegram arrived at his mam and dad's.

'I didn't know what a telegram was,' he says. 'It came through the door and my mam gave it to me and said, "You've got a telegram." It was a tiny little envelope with my name on and where I lived, Victoria Avenue. I was asking, "What is it?"

'I opened it and it said to report back for training on Monday morning. It never said anything else.

'Bob and Camille had a house phone and I rang it from the phone down the street. I spoke to Camille. She said, "Get the train back today." That was Sunday afternoon.

'I got the train at four o'clock. Bob picked me up. He said, "Have you got any idea what I got you to come back for?" I said, "Not a clue." I wasn't being funny. I didn't have a clue. He said, "You're playing on Tuesday." I said, "What?" He said, "You're going to play. The reason I've brought you back is so you can organise to get your family over." He said, "Don't tell anybody else."

'I'd played one full reserve game.'

On 21 September 1979, aged eighteen, Peter Beardsley played his first Football

League game against Blackburn Rovers.

'The first time I put the strip on was incredible,' he says. 'I was number ten. We wore blue strips with the little white trim and the red middle. We had the white shorts and the white socks. It felt great.' Howard Kendall, Duncan McKenzie and Derek Fazackerley all played for Blackburn.

The match finished in a 1–1 draw. Beardsley played 44 of the following 45 games, scoring 10 goals.

He played against Brentford the following season. Ron 'Chopper' Harris kicked him for ninety minutes. Johnny Giles was sat in the stands.

He sent a scout to watch Beardsley play in the FA Cup against Mansfield. Giles had won the league title twice with Leeds as a player. By this point he was the manager of Vancouver Whitecaps, who played in the North American Soccer League. Bob Stokoe, a Newcastle fan who had led Sunderland to one of their greatest triumphs, the 1973 FA Cup win over Leeds, had succeeded Moncur as manager at Carlisle. 'Bob called me in,' says Beardsley. 'He said, "We've had a bid from Vancouver for you."

'I discussed it with Sandra [Beardsley's future wife] and Pop Robson [the former Newcastle and Sunderland forward]. He said, "It's a brilliant opportunity for you, Peter. There's a lot of top people over there."

'The deal was already done. It wasn't a case of "What would you like?" It was, "This is what you're going to get: a two-bed apartment, wages and a Honda Civic with Vancouver Whitecaps splashed all over it." The deal was that I would move once Carlisle were safe from relegation.'

Beardsley moved his wedding to Sandra forward. On 21 April 1981, Carlisle beat Burnley 3–0 away. Gordon Staniforth scored a hat-trick. That night there was a stag-do in a Carlisle nightclub. The rest of the players had a drink, Beardsley, teetotal, did not. The following day, Sandra and Peter Beardsley were married. Staniforth was best man.

The following Saturday, Carlisle lost to Swindon but other results meant they could not go down. On the Sunday, Beardsley drove to London with his new wife and her family. The following day the pair flew 5,000 miles to a new life.

'What did I feel like? Excited, really,' he adds. 'I'd never been on a plane before. I just thought, this is big!

'When we stepped on it we were in first class – or whatever it was in those days – and I just thought, is this how people travel? I didn't know it was different to normal class. It was incredible. It was fifteen hours.

'We got well looked after. We arrived there and they put us in a nice hotel and we lived in the city for three weeks, downtown, which is where the stadium was.

'We trained on the pitch every day. It was easy because it was Astro-pitch. Sandra went to work in the office at the Whitecaps to give her something to do.

'We started going away to play the games, which was ten days at a time. She couldn't drive and it was really hard for her. To be fair, the other wives would invite her to stay round their houses, which made it easier.

'Vancouver is incredible. It would be in the top three places I've ever been. The Grouse Mountain, Whistler, it was like a holiday for us. I was going away to play football, playing three games on the road and I couldn't believe my luck.

'I very quickly became a driver. We got four station wagons whenever we arrived in an airport, Orlando, Miami or San Diego or wherever. You had four drivers and you were in charge of a skip each. I was a driver so the car was mine. I had to take four players with me to the hotel but after that the time was your own.

'The only time we ate together as a team was pre-match. You would get your money and eat wherever you wanted. Threes and fours would go off. The only time you were together was training, pre-match and games. Every three or four days you would do nothing, so I remember driving around New York on my own in the station wagon. It was like a different world, and it was exciting and there was me driving this automatic station wagon. It was a doddle. We'd go to Dallas on a road trip. The places I went, because I had the car, amazing.'

On 4 July Vancouver played San Jose, who had George Best in their team. Beardsley scored a hat-trick.

'He said to me after the game, "What part of Canada are you from?" I said, "I'm from Newcastle." He went, "You're not." I said, "I am, honestly." He said, "I'm going to ring Manchester United." As luck would have it, the next end of season Man United came over.'

In May 1982, Vancouver Whitecaps played Manchester United in a friendly. Gordon McQueen, the Manchester United central defender, made a mistake as soon as the game started. Beardsley scored after just thirteen seconds and added another one later as Vancouver won 3–1. Manchester United agreed a £250,000 fee to sign Peter Beardsley. He played one game for the Reds.

'I had a brilliant time, I was just unlucky,' he adds. 'Norman Whiteside had just come back from the World Cup and he was sensational. Frank Stapleton was playing alongside him. In them days there was only one sub and for thirty out of the forty-two games, Lou Macari was sub because he could play anywhere. I never really got a chance.

'I played in the reserves at Blackpool with Mike Duxbury, Arthur Albiston, Paul

McGrath, Martin Buchan, Ray Wilkins, Arnold Muhren, Steve Coppell and Mark Hughes. It was a brilliant education, but I wasn't good enough.

'I played one game against Bournemouth. Harry Redknapp scored an own-goal. That was where I was unlucky. The ball got squared, he came in and put it in the net before I got it. I was going to tap it into the net, on my life. Five minutes later I got taken off.'

He went back to Vancouver. Vancouver paid Manchester United the £250,000 back, as agreed in the deal. Vancouver had made £18,000 in interest.

Interest quickly turned back to Newcastle United.

'We were back in the apartment and I was having my tea when I heard,' he adds. 'I was listening to CFUN. I said to Sandra, "You're not going to believe this, Kevin Keegan's just signed for Newcastle." I was gobsmacked. I just thought, what a coup that is. It was incredible.'

Peter Beardsley couldn't afford to watch Newcastle play when he was a child. Instead he would walk the four miles from his home in Longbenton to watch the reserve side play at St James' Park.

'Jinky Jimmy Smith was my hero,' he says. 'I couldn't get to watch them, I couldn't afford to. I used to watch the reserves. I remember Man United winning five-one and I was in the Gallowgate End. I saw Bobby Charlton play in that win. It was free in them days. That's why I was there. There was about five thousand. That would have been 1977, something like that.

'The thing was in 1974 I queued up all night for the Forest tickets when there was the pitch invasion [in the fifth round of the FA Cup]. We went up after watching Match of the Day and queued all night at the bottom of the Gallowgate End. Tickets went on sale at two o'clock the next day.

'We got the bus to the station and walked up with our sleeping bags. We got two tickets each. Then my brother George sold my ticket. I was fuming. He had a mate he wanted to take. I was devastated. To play for Newcastle was always the dream but I never thought it was going to happen.'

When Arthur Cox phoned Peter Beardsley, he was sat in his Honda Civic outside a shopping centre in Vancouver. Beardsley thought it was a team-mate.

'We played in San Diego and I got set up by the lads. They sent me a message, "I'm watching you, I can't wait to see you, I've been waiting for this moment all my life. I'm in Row 5 Seat D and I'm looking at you." I was shitting myself. We used to wind each other up something rotten.

'Anyway, I was at the mall and Sandra was in the shop. I was waiting to pick her up when my phone goes – we had mobiles in the cars that were like bricks – and it's Arthur Cox. I was genuinely looking around, I thought they'd seen my car and the badge and thought, "We'll have a bit of Peter." That's why I thought it was a wind-up. I take this call and I'd never heard him speak.

'He said, "It's Arthur Cox here." There was a silence. He said, "I want you to come and play alongside Kevin Keegan."

'When Kevin Keegan had signed a year earlier I'd been talking about nothing else to the lads. I was saying, "KK's fantastic." I told them about his debut against QPR, I'd told the lads everything.

'I remember Newcastle winning five-one at Rotherham and he scored four goals. It was incredible. As much as it was possible, we were still getting the Big Match feed in Vancouver. We got the highlights. How him and Terry Mac changed the club was incredible.

'Arthur went, "You'll be playing for Newcastle United with Kevin Keegan, that must mean something."

Beardsley told Cox he would sign. His parents still did not have a phone. His two brothers still lived there. In September 1983, Peter Beardsley, still in Vancouver, bought a postcard.

'I put on it, "Dear Mam and Dad, Newcastle want to sign me. By the time you read this I might be a Newcastle player."

'Apart from the people at Newcastle, the first person who knew I was signing for Newcastle United was the postman in Forest Hall.'

Beardsley and Sandra flew back to London.

'We got on the shuttle, it was the last one back to Newcastle on a Tuesday night,' adds Beardsley.

'I spotted him when he got on. I nudged Sandra and I said, "It's Kevin Keegan!" She went, "What's wrong with you? You'll see him tomorrow." I'm thinking Kevin Keegan would never know me.

'When we got off the plane at the other end and went down the steps, he was waiting. He said, "You're the one Arthur Cox keeps telling me about. He rings me at two o'clock in the morning to tell me how good you are." He was brilliant. He went, "Welcome to Newcastle." From that moment he treated me like a king. He was incredible.'

Newcastle had a forward line: Beardsley, Keegan and Chris Waddle were enthralling. Newcastle United took off. Their fans were on the flight.

'The club had had a hard time,' Beardsley adds. 'Arthur said to me, "We're playing a different type of football. You'll suit how we play. KK will be great with you. We've got Waddle and Terry McDermott and there will be no negative football."'

Newcastle's first season with Keegan had been inconsistent, from a high of being joint top of the Second Division after their victories in the opening two games against Queens Park Rangers and Blackburn Rovers to a low of fifteenth in December. They rallied and finished fifth. Keegan scored 21 times. When Beardsley arrived back in the north-east in September 1983, they were seventh.

'When I went in to sign, the first person I saw was Joe Harvey [who had been manager when Newcastle had won the Fairs Cup]. He said, "Welcome to Newcastle, Arthur tells me you've got a good football brain. He also tells me you run around a lot. That will do for these people. This is their club."

'He said, "I was the captain when we won the FA Cup [in 1955] but that man across there, in the main stand, is even more special." It was Jackie Milburn.'

Milburn was the club's all-time record goalscorer with 201 goals. He had won the FA Cup three times in the 1950s. By 1983 he was a journalist. 'He was unbelievable,' adds Beardsley. 'He said, "I know all about you, son, you're a superstar. You're going to be brilliant, you're going to go down in history."

'In them days press men used to smoke and he would get a fag out as he was chatting away to me. I went home that night and told my dad I'd spoken to Jackie Milburn. He was gobsmacked.'

Beardsley's debut was away at Barnsley. He came on when Jeff Clarke was injured. Newcastle drew 1–1.

'My home debut was Portsmouth. Me and Sandra stopped in the Thistle hotel opposite Central Station. We walked up to the ground and thought nothing of it. I remember the atmosphere, it was amazing. The noise was incredible. All my family were there and so was Sandra's mam and dad. At two o'clock I just wanted to get out and play.

'Arthur would tell you the team at two o'clock and then he would give you the team talk at ten to three. For fifty minutes you were just sitting in the dressing room. There wasn't a lot of stretching or fitness coaches. You'd sit and read the programme.

'Terry Mac and KK would be in the player's lounge watching the racing. They'd come into the dressing room at ten to three with their suits on.

'We beat Portsmouth 4–2 and Waddler scored two twenty-five-yarders and Arthur took him off. We went in after the game and he said, "Why did you take me off?" Arthur said, "It's because you didn't care enough. Not many players get a chance to score a hat-trick for this club, son. You didn't want it enough."'

But he did. That front three wrote a glorious, season-long chapter in the history of Newcastle United.

'We scored sixty-five goals between the three of us,' says Beardsley. 'KK got twenty-seven, Waddler scored eighteen and I scored twenty. It was unbelievable. I only played thirty-four games and I didn't see myself as a goalscorer.

'My first goal was at Cardiff. We played two games in Wales. We were meant to play Swansea on the Saturday but because of the weather we played on the Sunday and then Cardiff on the Wednesday.'

Newcastle supporters who stayed the extra day slept on the beach and in shop doorways. 'Arthur was all for the fans and he had KK, Davey Mac [David McCreery] and Terry Mac putting pressure on him to see what we could do for them. KK even went, "Let them stay with us, put them in our rooms. They can sleep on the floor."

'KK was very much like that. He'd do anything for anybody. The club paid for the fans on the day of the game. After what the fans had been through, it made it double special that we could win both games for them.

'Keegan was amazing. The way he looked after me and Waddler was incredible. Would I have developed so much without him? No, definitely not. The first thing he said to me in my first start against Portsmouth when Carrsy [Kevin Carr] was shelling balls that were coming down with snow on them was, "Don't go for any long balls, I'll go for them, I'm finished, my career's coming to an end. You go for the flick-on. I'll do all the work."

'He was incredible, what a player, what an absolute superstar. It was KK who started calling me Pedro. He'd been in Spain for seven years.'

It was sunshine football. There were some magical days.

'We beat Man City five-nil and I got a hat-trick. I was really lucky in the sense that everything went my way. If you look at the goals, two or three I score are from people's mistakes or bits of luck.

'I couldn't do anything wrong. It was a huge match. Alex Williams was in goal for Man City. He walked off with me and said, "I'm happy with five."

'We played Portsmouth away and won four-two. My goal is the one I remember as the best I ever scored. It was the second one in the first half, just before half-time.

'I get asked a lot of times what my favourite goal for Newcastle is. It was that one. I'd gone past the keeper and the defender and then Sullivan the left-back comes across to try and tackle me and I can hear Terry Mac going, "Put it in, Pedro, put it in!"

'But I waited, he goes sliding by, at the time I thought at the worst if I don't score he'll score an own-goal. It was a last-ditch tackle and he went sliding past.'

Martin Tyler said in his commentary, 'Beardsley. Will he walk it in? He does!'

Beardsley continues: 'Arthur used to go down the tunnel at forty-four minutes. It was almost superstition. In his eyes we're one-nil up. He missed my goal because it was injury-time.

'We go into the dressing room and Arthur very rarely swore and he didn't this time, but he was really aggressive and he goes, "It's a bloody disgrace to only be beating these one-nil. You should have a look at yourselves." To be fair to Terry Mac, he spoke up and he said, "Arthur, Arthur, Pedro's just scored a wonder goal, it's two-nil."

'Arthur goes, "We're playing well aren't we?"

The good form continued.

'We beat Derby four-nil. I scored a diving header from Terry Mac, who was shooting! That was a brilliant game. We were almost there then. It was Easter time. That was when it was hitting home we were getting promoted.

'On the last away game of the season we played Huddersfield. They said Keegan had hurt his head against Derby, he actually hurt it playing cricket in the gym at Benwell. He was batting and the ball hit him in the eye. We kept it quiet.

'On the bus on the way down, Arthur came over and sat down next to me. He said, "You're going to wear number seven today." I said, "I'm number eight." He said, "Not today, you're not. You're the only person on the bus who can wear that shirt."

'It was brilliant. I kept the shirt. It was the silver one.

'Three sides of the ground were full of Newcastle fans. It was incredible. We drew two-two.'

That point guaranteed promotion back to the First Division. There were still two home games remaining, the final fixture against Brighton and Keegan's testimonial.

'Brighton was just incredible,' says Beardsley. 'It was the perfect ending. I had never scored twenty goals before. It was unbelievable. We all scored. KK gave me a poor pass and I chipped Joe Corrigan.

'Going round the pitch at the end of the game was as good as I've ever experienced, and I've won the league at Anfield – it was the best ever. I will never experience anything like that again.

'The way KK and Terry Mac were, you could act the fool. You didn't have to worry what people were thinking. The players were dancing. There were no inhibitions. Everybody joined in. I've never had a better day for the atmosphere. It will live me forever.

'We bowed to the fans. KK started that. He was God. He still is to these people. It was a dream. He changed the mentality of the football club.

'He announced his retirement on Valentine's Day [it was his 33rd birthday]. We were stunned. He was fit as a fiddle. There was no one fitter. Look at how young he was. He put it down to the four-nil game when we lost at Liverpool in the FA Cup.'

There had been 12,000 Newcastle fans at Anfield for the third-round match in January. It was a painful night.

'Arthur Cox was going to knock Graeme Souness out,' adds Beardsley. 'He did Kenny Wharton with a nasty tackle. In them days you got away with it. Arthur went up to him and said, "If you think you're big, have a go at me."

'Arthur always stood up for his players. He stood up for Kenny. It was a nasty tackle. KK and Terry Mac, who knew Souness, got in the middle and smoothed it over.'

Souness and Liverpool returned for the 'Auf Wiedersehen, Kev' night. As Keegan climbed into the helicopter, he took off his number seven shirt and handed it to a police officer. He told him to give it to Peter Beardsley.

'We all went to the Gosforth Park Hotel for a party. When I saw KK he asked if I had got the shirt. I didn't know what he was talking about. He was devastated. That shirt has never been seen since. There is still no sign of it. It does my head in. I only hope he didn't hear him because of the helicopter. I'm hoping he didn't steal it.

'The party was great, everyone was there. Leaving in a helicopter was perfect, I don't know whose idea that was. It's amazing how many people tell me that was the happiest time of their life. I was in the middle of it.'

*

NEWCASTLE HAD TO WIN. IT WAS NOW THAT SIMPLE. THE SEVEN-goal spectacle that had unfolded at Anfield three days earlier had left Tyneside drained. The nation was enthralled. The city that had provided the team was exhausted. There was now mental fatigue.

Keegan and McDermott turned the pressure at the training ground down to zero. There was a form of protection in the normality. It was a perfect escape. Beardsley and McDermott went to the Marks & Spencer close to the training ground as they did every Friday lunchtime and loaded the car with the sandwiches players had ordered, and chocolate.

McDermott joked. Keegan smiled.

By half-time the following day, it was still 0–0. Nobody was laughing. Queens Park Rangers were eighteenth. St James' Park had become anxious. This could not happen. It had to stay as a fortress.

Peter Beardsley went to the toilet, as he did midway through half-time in every game of football he played. Keegan followed.

'I would never drink anything in the build-up to the game but I used to have a pee before I went out and I would come in at half-time and it was the same then, I always had a pee before I went out,' he says.

'He always knew when the buzzer went that was when I went for my pee. Everyone was done by then. He followed me into the toilet and he said, "Here we go, Pedro, this game is made for you." He was so positive.

'He just said, "You can do this, Pedro, I know you can." It was like he willed you to do it. What the man thought of me was more than I thought of myself. Honestly, he made you feel ten feet tall.'

Beardsley had not felt ten feet tall when he had sat down with Willie McFaul in 1988. Arthur Cox had resigned in 1984 after promotion because the Newcastle board would not sanction the signing of Steve Bruce, Mark Hateley and Kevin Sheedy.

Jack Charlton had taken over. He signed Tony Cunningham and George Reilly and put Waddle and Beardsley on the wings. He resigned in the summer of 1985 after criticism from Newcastle fans during a friendly. McFaul had been at the club for nineteen years, first as a player during the Fairs Cup success and then as a coach. He was the safe pair of hands to take over. Newcastle rediscovered their flair, but they were a team on the periphery.

Waddle moved to Tottenham for £590,000 and Beardsley was increasingly carrying a team. There were two years left on his contract when McFaul arranged a meeting, away from St James' Park, at the George in Chollerford.

'We had a meal and he said, "I want you to sign a new deal," says Beardsley. 'I said, "I don't need to, I've got two years left." I asked him what his thoughts were. He said, "If you don't sign, they'll sell you." I said, "Something must be going on."

'He said, "There's definitely interest, Liverpool want to sign you." I said, "You're happy for me to go?" He said, "If you won't sign, we are happy for you to go." I said, "I won't sign because I don't need to. I could commit and you might not buy a player." He said, "I can't guarantee that."

'I don't know whether the club wanted to sell me or whether it was a double-bluff, I really don't know. Willie was almost piggy in the middle. He wanted me to stay and he was as good as gold. I hadn't spoken to Kenny Dalglish then, I wasn't even aware of their interest.'

Beardsley moved to Liverpool for £1.9 million in 1987. It was a new record for a British transfer. Newcastle built the Milburn Stand, which replaced the old West Stand, with the money. Despite the sale, they finished eighth. The following summer they sold Paul Gascoigne to Tottenham Hotspur for £2.2 million.

They signed Dave Beasant, Andy Thorn, John Hendrie and John Robertson.

After seven games McFaul was sacked. By the end of the season Newcastle were relegated. Beardsley won two league titles with Liverpool. There was also an FA Cup success. However, by 1991 he had moved across Stanley Park for £1.5 million, sold by Souness.

In the summer of 1993, Howard Kendall called Beardsley into his office. Everton needed to sell a player for a decent fee and the only other one who could command a substantial price, Dave Watson, was the club captain. Beardsley went to talk to Arthur Cox, who was by then in charge at Derby. It was a league down the ladder and he did not want to go.

Beardsley went back to Kendall. 'Howard said, "I've got one or two more interested in you." I didn't know that. I said, "Who's the two?" He said, "I'm only going to tell you one. It's Newcastle."

'I said, "So what's the story with Newcastle?" He said, "Kevin Keegan came for you a year ago, before they got promoted. He asked me if he could have you and I said no. Kevin said, 'Don't tell him, I promise you I won't tell him.'" And he didn't. I didn't have a clue.

'He said, "I'll ring KK. So he rang KK, or he thought he was ringing KK. Terry Mac answered. KK was on holiday. They used to call it the bat phone, you knew something was happening when the bat phone went off.

'Terry Mac answered the phone. He was on speakerphone. He goes, "It's Terry, Kevin's away, who's this?" Howard goes, "It's Howard Kendall." Terry goes, "Howard! How have you been? We've been waiting for your call. Are you ready to sell him now?"

'Howard replies, "Well, yes and no. I don't want to sell him." Terry goes, "How much do you want for him?" Howard goes, "One-and-a-half million." Terry said, "Yeah, we'll give you that."

'Howard went, "Do you need to speak to Kevin?" He said, "No, it's all sorted." Terry Mac was amazing. He didn't know I was listening. "No, we'll pay it," he said. "We want him."

'I was in Southport later and KK called. He goes, "Pedro, Terry Mac told me the good news. Meet me on Sunday night at the hotel in Wetherby, just off the motorway, at six o'clock."

'I drove over from Southport. I got there and the hotel told me, "Your meeting room is here." Kevin was late. He was trying to sign a Russian player in another room.

'KK came in and said, "Sorry for being late, Pedro. I'll give you a testimonial and that will get you up to near to what you're getting at Everton. Are we sorted?" I said, "Yes."

'He said, "We start back a week on Monday, I'll see you at Maiden Castle then. I'll go and try and get this Russian sorted now."

The Russian never signed and in a pre-season friendly Neil Ruddock smashed Beardsley's cheekbone in an aerial challenge. He was out for seven weeks.

'Eventually I got back in. KK said, "Do what I did, Pedro, come back, run the team. You're not the captain, but you run it." He said, "Andy Cole will be good for you, you won't have seen a lot of him. He'll make you look good."

'I remember I came up to be on television for the final game of the previous season, when Newcastle were promoted and beat Leicester seven-one. I spoke about Andy Cole's movement. I never dreamed I would be playing with him. We scored sixty-five between the two of us, having done that between the three of us in 1984. For him to score forty-one goals was phenomenal. For me to score twenty-four was something I had never done before.

'When I came back KK said, "You'll get back in the England team," and I was going, "Nah, no chance." He said, "You will. I'll have a hundred-pound bet with you." Terry Mac goes, "I'll have some of that. I'm in for a hundred." I didn't know they'd already spoken to Terry Venables. I was back in the squad. The bastards, they took me for two hundred quid!

'Everything about the season for Newcastle, the way we were as a group, the atmosphere in the group, was incredible. KK was incredible. We deserved to finish third.'

Two seasons later, with seven games to go, there was the prospect of doing better, much better.

'Les looked like he was born to wear the number nine shirt,' adds Beardsley.

'When Andy Cole went, I thought KK must have something for it to happen. I thought it would be in the next day or two. We had to wait until the summer but then he got big Les.

'He was the best header of a ball I ever saw. I genuinely mean that and David Ginola was frightening, seeing some of the things he did, and then we got Tino and you watch him and go, "Fackin' hell!" It was the best team ever in terms of football. I was the number ten, I was in the middle of everything.'

Beardsley was stood in a toilet when Keegan told him the QPR game was his for the taking. Newcastle, The Entertainers, had not found the net in three of their previous five games. It was 0–0 against QPR. Within eight minutes of the second half, it got worse – Ian Holloway scored.

'We could sense nervousness from the crowd,' Beardsley says. 'I think the crowd were stunned more than nervous because of what had happened on the Wednesday. A lot of them were more negative than we were. We'd lost an important game but we weren't as affected by it.

'They were starting to see the signs that we might falter and QPR was a game we should win comfortably. They were in serious trouble at that time. We were thinking we had to win and then they scored.

'Peasy [Darren Peacock] was saying, "They'll crumble, don't worry, we'll get the goals. They'll throw the towel in." He'd played for them and he was trying to be positive.'

Tension was everywhere. With thirteen minutes to go, Newcastle were still trailing.

'The ball came across the box to me and I suddenly thought, Christ! That goal doesn't look very big, I could miss this,' adds Beardsley. 'That went through my mind. It's funny when the pressure is on and you need something. "Is that goal smaller?" That's what you think. As that ball came across, I thought, "Is that goal shrinking?" It felt like the goal was moving and getting smaller.'

It hadn't. Beardsley equalised.

There were thirteen minutes to find a winner. Four minutes later Beardsley got the ball and started dancing with it.

'The position I end up in, I can't get the ball across. If you look at the people around me, I literally can't pass the ball. I really can't. It's so tight, I thought I'm going to have to try and go in and out and go for the far corner.'

Beardsley held off Andy Impey and used his dancing feet to cut inside David Bardsley. There did not seem enough space before he struck a shot from ten yards into the far corner of Juergen Sommer's goal.

'The roar was unbelievable when it went in,' he adds. 'It kept us in there. Everybody knew it.

'It felt like a good goal but I knew it was massive in terms of what it meant.

'People after were saying what a goal it was. I never thought it was special. I thought what a goal in terms of the timing but it was better than I thought. It would be in my top twenty but it was in my top three in terms of importance. It was massive.'

Nine minutes still remained. For the first time, with the scars of Anfield still fresh, there was consternation on the pitch.

'We had a problem,' says Beardsley. 'Do you keep going, which was the Newcastle way, or having lost the way we did at Liverpool, do you think, they could still score here. The people at the back were telling us to come back. The people at the front thought we could get another. That's what we thought, we could get another. They got a chance and they could have equalised – phew, it was close, you just wanted the whistle to be blown.'

The whistle blew. Newcastle had won. They were three points behind Manchester United with a game in hand.

The race was back on.

GRAHAM FENTON – WICKED GAME

IT WAS THE FRONT ROOM OF A SEMI-DETACHED HOUSE IN GREAT Harwood, but it did not look like it. Wherever your eyes went, there was mess; sleeping bags, eight of them in all, sports bags, jeans, T-shirts, trainers and cans of beer.

Whitley Bay is, in the main, black and white. It is the seaside town that no one will ever shut down. Two cars set off from Whitley Bay at lunchtime on Sunday, April 7, en route to their mate's house in Harwood, northern Lancashire, about eight miles from Ewood Park.

Newcastle's push for the title was back alive. There was a determination to go again, that it was not over, that this was how you won the league, probably. It was all guesswork by now, but then, it always had been. The title had not been won since 1927; there was no one with a tried and tested blueprint.

Each car had four Newcastle fans in it. The plan for Sunday and Monday was simple: drive, drink, sleep (optional), match.

Spirits were understandably high. The journey down took less than two-and-a-half hours. Newcastle were playing Blackburn Rovers on the Monday night. The game was to be televised live on *Sky Sports*. They were going to get drunk and have a ball. What could possibly go wrong?

Their host for the two-day trip had to squeeze his eight friends into the front room of the house he shared with four others. Then he had to find cigarettes and alcohol. Twice he taxied them to shops. Later on, the eight headed out. When they returned there was noise and chaos. Their host, their lifelong friend and now Blackburn Rovers player Graham Fenton, had not gone with them. He asked for peace and quiet. Upstairs Shay Given and three others tried to fend off the noise.

Fenton was given slurred assurances that all was fine. The carry-outs contradicted the promises.

'I think I got about an hour's sleep,' Fenton says. 'I dropped them off in Accrington in two ferry loads, I said, "I'm not coming out later on, get taxis back." Lads being Geordies, they thought it was a good idea to bring cans of lager back at the end of the night.

'This was the day of the game now because it was Monday morning. I planned to get some sort of sleep, but there was no chance of that, and then I was sent out on fag runs and all sorts because they were too drunk to drive. I was basically a gofer for the night when they came back.

'They didn't say anything about the match. I genuinely think they just thought Newcastle would win. They didn't say anything probably because they knew I wasn't playing.'

When Jim Smith had taken over at Newcastle in 1988, he appointed Derek Fazackerley to become reserve team coach. Fazackerley, who had played more than 300 times for home-town club Blackburn, survived the departure of Smith.

When Ardiles arrived, he was promoted to first-team coach.

When Ardiles was sacked, Keegan, with little experience, retained his services. By 1995, Fazackerley was homesick. Keegan honoured his wish to return to Blackburn, where Ray Harford had succeeded Kenny Dalglish as manager.

On Sunday, 7 April, as two cars were setting off from Whitley Bay, Harford was informing Fenton he would not be starting the following day's game against Newcastle. Instead, he would be expected to undergo a light finishing session in the morning, by when eight men had drunk themselves to exhaustion in his front room. The man who would lead the young Geordie forward for that hour's training was Derek Fazackerley.

'It was a good session,' says Fenton. 'It was light work really, just on the legs. I went in for a quick hour and then came back and tried to get my head down for an hour's kip in the afternoon. That didn't really happen. They weren't drinking during the day but they were making a racket.

'The lads were still there when I left to go to the game. They said nothing to me. One of them might have said, "Please don't score," but they were just joking around. They didn't say anything like, "We'll kill you if you do."

'My mam was at the game, my dad wasn't, he was working. He was self-employed in the construction service. He did all sorts of stuff. He was working so he couldn't get down. My mam was stopping in a hotel.

'Before the game, after I left the lads in the house, I spoke to nobody from home.'

Home had always been Whitley Bay.

Fenton played for Whitley Bay Boys Club until Under-13 level. He had a brief spell at Wallsend Boys Club, left, and then flourished at Cramlington Juniors. 'It was one of the best things I ever did,' he adds. 'They had fantastic coaches.'

He was being watched.

'Sunderland were sniffing around me, so were Middlesbrough, but Newcastle didn't. Why? I don't know.'

Instead Aston Villa's scout Dave Richardson spotted Fenton at a youth tournament in Ayr. He had already been to Doncaster, Ipswich and Brentford. He went for a trial.

'From the first day I wanted to stay there,' he says. 'I loved the place. There was a real family atmosphere. I went on loan to West Brom and loved it there. I scored three goals in seven games and we stayed up.'

He played in the 1994 League Cup final at Wembley when Aston Villa beat Manchester United.

'The cup final was brilliant,' he adds. 'I played the full game, just. I cramped up at the end. It was against such a good Man United side that went on to win the double. We thoroughly deserved to win. I was put in there to run round and kick people and give Kev Richardson and Andy Townsend a break. It was my fourth game for Villa. My mate said at the time it would be downhill from there!

'I played for the England Under-21s; I might have just turned twenty. It was 1994 at St James' Park. My family and friends were there, everyone was there.'

This was Fenton's introduction to Keegan, who was in temporary charge of the Under-21s at the time.

'Jamie Redknapp pulled out the day before the game. Kevin [Keegan] was manager, I'd heard a lot of different things about how good a manager he was. He was fantastic. He was relaxed around the training ground, very approachable. He made sure you were confident before you went out.'

There was no desire to leave Aston Villa. Brian Little, from Horden in County Durham, the new manager, saw things differently.

'Kenny [Dalglish] had just gone upstairs at Blackburn,' he says. 'I had a meeting with Brian who had just taken over at Aston Villa and I put across what I was expecting because I had played in the first team for a couple of years by then and I thought the offer we talked about was quite derogatory for what I had done.

'I decided I wasn't going to sign a contract and he said, "Well, Blackburn Rovers want to sign you."

'I was thinking, "Do I sign for a club on a not great amount who don't really want me or do I go and sign for the champions?"

'I went there to meet Ray [Harford] and straight away I knew it was the right club for me, because of the person Ray was. He was a lovely fella. He was a big bloke but very softly spoken. He was a nice person to be around. He was a good coach.'

Harford was the Blackburn manager that night, in April 1996.

'I remember coming out before the game and behind the goal to your right as you came out was split, it was all Newcastle fans to the right and the top was filled with them,' says Fenton. 'They were making a right noise. The atmosphere home and away for Newcastle games was absolutely tremendous. They were the best supported club in the country at the time.

'How many people couldn't get a ticket on a match day at home? Yeah, they were making a racket before the game and even more of a noise when David Batty scored. It was a good goal. He stepped inside and hit it with his left foot and it went past Tim's right hand.'

It was at the far end of the ground. There is always a second of disbelief when it's that far away. Tim Flowers' towel flicked outwards. It was tied to the side-netting, and that meant it was in. There were less than fifteen minutes remaining and Newcastle were winning.

In the away end, the new away end at the Darwen End, people jumped and writhed and bounced into and off plastic seats. All around you was joy. Everyone knew how big a goal had been scored.

It was breathless celebrating. It was a roar from the heart. You jumped and fell over seats until your lungs gave out.

Fenton had been on the pitch for a minute. Newcastle's push for the title was alive. It was Batty's first goal as a Newcastle player, in his sixth game since his arrival from Blackburn Rovers at the beginning of March. It was the 76th minute.

The game had felt near to finishing before Batty scored. As soon as he did, when your head cleared and you could breathe again, there was ages left. Absolutely ages.

The Liverpool game was still fresh. The wounds were still raw.

Those away fans kicked every ball, because that's what it had come to. This was not entertainment, it was slow torture.

Newcastle's players were being implored, begged even. Come on, man. It's all on the line here. Give it everything you've got.

With four minutes of the game remaining, Alan Shearer, by now a Premiership title winner with Blackburn, the club he moved to from Southampton for £3.3

million, then a British record transfer fee, shot for goal. The ball was blocked.

'Al got it, hit it and it didn't go in the back of the net,' says Fenton. 'The deflection happened and I read it just before any of the defenders. I kept myself onside.

'Then it was a case of getting any sort of contact on it. It's just numbness when you score. I wasn't thinking anything. It was back to one-one. I don't really want to celebrate so let's get back to the halfway line, but there's only four minutes to go.'

Newcastle went on the offensive.

Going backwards was never an option. It was about a city, an overlooked city, stuck out of the way, in the very furthest corner, in the north-east. Keegan made that city move forward, not back. He filled its people with pride. He made the supporters believe in taking people on and his team were the embodiment of his philosophy.

In the final minute they were still trying to score a winning goal. Keith Gillespie shot from a narrow angle and it took a fine save from Tim Flowers to stop him. At that point, Graham Fenton wrote his name into the history of the club he had followed since he was a child.

'It was the eighty-ninth minute and Newcastle were on the attack, again I think Tim might have made a good save and someone absolutely launched it down the pitch,' says Fenton. 'We had left two up top. I've tried to put Al in, I didn't get the pass right and it pops back to me.

'The pass was cut out but it fell back to Al and I carried my run on. He managed to get me in. I was through and then I dinked the finish. It was a dink. It was a dink and it went in.'

*

THERE WAS NO WAY BACK. KEEGAN'S FIRST AWAY GAME AS A manager had been at Ewood Park. Newcastle had lost then as well. The away end had changed, and so had the pain. This time it left you numb.

Keegan's first away game as manager was about energy and thousands flocking all over Blackburn, like a plague the town had no idea how to repel.

Energy was everywhere, dangerous, crackling energy. The bloke who had called 606 four years earlier was spot on then. The power had been unleashed all right.

On that Monday night, when the final whistle blew, the 6,000 from Tyneside searched desperately for the unleashed power.

Those goals hurt, in a physical way. You felt winded, like you'd been punched in the stomach. The people of Newcastle looked defeated. There was a collective disbelief. Did that just happen? But no one spoke. There were no words. Six thousand people said nothing and thought everything.

Mostly, they wondered how football could be quite so cruel. When David Kelly had scored in 1992, the away end had gone wild. It was not quite Keegan's goal on his debut as a player, but it was not a million miles away. David Speedie scored a hat-trick and Newcastle lost but there was enough energy and desire and belief to brush it off.

When a Geordie scored two goals, so late, so much further down the road, there was exhaustion. We've come this far for this? Jesus, you're kidding me. A lad from Whitley Bay?

The walk to the endless rows of buses and cars hidden in the Blackburn night was made in silence.

'Where do you go from that?' asks Fenton. 'I did the Sky interview. You don't have much time to think about it. I walked into the changing room and Alan [Shearer] burst out laughing at me. I think he was just glad that he hadn't scored. He said, "What have you done?"

'It was tongue in cheek. Derek looked over and went, "That finishing session worked then, didn't it?"

'I guess after that I had a good night with some of the lads back at the hotel. My mam was there. The first thing she said was, "Well done."

'My cousin phoned me the next day. He said the same as Al: "What have you done?"

'I realised there was a problem two days later when I got a death threat. I knew then how serious it was. It was a letter sent to the training ground. That wasn't nice. I thought, this is getting out of hand now.

'The worst thing about the letter was there was a threat to my mam and dad, who were back in the north-east. I don't even know if they know now. My dad has passed away. I don't know if my mam ever knew.

'That was horrible. I came back that summer to the north-east not long after and sensed a really negative vibe, and didn't stay long. Whenever I finished football, at Villa or at Blackburn, I would spend six or seven weeks in the summer back home in Whitley Bay. Just knocking around with my mates, seeing my mam and dad, playing golf with my dad.

'Pretty much within a couple of days I decided to go back. I was really, really concerned. I have a good group of mates but they're not fighters. If anything had happened it would have been pacify, pacify. I think it was the right thing to do.'

It did not end there.

'My mam and dad's windows didn't get smashed, but someone else's did,' says Fenton.

'I've heard through someone that a bloke was in a pub in Wallsend watching a Newcastle match. For some reason the information on me, under my place of birth, was Wallsend. I was born in Willington Quay. In Wallsend someone has gone, "He's from Wallsend," and they've looked for a Fenton in Wallsend in the phonebook.

'There was one apparently at that time. They went to that house and smashed the windows in and it was obviously nothing to do with me. Some Fenton in Wallsend had their windows smashed in just for their surname.

'There was another one. A survey was done a little while later in the north-east for the most hated men in history. I came second. Saddam Hussein won. The best one is who came third. It was Adolf Hitler. In a vote for the most hated man in history in the north-east I beat Adolf Hitler.'

In the ten minutes that followed Batty's goal, Newcastle had moved level on points at the top of the Premiership table with Manchester United. If they had scored twice more they would have gone back to the summit. Instead, the two goals came from a Newcastle fan, rather than a Newcastle player.

There was, however, a title still to be fought for. It had not gone, despite the pain. Newcastle had lost their game in hand but they were still only three points off top spot.

'I was still desperate for Newcastle to win the Premier League,' adds Fenton. 'My dad took me to my first Newcastle game. I remember Ray Houghton scored, so it must have been Fulham. I'm talking about a vague memory. My first emotion as Newcastle fan? Disappointment. Get used to it! It was your local team. Get the interest going.

'After that I started going to watch Whitley Bay. Then, when I was about thirteen, me and my mates would go on the Metro to watch the likes of Mirandinha. That was me for the three years before I went away, going to St James' if I wasn't playing.

'I was still a fan. Of course I wanted them to go on and win it.'

JOHN BERESFORD – 24 HOUR PARTY PEOPLE

'I FUCKING TOLD YOU!'

*

JOHN BERESFORD WAS SAT IN HIS CAR OUTSIDE ANFIELD THE FIRST time he spoke to Kevin Keegan. He was already in tears.

Beresford had missed a penalty for Portsmouth in the semi-final of the 1992 FA Cup at Villa Park, against Liverpool. His rising star had not faded with the miss. Instead, Graeme Souness, then the Liverpool manager, called him four days later.

'The phone went and this bloke goes, "Hello, is that John Beresford?"' says Beresford. 'I said, "Yes." He went, "It's Graeme Souness." I thought it was someone having a joke. I was like, "Yeah, OK mate, hi, Graeme." After a bit of that, he goes, "Is there something wrong here?" I realised then it was him.

'He went, "I've agreed £650,000 for you. I've been impressed with what I've seen. Do you want to come and join us?"

'From being lower than a snake's belly, I'm on my way up now. Done. I went up to sign and failed the medical. It was on my ankle. I'd had cortisone. Probably because of the damage I'd had it would have shown up but they were saying it was from an old fracture that had not set properly from Barnsley and that was rubbish. I later found out when I spoke to Graeme that he had a problem with the board and they were never going to sign anyone unless they were a hundred per cent.

'I came out of Anfield and I was in tears. I'd gone. I was devastated. I thought nobody would touch me. I phoned Jim Smith up, who was my manager at Portsmouth, and told him what had happened and he went, "Ah, bollocks." I went, "Jim, he ain't signing me." He said, "There's somebody else who wants you, but once he knew Liverpool were interested, he thought he'd have no chance. It's Kevin Keegan."

'You have to remember I'd played Newcastle that year and they'd just survived. Newcastle weren't a great team but Keegan was a boyhood hero of mine. For me, he was the one, he was the poster boy. It was when he was at Liverpool, I wasn't a fan of them but they were the only team on the TV. It was them and Ipswich. I was a Sheffield United fan.

'I bumped into him as a kid when I went on trial to Southampton. He was there and they were using him to say come to Southampton. I remember going, "Wow, it's Kevin Keegan in his Patrick boots!"

'Anyway, I was outside of Anfield and Jim said to give him a call. I called Keegan. He went, "Hello, who's this?" 'I said, "It's John Beresford." He went, "Oh, great, thanks for calling. Get yourself up here and come and sign for me." I'm like, "Hang on, do you know what's happened?" He said, "What?" I said, "I've just failed a medical at Liverpool." He said, "Don't worry, I've just signed Paul Bracewell, you'll piss ours."

John Beresford's dad was also called John. In 1966, Brian Clough called. He wanted Beresford, then a defender with Chesterfield, to move to Hartlepools. Clough's fire was beginning to burn. Beresford's wife, Carol, a hairdresser, was pregnant with a son, John junior. It stopped the move. The Beresfords stayed in Sheffield. John (senior) went to Notts County and six months later he wrecked his knee. They were career-changing injuries at the time.

'I grew up in the centre of Sheffield in a high-rise flat, a concrete jungle, call it what you want,' says Beresford. 'It was one of the best things that ever happened to me. You'd just go into what we called the rink and it was somebody playing football, and your best mate was the lad who got the ball.

'My old man had been a decent player. My mam was a hairdresser. I had all the stupid haircuts you can think of. When you played football, you'd get bumped around. My schooling wasn't the best, but that's where I learned to play football, in the street, in them flats. As you got better, people wanted you in their team.

'I joined a Sunday team called the Throstles. That was a great experience. That's when I started to realise I was decent. I remember being twelve and we saved up and went to America. We just went over as kids with a coach and you lived with a parent. I remember going over and thinking, how good is this? It was a great experience. It opened my horizons. Because we were successful we played in Holland and you start to learn your trade. I thought, I want more of this.'

He had a trial in Howard Wilkinson's back garden to see if he was good enough at keepy-ups to take part in a ball-juggling contest before the 1978 FA Cup final between Arsenal and Ipswich Town. He was. 'There were five of us from around the country. It was amazing.'

He told his mam he would sit his exams at school but instead went on tour with Manchester City to Germany, having been given terms. He went on to represent England Youth and established himself in City's reserve team, but then came a spectacular fall-out with the then City manager Billy McNeill after he asked for a first-team chance. 'I can't tell you how bad he was after that,' he adds. 'He decimated me. Every training session after that he said, "Who do you think you are, you little fucking upstart?"'

One morning there was a letter on his peg at training.

'All the lads were looking at me and I said, "What's up?" I saw the letter. I knew what it was. He hadn't even come to me face to face. I wish I'd kept it. I opened it and ripped it up and threw it in the bin. Mick McCarthy found out about it and put a word in for me at Barnsley [McCarthy's home town and former club].

'I phoned Newcastle before I went to Barnsley. Willie McFaul was in charge. It was 1985. I phoned him up and said, "I just want a year's contract. I'll show you what I can do." He said, "No, I'll give you a week's trial." I went, "No, sorry, I need a bit more than that!" Barnsley had offered me two years.

'I called McFaul because Newcastle had won the Youth Cup. I'd played against Gazza, Joe Allon, Paul Stephenson and Ian Bogie in the Youth Cup with City. We were favourites to win it and we lost at St James' Park. I'd played with Gazza and Joe for England Youth and I was thinking they had a great youth set-up. It might have been a blessing in disguise because I don't think they did!

'I went to Barnsley and it was a shock to the system. They were skint. It benefited me because if you do all right you know you'll get sold on, but it was hard work.

'We were bottom of the league. We had some decent lads but if we finished midtable we'd won the league. I was there for three years and then they sold me to buy some new floodlights.'

He went to Portsmouth. Then to Liverpool. And then John Beresford called Kevin Keegan.

'He said to me, "Where are you next week?" I said, "I'm back in Portsmouth."

He said, "Great, I'm in Ascot." I met him at the Holiday Inn hotel, off the M25 going into Heathrow. I will never forget that day. He had a top hat and tails on and everything.

'He was stood there dressed to the nines, he shook my hand and said, "Look, failing that medical will be a blessing in disguise. We'll get promoted this year, we'll be in the Premiership next year, we'll be in Europe the year after and I'll get you in the

England squad." I stood there thinking, he's off his head.

'Then he put his hat on and went to the bloody races!

'I came up to Newcastle for the first time and the old doc at the medical went, "Which is your ankle you've got a problem with?" I went, "You fucking find it! I'm saying nothing."

'He twisted it round, did a couple of x-rays. I thought they were going to find something. Nothing came up.

'Keegan told me he'd signed Brace [Paul Bracewell] and Venners [Barry Venison] but they were older and he wanted to make a statement. He said to me, "Bez, if I sign you, I know people will take us seriously and players will look at us."

'There was something else he said which was brilliant. I couldn't tell you how good it was. Sheffield Wednesday had been in for me as well and were ready to match Liverpool's salary. They only offered me half when they heard what had happened. I told Keegan when I came up here for the medical.

'Not once did I speak about money. Keegan never mentioned it. I met him at the Gosforth Park Hotel and he said, "Right, OK, bit curious, you've not asked anything about money."

'I said, "Pay what you think." He said, "I like that." I said, "My head's gone, I just want to play football. I don't know what your structure is." He said, "Leave it with me." He phoned me up the following day and called me into his office. He said, "There you are," and he put the contract in front of me. He said, "I've spoken to Graeme Souness and I saw the contract you would have got at Liverpool and I've matched it." For me, I was like, I'll jump off the Tyne Bridge for you if you're going to do that for me.'

John Beresford was 25, confident and tipped his hair when he first went for a drink as a Newcastle United player on the famous Quayside.

'I just remember walking into Jimmy's and pressing this button for half-price drinks,' he adds. 'I thought I was in Magaluf but it's colder! I'm on holiday. That's how it felt. You'd be getting into clubs straight away. You'd walk straight to the front of the queue, but there was never animosity, no punters calling you. They were slapping you on the back as you went in.

'Then you'd get the female attention, which was fantastic. You'd be standing there thinking, I'm looking great tonight! I could have been wearing anything. It was like that. You get caught up in it. I was twenty-five and it was fantastic. Yeah, I got divorced, yeah, thank you, Quayside!

'You were just having a laugh and a joke. We'd go into Julie's and you'd get a round of girls coming up. I remember my mate came up from Sheffield once, and he said, "This is ridiculous!" I said, "Say you're a player." He went, "Shut up." I said, "Say you're a foreigner. Just do it." Twenty minutes later he came over and he goes, "It's fucking brilliant up here!" He was with a woman. He'd said he was an Irish international.

'It was the best job in the world. You knew it was different. I loved every minute of it. I loved going into training. I loved the lads. It weren't like a job. Normally as a player you go in and you do stretching and work to Saturday. Keegan didn't make it that way. It was just fun. We'd go in and play head tennis, we'd have games, the banter was flying and people laugh when you say what Keegan's team talks were like but seriously, he would look at their team sheet and he'd pause and and go, "If we're not two-nil up in ten minutes there's something wrong."

'When we did training it was short and sharp. The small-sided games were done at such a tempo. That team, that era. It was ready to go. Keegan was a very deep thinker, how he saw things. He did a lot on positive thinking and he would talk about the snowball going down the hill getting bigger and bigger. He knew I was quite chirpy and I'd go, "Yeah, but it could smash." And he would go, "No, if you build it big enough and strong enough it will go through it."'

Aston Villa came to Newcastle on another Sunday. Sky by now had their teeth into Newcastle. The day before the game, Keegan had pulled Beresford in training.

'He never did any tactics as such but he said to me, "I want you to do something a little bit different tomorrow." I said, "What's that?" He said, "Tuck in." I said, "OK." He said, "Tommy Johnson and Dwight Yorke are quick, they'll try to get down the sides, so help Philippe."

'I said, "OK, fine." He said, "Good." I said, "But you've got a problem as well." I knew Gary Charles from England Under-21s. I said, "He will not want to defend against Ginola, no chance. He's a great athlete, he's quick, he'll bomb on." Keegan went, "I know, I'm going to have a word with David to drop back."

'I thought he was having a laugh. He saw my face. I went, "Gaffer, he won't, he'll say it but he won't. You know what he's like." Now I could sense things were a bit prickly. He went, "Do as you're told." I said, "Fine."

'The game kicks off and then I remember it happening. I've tucked in and the ball gets pinged from Alan Wright. We were attacking the Leazes End so I was right in front of the dugout. The actual attack broke down but now I'm fuming because I knew exactly what had happened.

'I remember Keegan coming to the technical area but he's shouting off to somebody and then he turns to me and I turned and I said the worst thing, I went to Keegan, "I fucking told you. I fucking told you he wouldn't come back." It was the worst thing to say because you can't swear to Keegan, it's a big taboo.

'He turned and he started shouting at the dugout. I turned away and I thought, ooh. So I started ignoring him. It was early in the game but I turned and I can see Robbie Elliott warming up and I could see Derek Wright getting the numbers.

'I started thinking, I'm in trouble here, and then I thought, no chance, he won't do this. We were live on Sky. He won't do this, we're going for the title. But then number three has come up and the red mist has come down now, little-man syndrome and everything like that.

'I remember walking towards him, and me and Robbie got on great, I shook Robbie's hand and Keegan blanked me and I just went, "Shit decision." I remember sitting down and raging, and then after five minutes it started to clear.

'I sat there and I thought, I'm fucked. I am finished. Arthur [Cox] was standing on the side. It came up to half-time. I went, "Arthur," and he went "What?" I said, "What do I do?" He said, "You'd better hope and pray we win, son."

'I went into the changing room at half-time and I sat there with my head down. A couple of the lads were looking at me but they weren't getting involved, so in the main I got blanked.

'We won the game one-nil and Les scored. I sat in the dugout. Back in the changing room Keegan does his, "Well done, boys" and they were all celebrating. I went back up to Arthur and I said, "What do I do now?" He went, "Get in there and beg if need be."

'Keegan had his little coaches room and he had a television and a couple of seats. I knocked on the door and he said, "Come in." I said, "Hi, gaffer," and then I got down on one knee. I said, "Gaffer, I've come to beg for forgiveness."

'He went, "Get up." I said, "Gaffer, I'm so sorry, it was heat of the moment, I shouldn't have said it, I was bang out of order, it'll never happen again." He went, "Don't worry about it, it happens. It's one of those things, it happens to us all. Let's just carry on as though nothing has happened. We won the game."

'But he made me pay.

'I didn't go out that night. Everyone was asking me. I can remember thinking, "Why did I say that?" My parents had come up from Sheffield. They said, "What's happened?" and I told them. My dad said, "You've just got to work hard." That's what I did.'

Three months later, on a pre-season tour to Asia, Keegan turned to Beresford, who, in his own words, had never worked so hard in a pre-season, and said, 'You're back in.'

For the rest of the 1995/96 season, however, John Beresford did not kick another ball for Newcastle United.

17 APRIL 1996

ROBBIE ELLIOTT – WONDERWALL

THE BIGG MARKET WAS FULL, FULL ENOUGH TO BURST. TYNESIDE was celebrating. The songs of victory filled the night air. There was a fizz of energy, excited voices broke through in between chants. It was a balmy night and everywhere you looked people were smiling and hugging each other. It felt like the Ramblas: short sleeves, drinks in the street – this is what it feels like when Newcastle win something.

Take a slow, ten-minute walk down from St James' Park, past Rosie's Bar, the Tyneside Irish Centre and the Newcastle Arms, do a right and follow the curve of the road, as it leads to your left, and you will walk into Newcastle's Bigg Market, so called because of a barley grown locally, renowned internationally because of what is drunk there. It held markets from the Middle Ages, selling all kinds. It is littered with pubs and in Balmbra's – when it was the old Balmbra's Music Hall – they heard the first airing of the 'Blaydon Races'.

You could hear the anthem of Newcastle on the streets that night, on Sunday, 9 May 1993, when Newcastle opened its doors to celebrate winning the Division One Championship – the team's first major silverware since 1969. Twenty-four years had passed. For many it was the first experience of a trophy. The huge flag a fan called Keith Barrett had collected for was being paraded through the streets. It was impossible not to be swept up in the euphoria of it all.

The Bigg Market is a largely open area, bordered by buildings that have stood for centuries. Those buildings were being climbed that night, such was the volume of people at its heart and the desire to celebrate. Some supporters were going high enough to jump across to the top of lampposts.

It was another leap of faith.

Robbie Elliott wasn't swinging from lights that night, but he was climbing up a wall to stand on a ledge and sing and shout and marvel at what it all meant to the fans.

That in itself was hugely significant. Two years earlier, Elliott suffered a cruciate injury. His career was in the balance. He went to Lilleshall as part of his recuperation. He was one of nine players, from a variety of clubs, who had undergone an operation on their knee. The surgeon in each of the other eight cases had used a part of the player's hamstring to repair the damaged cruciate. Newcastle United's own surgeon instead used part of Elliott's patella tendon to repair the cruciate. The other eight never played again.

Elliott's knee, by contrast, was fine. It had to be. In 1996, with four games to go, he was now the Newcastle left-back in a team bidding to create history and win the English title for the first time in 69 years. He had come on as substitute when Beresford had been hauled off by Keegan for his outburst. Now he would be starting against Southampton at a time when the option of any error, even the slightest margin of one, had past.

That, in 1990, had been the case for his Newcastle surgeon.

'He had a great name, Dr Beverage!' says Elliott. 'He was unbelievable. A lot of them were doing the operation where they take part of your hamstring. Dr Beverage took part of my patella tendon. He passed away a few years back but we kept in touch. He was from the north-east and he was the club doc. We didn't fly off for operations in London.

'If he had used the hamstring like the other doctors, it's possible I wouldn't have had a career. You can't say for sure, but without a doubt I owed him a lot and I let him know that. I told him what he did for me and I'm glad I did.

'I did my ACL [anterior cruciate ligament] in a cup game against Middlesbrough. I did my cruciate but it wasn't spotted straight away. I ended up playing again with an ACL. I was seventeen. Then I broke down a couple of times and spent a lot of time at Lilleshall and I ended up having the operation.

'Rehab was frustrating, being at Lilleshall as a young lad wasn't great. The group you were with was really important. I had John Barnes, Michael Thomas and Richard Gough. They were all good professionals. They talked you through the injuries. If it had been a bad group with the wrong people in it then it could have gone different because I used to spend twenty-four/seven with them, Monday to Friday.'

It was a lot to ask of a seventeen-year-old.

'I was out for fourteen months,' he says. 'It was a long, long time. I was in plaster for months. Yeah, there were lonely periods. I was back at the club and I wouldn't be playing for another six months.

'It was long hours. You have to be strong mentally. You always think you'll be OK at the end. I never thought I wouldn't come back. That was naivety. When I was at Lilleshall there were eight lads with the same injury as me. Looking back, I was the only one who got back playing.'

Elliott had been spotted when he was nine, playing for Gosforth Park First School. He went to Wallsend Boys Club and met Lee Clark, Steve Watson and Alan Thompson.

'Back then you had to be within a certain area to play for a boys club and I was right on the brink,' he adds. 'I used to think Gosforth was miles away from Wallsend. It was a real trek going to the game. Yeah, I was the posh one!'

Elliott, naturally, was another centre-forward.

'We were winning by too much in one game, and I got moved to left-back because the left-back had gone off,' he adds. 'That's how it happened. I was a left-back from then on. I was fourteen.

'It's one of them where you do as you're told. I was never one to complain about being on a football pitch. At that time as well, I was at the Southampton Centre of Excellence at Gateshead Stadium.

'That was through Jack Hixon. I think I was twelve when I started going to the Southampton Centre of Excellence.' Hixon was Southampton's north-east scout, famous for discovering Alan Shearer.

'Alan was older, his name always got mentioned. Jack came to our house and made you feel special, even at that young age, and my family loved Jack as well and had a lot of respect for him.

'I was twelve or thirteen, I was there for a year. Sheffield Wednesday took over the centre of excellence at Gateshead. That's when I moved to Newcastle and I signed schoolboy forms.

'I used to go to watch Newcastle games at St James' Park. My dad, George, wasn't a shout-from-the-rooftops Sunderland fan but I used to go to Roker Park sometimes with him as well. Not every week. I was Newcastle, being from Newcastle.'

Robbie, spotted, like his young team-mates, by Peter Kirkley, was listening to the advice of Stan Nixon, a youth team coach at Newcastle, and was about to push for a first-team spot closer to home.

'Peter took me to Newcastle,' adds Elliott. 'He was scary at times. He was a great guy but if he lost it you wouldn't want to be the one he lost it to. He used to have a big link with Wallsend. It was a case of, "We'd like you to come." When Newcastle come knocking you don't need much encouragement to get there.

'He obviously had an eye for a player and we had Stan Nixon, who was incredible on the coaching side. Stan took us on to the next level. He was part of everyone's path.

'You owe them massively, Peter for spotting you and giving you the opportunity and then Stan as a coach. He was fantastic, he really was. He was hard on you, even when you were young, but he used to give you a lot of pointers when he came to watch the games. I would ask him in the next session how I could get better.

'To be honest, he used to push you on. Peter got the players in and then Stan would work with them. I was a very laid-back kid and they wanted me to do more on the pitch. There was always more that I could give. They would say, "Go out and do it." After what Stan instilled in us, it's no coincidence the players went on to have successful careers in the game.

'You signed schoolboy forms at sixteen. The centre of excellence was once a week and there was an extra special night where a few select ones would go.

'The one good thing about training was we used to train in the same area as the first team. If anyone went down injured you might get called over. Because I was left-footed I used to have to warm Budgie up before training. That was scary. To be sixteen and have him bawling at you was terrifying.

'It probably put me in good stead. As mad as he was he would talk to you about the professional side of the game.'

Elliott made his debut on the same night in March 1991 as his pal Watson was doing somersaults at Ayresome Park.

'I was obviously doing the right stuff, they put me on the bench and, as bad as the game was, they thought there was nothing to lose so they gave me a run-out,' he says.

'It's one of them, you blink and it's gone. That's how quick it is. You don't even know what's happened.

'It all kicked off in the dressing room after the game. I'd not been involved in anything like that. Then you're actually part of it. The likes of Roy Aitken and Budgie, big characters you'd expect, and the gaffer at the time, Jim Smith, all going for it.

'You're too young to take it in. The next day I was cleaning the boots of the players I'd played with the night before. You didn't have time to go the wrong route. It was back to reality, and rightly so.

'You don't really notice a reaction from people. I was still going to high school doing an A level when the kids were going to college. I had started doing an A level in graphic design but I had to drop it because I couldn't take Thursdays off training.

'Then Ossie took over from Jim Smith and everything changed for all of us. He put six or seven of us in there. It made it easier. It made it natural. You'd be in the dressing room and you'd see familiar faces.

'It's funny, in the dressing room as an apprentice, you're all fighting each other because you all want that pro contract, but it never felt like that with our lot. I don't know if it's because we were all confident we were going to do well or just because we were good friends. We always had each other's back.'

Then he got injured.

Newcastle took off and Elliott was watching, rather than playing.

He started going to away games with his mates. When David Kelly and Andy Cole scored a hat-trick at St James' Park and Newcastle beat Leicester 7–1, Elliott went and celebrated at the heart of the support.

'The whole city just took off,' he adds. 'That was the start of the ride that we went on. To be there, to actually feel it, is something you just can't put into words. It still sends shivers down your spine. It was phenomenal.

'The scenes in the Bigg Market were incredible.

'The big flag was going through the streets and those flags were amazing.

'I'm halfway up one of the buildings on the window ledge. "Eee aye, eee aye, eea aye oh, up the Football League we go!" That was the song! It's night-time. I didn't even know what I was doing. I can still picture the building, it's got the grooves in that you can climb up. I don't think it's as easy to get down! I wasn't jumping onto lampposts. That wasn't me! You look back and you think it's crazy.

'It was like a bottle of pop that had been shook up and shook up and it just exploded.'

Elliott stood on his perch and watched the explosion. He would be at the heart of it when the nation realised what was going on. After fourteen months on the sidelines, Elliott made his return at Boundary Park.

'I remember the first behind-closed-doors game I played when I was fit at Maiden Castle,' he adds. 'Derek Wright was concerned, and then after thirty seconds I wiped someone out and he walked off.

'My first game back was Oldham away. That was like my second debut. Aye, it wasn't a bad game to come back for. I didn't plan it like that!

'Coming back that night was what dreams are made of. When I was injured I used to travel to away games, just to see what it was like. It's a different animal being a Newcastle away fan.

'Just to be playing against was special. I used to look around the dressing room and it was my friends and when I went back I was looking up and it was Peter

Beardsley and Andy Cole. "This is getting a bit scary, what am I doing sat here?" That's what I thought. You think you're sat in the wrong place.

'It was just incredible to be part of that and to be made to feel part of that as well. Obviously Kevin saw something in me to give me the opportunity when I was recovering. My contract? It sounds weird, but that's not why you're doing it. Jesus, they didn't have to break the bank to keep me involved!'

The start of the following season was at Leicester, when Albert made his bow in English football. Elliott came on and scored, and when he did, he ran in front of the celebrating visiting fans, in the same end they had been housed when David Kelly sat with them because of the fighting, and he danced like a chicken.

'I went on holiday to Turkey with Hunty [Andy Hunt] and obviously there had to be drink involved and we were sat on a bar stool and he was trying to take off and started flapping his arms,' he says.

'I went, "What are you doing?" We had a bet there and then. Whoever scores first in the season has to do the chicken dance, that was the bet.

'I knew I was ready to be involved, and to play, and it was great to get the opportunity at Leicester. I just didn't expect to score, but when I did I danced like a chicken! It was memorable.'

Newcastle were back in European football by then. Now he was being watched by the supporters with the big flags who had climbed alongside him in the Bigg Market.

Like Albert, he would not forget the first trip to Antwerp either.

'None of us had really experienced it before,' he adds. 'We went to Antwerp and the fans took over. I'm struggling to say how good it felt. You were coming through a foreign city on the bus and there were just Geordies everywhere. It was really something proud. To go to a place we'd never heard of and play was just unbelievable.

'Did it mean more being a Geordie? I can't answer that because I know it meant a hell of a lot to the other players, but I can't imagine it can have felt any better than it did for me.

'Antwerp felt like a home game. It was one of the great experiences. Just to travel abroad and fly with the team was something we'd never done. It brought us closer together. Obviously we reaped the rewards in the season after.'

Then Elliott was brought in from the cold, first as a substitute against Aston Villa, and then to start against Southampton, whose centre of excellence he had been in ten years earlier.

'I was just honoured to be trusted with the place,' he says. 'I know Bez and Kevin had the argument before I came on against Aston Villa but it meant a lot to me to be picked. To keep me in for the next game against Southampton spoke volumes for me personally. I just wanted to go out and do him proud.

'People thought it was funny when they saw me and John out as friends. We were friends – he didn't pick the team. We used to train together. Bez looked after me. There would have been better ways to get the opportunity but I wasn't going to complain. I was in there, of course it was great for me.

'I wanted the opportunity. I wanted to play. Newcastle were going for the title. I was in the team.

'We were playing Southampton, there were four games left and I was picked. With Kevin, whenever you left that dressing room, you always thought you were going to win, it was never in doubt.

'Three points. That's what you expected. You'd never even think about anything else because when you went on to that pitch you were ten foot tall. He did an incredible job of making you think you were the better team.

'He would go through the opposition and say, "I wouldn't have any of them." He would speak briefly. There wasn't a high amount of team meetings, but then you'd be one on one as you go out on to the pitch and he'd put his hands on your face and say something to you and you felt invincible.

'How he did it I have no idea but it was magic for the team and for the individual. Kevin was a phenomenal man-manager. He could have been a politician. We used to laugh when we were young lads, and we would go in to see him because we were unhappy and we'd come out saying, "Yeah, you're right!" I don't know how he did it.

'At the time, it wasn't just the playing staff, it was the medical staff, it was the coaches, even the people who made the meals at the training ground. Kevin instilled a spirit that people had never experienced before. Once you're in a team that is doing well with that spirit it is only going to get stronger.

'When you look on the bus or in the dressing room it was world-class players to the left and right of you and there was the likes of us sat there going, "Jesus, is this really happening?"

'It was vital we beat Southampton.'

Newcastle did. Asprilla fed Lee to his right in the tenth minute, Lee cut inside and drilled a shot past Dave Beasant. It was the only goal of the game.

'There were nerves in that game, nerves in the stadium as well, but it felt great to be back in,' adds Elliott.

'It wasn't the way we usually did things but after the way it had gone, to get the win and to get the three points was the important thing.

'We had blown teams away all season then we beat Southampton one-nil. We'd beaten Aston Villa one-nil.

'The defence got caned for however many seasons. You brush the criticism off. Man U were known as stalwarts at the back with brilliant centre-backs and an unbelievable goalkeeper.

'The way we played and the way Kevin wanted us to play, we were going to concede goals, but we won and we were still in for the title.'

By the time Robbie Elliott shook the hands of Southampton's players and hugged his team-mates and ran down the tunnel, Newcastle had conceded 35 goals for the season.

Exactly the same as Manchester United.

KEVIN KEEGAN – LOVE WILL TEAR US APART

THE HEADSET WAS ADJUSTED INTO POSITION, THE RED LIGHT ON the camera flashed, and then the manager of Newcastle United was asked about comments Sir Alex Ferguson had made.

Keegan started calmly, but then the fire inside roared into life. He was about to make a piece of television history.

*

KEEGAN HAD BEEN IMMERSED IN NEWCASTLE UNITED FROM A young age. He was not from the north-east – Keegan was born and bred in Doncaster – but his grandfather, Frank, and his father, Joe, were. Frank had lived in Stanley and worked at the Burns coalfield, as an inspector.

In 1909, the West Stanley Colliery was hit by an underground explosion. There were 198 men and children down the mine that day. Only thirty survived. Frank Keegan had been one of those rescued and that no more than 168 had died was in part due to his desire to keep returning to the 'fiery hell' to save those who were dying.

His father Joe – Keegan's first name is the same as his dad, a family tradition, Kevin being his middle name – had fought in Burma and would suffer from bronchitis and silicosis as a result of his time down the mines. He moved the family to Doncaster for work. Kevin Keegan grew up in a home with no electricity, no inside toilet or bathroom. He cleaned cars with a friend to make money and grew to love horse racing through the St Leger, run every year at Doncaster. Entry was free and he met Jean, his eventual wife, on the waltzer.

He got his first pair of football boots after his dad had won a bet. He started in goal but was moved outfield by a teacher called Mr Teanby because he was too small. That would also stop him from being picked for Doncaster Boys.

All the while was a drip, drip effect of the history of Newcastle United. Keegan's family would head to his home and the stories revolved around one thing.

'My father was a Geordie born in Hetton-le-Hole, the same place as Bob Paisley,' says Keegan. 'Although I'm a Yorkshireman born in Doncaster, all his family used to come down. They were all from the mines, they used to speak with this crazy accent and I learned to understand it. They all used to talk about Newcastle United and Hughie Gallagher.

'Without ever being to Newcastle I felt this thing inside me, also in my genes, that was a pull. Whenever I went to play up there, with Liverpool, it felt something really special. I could relate to it, with the fans, because I'd had it imbedded in me since I was young boy.

'They were talking about Newcastle, the Geordies, how big the club was, what it was like in the Toon and I didn't even know what that word meant. It was imprinted in me from being four or five. The one thing I would say is that it wasn't until I went there that I realised what it all meant.'

Keegan would be snubbed when he went for a trial at Doncaster. He was told to be a jockey. Instead there would be a six-week spell at Coventry. He was rejected and, after leaving school, started working in Pegler's Brass Works for six pounds a week. Keegan was a tea-boy and a messenger.

He was playing work football, youth football and pub football, for the Lonsdale Hotel. The Lonsdale played Woodfield at Hexthorpe Flats on a Sunday morning. A man called Rob Nellis was playing for Woodfield. He knew a Scunthorpe scout, he spoke to Keegan after the game and said he could make it as a professional.

Nellis would pick Keegan up in his furniture van and drive him to Intermediate games for Scunthorpe, where Keegan was a guest player. He trained with the first-team squad, played a game in a car park and was asked by Ron Ashman, the Scunthorpe manager, if he would like to sign as an apprentice, on £4/10 [£4.50] a week. He signed.

His day would start at six o'clock in the morning: he would leave home an hour later, take two buses and then hitchhike the final fifteen miles. At seventeen his wages rose to seven pounds a week and he was put in digs. He made his debut on 16 September 1968 against Peterborough, in Division Four, on the right wing. He played twenty times. When he wasn't playing he was running up and down steps with weights in his hands to get stronger.

Keegan played 91 of 92 league games in the following two seasons. He had become indispensable, but his pay still went down from fifteen to ten pounds a week in the summer. He got a job as a plate-layer in the steelworks and drove an old Morris 1100.

His world was about to change. Liverpool and Bill Shankly offered Scunthorpe £32,500. Preston and Alan Ball senior (with Arthur Cox as assistant) offered £5,000 less. Shankly had watched Keegan in an FA Cup replay against Tranmere that was played at Goodison Park. It was 1971 when Keegan moved to Anfield. He bought a red tie for the occasion.

'I never went on the pre-season tour with the first team,' he adds. 'I played little games in New Brighton and Southport, until the Thursday before the Saturday game, when Bill Shankly threw me a shirt for the practice matches and it was red. It was the first team. I played with John Toshack

'After 25 minutes he stopped the game, we'd scored five goals and I'd got two and Toshy had two. I was walking off the pitch, I was playing with guys I'd seen on the telly. Shanks came over and said, 'Son, where would you like to play on Saturday, the first team or the reserves?' I didn't know what to do, I said, 'Mr Shankly, I've not come to play in the reserves.' He went, 'Good, son.'

'The reserves were at Birmingham and the first team was against Nottingham Forest, at home. I couldn't believe it. When I drove to the ground, my name wasn't in the programme. Near the ground they stop you, and the guy said, 'Yes?' and I said, 'I'm playing.' He said, 'Pull the other one.' He walked away and I went and parked in Stanley Park. Before I knew it I was out on the pitch.

'Bill Shankly came over to me a week after playing against Forest – and I got a very lucky goal – and he said, 'Son, you'll play for England in a year.' I knew then I'd play for England, one man believed in me. I'd had rejection in Doncaster. This guy's size didn't matter, it was the size of your heart that mattered with Bill Shankly. He was from mining stock as well, same as my family. He felt an affinity with me. 'You're a bit like I was,' he said to me.

'Bill Shankly used to say to me, 'You're privileged to play for these people.' Shanks said to me once, 'Just go out and drop hand grenades all over the place, son. Cause problems wherever you can.' It gave me a licence to do what I wanted to do.'

He did. Keegan won the league title three times with Liverpool in a five-year spell. He was runner-up the other two. He lifted the European Cup, the FA Cup (beating Newcastle and scoring twice), the UEFA Cup (twice) and the Charity Shield (also twice).

Then he went to Germany and signed for Hamburg. 'It was a sleeping giant,' he said. 'They hadn't won the league for nineteen years.' They did with Keegan, finishing first and second in his three years. Keegan was twice voted the best player in Europe.

'It was a great three years for me,' he added. 'I really enjoyed it. It was a challenge. The people were very respectful. They thought I had the German mentality, work hard and give everything you've got.'

He returned to England with Southampton for two years, and then, finally, at the age of 31, signed for his family's club.

'This was a move that was me saying I wanted to go and see what Newcastle is like,' he says. 'The first time I'd been to St James' Park was with Liverpool. The stadium was still fantastic but in a different way. It was very old, the old stand was still there, with a corrugated stand on the end there.

'I don't know how, it just had something. It always has had, it always will have. They can change the buildings around but basically it is the people inside who make it special, not the building.

'I'd had all those Geordies coming down to Doncaster from when I was a child and my dad's accent always got stronger when they did. When they get together you'd notice an accent change. You can have a Geordie in London and if another couple of Geordies come in, you notice the conversation change. I used to struggle with a couple of my relatives. They spoke quietly as well. They had very broad Geordie accents. They'd use words like canny, and they didn't say that in Doncaster. My dad's favourite word was champion. Even when he was dying. I'd go, "How are you, Dad?" He'd go, "Champion, son."

'They spoke about Hughie Gallagher and Jackie Milburn. There was such warmth. I thought I have to go and sample this, while I still can. I was thirty-one and was still fit and England captain. It was a fantastic challenge. Arthur Cox was very instrumental.

'I probably had two or three years left at the top level. I just said, "Yeah". It was fixed up very quickly. I wanted to go there to finish my career at Newcastle. You know, I just jumped at the chance. I didn't know any of the players, I didn't know Arthur, I'd heard Stan Seymour's name but I'd never met him. It was just one of those things where I thought, yeah, this could be great. It was somewhere in my genes. I was always going to go and the time was right.

'There were people all around Gosforth Park when I signed. I was surprised by the level of interest from the Newcastle fans. You've got to remember, I was still England captain. It was a big signing for them. I was amazed but it was the last time

I was amazed about Newcastle fans.'

Then came his first game in a black and white shirt, when Tyneside came to a standstill.

'Whatever you thought it was going to be,' people said, 'you're not going to believe what it's going to be like tomorrow.' I was thinking, 'I've played at Liverpool, in a European Cup final in Rome, I've played at Wembley, I've played in Hamburg, I've played at the Maracana.

'They were right. I'd never known anything like it, and I still don't. If someone had said there was 100,000 in there, you'd have said, 'I'd have thought there was more.' The noise, I remember as you were jogging out, you're thinking, 'I haven't got to let them down!'

'It just gets harder. That is why a lot of players struggle at Newcastle. Sometimes, because of the passion of the people, players find it difficult to think about it and they go, 'The responsibility of this club is too big.' I remember coming out the tunnel and there was all the people there patting you on the head as you come out, it felt like there were about four thousand of them hanging over the top, you came up the steps, and you can't help but remember these things.

'I remember everything about the goal. I remember flicking the ball on and Imre Varadi flicked it back, and I knew when he flicked it and with the run I'd made that I was going to get one-on-one with the keeper. I knew no one would catch me.

'I had to make sure I did it, things go through your mind, but I never thought I wouldn't score. I just sort of rolled it and it went under the post and then I ran to the crowd. It was just unbelievable. For me, that relief when people come with such expectation, sometimes it can be unrealistically so.

'They want to see you win, they want to see you score, they want to remember the day forever, and you think, 'Well that's great, but we're not writing a book here, this is real life, you know,' and for it to happen was just incredible. I mean, I can't remember anything else about the game, I can't remember if we played well, did we deserve to win? I can't remember, but I remember the goal, I will remember that goal for the rest of my life.

'I say to people, 'Go to St James' Park.' I don't think anywhere else in England I know gets near. It's something to do with where it is in the city. Other cities have cathedrals sticking out – that is the cathedral. You can see it from anywhere. People who I know say, 'There's the cathedral,' it's a religion.'

Keegan changed the feel of a football club forever. The DNA was altered. He was not used to losing – Newcastle were. Within two years Newcastle were up and Keegan flew off and then flew back when it had relapsed.

'You've got the vision and I've got the money,' Hall said to him.

'When someone says something like that in your life, I said, 'Wow,'' adds Keegan. 'I met him at Kew Gardens because he was there with Lady Mae and I said, 'What's your vision? What do you want?' His vision was even better than mine. I thought, 'Wow, if we can achieve that for this city, it will be fantastic.'

'I think anyone who knew anything about football knew it was a massive club because of the support. That's the only reason it is a big club, because of its support. It's not a big club because of its history. They won the cup a couple of times in the 1950, and people talk about the Fairs Cup but they finished tenth to get there. The history for fifty years didn't make it a big club. It was the fans.

'What we had to, we all felt, is make it huge by its performance on the field as well. As you know, that's always been the biggest challenge there. I trained with the players on my first day and played in a five-a-side. I got in the bath and thought, 'I should still be playing'; the quality wasn't great. That was what we had. I got Terry Mac to come and he thought the same, it would be a struggle.

'When a football club goes into decline, a lot of people make bad decisions, 'These players don't deserve to play for this club so we're not going to book hotels, we'll go down on the day of the game. The players can wash their own strips,' that sort of thing. Some of their black and white strips, because of the washing powder their wives used, were grey. This was Newcastle United.

'I wanted them to feel like they were coming into a different club. It cost £6,000 [to refurbish and fumigate the facilities] for a club that could have got relegated. The players came in and you could hear them going, 'Bloody hell, what's happened?'

'There was a lot of disappointments going back, seeing the club had not made a bit of progress and if anything it had gone backwards, but we started from a low point and then we took the view, all of us, the players and the staff, that this place could really only go one way, it wouldn't take much to turn this club around. 'When you turn Newcastle around,' I said to the players, 'it will be like a ship. Once you turn it around you won't be able to stop it.'

'That's what we tried to do, bit by bit. We were signing players who could grow with us. We won the first eleven games the next season. We'd have meetings and say, 'What can we do now?' We need to see the board and say, 'We'll be in the Premiership next season so we need to buy players now or next season they'll cost you a lot more money. That's why we bought Andy Cole for what looked like a lot of money but they were bargains. We knew we were better than the normal teams that came up.

'We ran it on the grounds when I was managing, 'What do these people [the fans] want?' Having played there for two years I knew exactly what they wanted. When I was playing we couldn't give them what they wanted, we weren't good enough. We didn't have the money to spend. We didn't have the players in our squad.

'It was very obvious what they wanted. It's very simple really. They work hard all week, they have a couple of brown ales and they want to go to the match and they want to see a team in black and white give everything they've got to win a football match and entertain them.

'You can lose three-two and they will not boo you off, they will not walk out. They will go to that pub and say, 'Wow, I'm glad I went to the match today.' That's why they're very special. Winning is great, they want to win something, but it's more than that. All we did with my team, we kept saying, 'Who can we better it with?' It's like putting a performance on at the theatre. 'We've come a long way but we must not stop here.' That's where the Halls were very supportive.

'We kept trying to improve the squad. We were close. We knew we were close. If you're in that position you try to improve it. We went for the signing that would make us that bit different. That's what Man United did with Cantona, he was the one who made the difference. They had good players but he made the difference.

'We knew it would not be easy, but we had the ability. We had quality and we had belief. When we had signed Peter Beardsley it sent a message to the Geordies, not only are we not going to sell our best players, we're going to bring them back.

'Waddler had gone. Peter had gone. Gascoigne had gone. We all know the reason. It was always financial; the club couldn't offer what they could there and we understood that. We went, 'Let's reverse that.' Once we got so far they didn't say, 'Let's consolidate and get a few out.' The Geordies don't care where the players are from as long as when they put that shirt on, they give it their all. They will come every week and support them every week until the day they die.

'The greatest thing I took from Shanks to Newcastle was the belief that a football club is for the fans. What makes Newcastle United so strong as a club in terms of its support is that it is a one-town, one-city football club. Sunderland is ten miles away. It doesn't matter. Newcastle is not like Manchester or parts of London. You're black and white and that's it. You're privileged to play for the club.'

Manchester United's victory over long-term foes Leeds United on 17 April had been scrappy and tight. The Reds had won 1–0 for the eighth time in the campaign.

Alex Ferguson did not have a headset on and he did not wave a finger, but his anger looked real.

'For some it's more important to get a result against Manchester United to stop us winning the league than anything else, which to me, they're cheating their manager,' he said to the camera. 'That's all it is. Of course, when they come to Newcastle, you wait to see the difference.'

When the Newcastle team coach pulled into the car park next to the South Stand at Elland Road, it was mobbed. Mostly they were Newcastle fans who waved bits of paper in the air, but some wore the white of Leeds as well.

Keegan could not get off the bus such were the numbers. He began signing autographs as Newcastle's players made their way to the stadium, for such a huge game.

Keith Gillespie had, in his mind, proved an easy target to leave out. There was a numerical problem with the signing of Faustino Asprilla, as much as a logistical one.

Keegan had six forwards he wanted to play and he could only pick five, so Peter Beardsley had been moved to the right side of midfield, which did not suit him, and Gillespie had been moved to the bench. If there had been a legacy of the shocking challenge from Phil Neville at Old Trafford on 27 December, it had been that Keegan had got used to playing without his fearless right-winger. The team was going so well at the time that the change in balance did not overly affect it. David Ginola thought it increased the onus on his side of the pitch.

'That made it more difficult for me because the opposition concentrated their efforts on my wing,' he said.

Newcastle were imbalanced.

There was a clamour to put Gillespie back in the team, to finish with the same players who had swept everything before them at the season's start.

'I always felt that I was going to be the one that was left out,' adds Gillespie. 'It was an easy decision for the manager, I was young and I won't say anything. I'm twenty-one. I always felt that I would be the one and Peter moved to the right.

'A lot of people do say it upset the balance. We got ourselves in that position at the top of the table by playing four-four-two with two wingers; get the ball in the box and job done, Les will score.

'Peter's a great player but he wasn't a right-winger, he wasn't going to beat a couple of men, go to the by-line and put a cross in. Leeds was my first game back in the team. Maybe I had a point to prove.'

David Batty was also back where it had all started. He was an uncompromising Yorkshireman who had been signed for £3.5 million. Batty had come through the ranks at Leeds. He had won the title. He went to Blackburn in their title-winning season as well but hardly played through injury.

In 1996, he slipped into St James' Park almost unnoticed. There was no fanfare. Ferdinand, Ginola, Hislop and Barton had arrived for £14 million and within a month were marching down a catwalk in the middle of the St James' Park pitch for a fashion show. Eight months had gone by since then. Much free-flowing football had passed under the Tyne Bridge. Keegan was being given advice he neither wanted nor needed as to how Newcastle should change, and evolve, and progress. Asprilla's clash with Keith Curle at Maine Road had brought much criticism.

When Batty moved to Newcastle, with eleven games remaining, there was not even a press conference. It suited David Batty. He was not one for words. He was not brought in for his eloquence or his flamboyance (though he surprised Keegan with his ability). It was a nod towards adding steel to the team, if not the central defender Hall had urged him to sign.

Batty's debut had been on the white-hot night at St James' Park when Newcastle lost to Manchester United. He had missed a tackle on Giggs in the run to the goal.

'The Newcastle team, with David Ginola, Peter Beardsley and Tino Asprilla was the best I ever played in,' he said in his autobiography.

> There was a tremendous team spirit, and it was down to Kevin and Terry.
>
> With our lead slipping away, we were running through the woods in training one day when Kevin suddenly announced: 'Anyone who goes out tonight won't play for this club again.' It was the only time I saw him clamp down.
>
> It was good to be part of a set-up where the spirit was so strong and the socialising such fun, but it was equally important to keep a balance between the lighter side and the serious side.
>
> Kevin really wanted to produce attacking, entertaining teams. I remember how he raved down the phone to me just before I joined about 'this guy Ginola'. Ginola was one of those flair players who can disappear when the heat is on, especially in away games.
>
> That isn't a big problem to me as long as he's doing what's required in attack. I've always loved the entertainers, the guys who can appear to be contributing very little and who then suddenly produce a moment of magic to turn a match in your favour.
>
> The manager must have a different perspective. His job depends on results, not performances, and that is why the Ginolas of this world can be a weak link for the man in charge.

There were 5,000 Newcastle supporters in the John Charles Stand at Elland Road. They had barely settled in a fixture in which there was historically no love lost between the supporters of both clubs when a cross came over from the right and Gillespie headed the ball back across the face of the goal and into the top corner of the Leeds net.

It was a scrap. Wilkinson had been given everything his struggling players possessed. It was still not enough to stop Newcastle, who were finding resilience at the right time.

The gap to Manchester United was back down to three points.

'It's always nice when you score a winner in a game like that,' adds Gillespie. 'I don't score many headers, but it was nice to be back in the team. Scoring the winner was the icing on the cake. I did have a point to prove. I was disappointed I hadn't been playing. I had played a big part in getting us to where we were. It was a very important game and we'd won.'

Keegan walked down the cinder track with Wilkinson and the pair chatted. He went to his players in the dressing room and said well done.

'It's funny really,' adds McDermott. 'He came on to the coach, he was going home in his car, he lived over in Yarm, he wasn't far away and he got on the coach. "I'm just going to do the TV," he was laughing. We'd won one-nil. He was happy as Larry. "I'm going to shoot," he said. "I've got to do the press and I'll speak to you later, if not in the morning." I went, "OK, mate, see you later."'

Richard Keys and Andy Gray were in the Sky studio.

What followed will never be forgotten.

> Richard Keys: *Why do you think all that was happening, Kevin, tension on the night?*
>
> Kevin Keegan: *I don't think you can discount it. We just want to keep our hopes alive and a lot of things have been said over the last few days, some of it slanderous. We've never commented. We've just got on working, trying to pass the ball like we do in training.*
>
> *I think you've got to send Alex Ferguson a tape of this game, haven't you? Isn't that what he asked for?*
>
> Andy Gray: *Well, I'm sure if he was watching it tonight, Kevin, he could have no arguments about the way Leeds went about their job and really tested your team.*
>
> Keegan: *And . . . and . . . we . . . we're playing Notts Forest on*

Thursday . . . and he objected to that! Now that was fixed up four months ago. We're supposed to play Notts Forest. I mean that sort of stuff, we . . . is, it's been . . . we're bet– we're bigger than that.

Richard Keys: *But that's part and parcel of the psychology of the game, Kevin, isn't it?*

Andy Gray: *No, I don't think so.*

Keegan: *No! When you do that, with footballers, like he said about Leeds, and when you do things like that about a man like Stuart Pearce. I've kept really quiet, but I'll tell you something, he went down in my estimation when he said that.*

But I'll tell ya – you can tell him now if you're watching it – we're still fighting for this title and he's got to go to Middlesbrough and get something, and I tell you honestly, I will love it if we beat them. Love it!

Keys: *Well, quite plainly the message is, it's a long way from over and you're still in there scrapping and battling and you'll take any of these as long as you continue to get the results.*

Keegan: *I think football in this country is so honest and so, honestly, when you look abroad you've got your doubts. But it really has got to me and I, I, I've not voiced it live, not in front of the press or anywhere – I'm not even going to the press conference, but the battle's still on and Man United have not won this yet!*

The reference to Nottingham Forest's Stuart Pearce was because Keegan had agreed to take Newcastle to the City Ground for his testimonial after the season had finished. The game would take place eight days after the two teams met in Newcastle's penultimate game of the season. That was enough to irk Ferguson.

The first Newcastle fans who were there knew of the outburst was on the Radio Five news. It led the programme. The car park at the back of the John Charles Stand was strangled by traffic trying to get home. Keegan's tone went up in the car speakers. Nobody said a word. As soon as the piece had finished, there was a roar in that car. 'Come on!'

To supporters it was a rallying cry. Nobody wanted to give up.

As soon as the interview had finished, the players of Newcastle United on the team bus found their mobile phones heating up.

'"Fucking hell, have you heard Kevin?" that's what we were told,' says McDermott. 'Listen to this. We had the telly on. Fucking hell, I couldn't believe it. "I'd love, it love it. This is not finished yet, we can still go and win."

'He was right as rain going into the interview. He wasn't saying, "I'm going to show that bastard." We'd just won, he was in good fettle. I was more shocked than anybody.

'He phoned me, I said, "What the fuck was that?" He said, "Ah, sod him." At the time he didn't really like Ferguson.'

Keegan was unrepentant, as he told Steve Harmison on Sky's *Sporting Heroes* in 2014:

> *Where Alex Ferguson annoyed me, it wasn't anything about Newcastle, it was about football.*
>
> *He more or less said other teams wouldn't try as hard against us as they would against Man United. Call it mind games, call it what you want. It got beyond football that.*
>
> *It's insinuating in my mind that teams won't try and they will throw games. At times it's hard to go after a match. We'd won that match at Leeds when I did the interview. I had the cans on and I didn't realise how loud I was shouting.*
>
> *You have to look at it and say it was part of that season, the emotions of that season, the roller-coaster ride.*

Ferguson had been on a long lunch with Roy Evans and two journalists by the time he sat at home, in front of his television. He was more concerned about the wrath of his wife, Cathy, than the mood of Kevin Keegan.

'I sat in my favourite seat to watch the closing minutes, hoping that Leeds would snatch an equaliser,' he said in his autobiography.

> *After the final whistle, I started to attempt an explanation of why I was so late and was stopped dead in my tracks by Kevin's outburst. God, I felt for him. Looking at replays later, I was better able to digest what he said and at first it made me feel a bit guilty.*
>
> *Then I thought to myself that I had done nothing wrong. I had said something that related to the honesty of the game, which I had a right to do.*
>
> *I stress again, my words were not directed at Newcastle or Kevin but at Leeds players. I had always got on well with Kevin and had given him some advice in his early days at Newcastle.*

Although I was a little disappointed he attacked me, I just put it down to pressure. There was plenty of that still round.

McDermott concurs.

'Mind games?' he adds. 'Load of bollocks, absolute bollocks. Mind games don't score a goal, a player does. Do you care what your manager says? No you don't.'

Keith Gillespie got off the team bus in Newcastle and went to a nightclub.

'We were on the coach and somebody was speaking to a girlfriend,' he says. 'That was when somebody said what had happened. We watched it on the bus. I loved the passion he shows, not many managers would do that. He was so for us winning the league.

'Him showing that sort of passion was great for the fans. I know people take the piss about "I'd love it", but to me it was an absolutely brilliant reaction. I don't think any of the players would say it put any pressure on us.'

2 MAY 1996

LEE CLARK – LIVE THE DREAM

THE DINING ROOM OF THE HOTEL IN THE EAST MIDLANDS WAS FULL of Newcastle players. It was breakfast time. David Batty turned to Kevin Keegan. 'I'd love it if you gave me a bit of bacon, gaffer,' he said. 'I'd love it!'

Keegan laughed. The ice was broken. Everyone laughed. Batty got his bacon. Newcastle were ready to roll again. There would be no hangover from Elland Road.

'We made a good joke of it, it was a good laugh,' says Lee Clark. 'I think what the gaffer did at Leeds, he took away some of the pressure from the players because it was all focused on his reaction.

'It felt like he'd done it on purpose. No one had seen it at the time. We saw the footage on the coach. It never did anything negatively to the players.

'The reaction of Kevin during that interview did not affect the players, not at all. The opposite in fact. We made a good joke of it. Batts said he'd love a bit of bacon and the gaffer took it great.

'We had Forest away and it was never going to be an easy game. There were more than 5,000 Newcastle fans heading to Nottingham. It was the third game in six days but we were ready.'

Clark's relationship with Keegan went the deepest.

He had been there, that day, on 28 August 1982.

The nine-year-old Lee Clark was a regular at St James' Park, but he was there for Keegan's debut, in the West Stand paddocks with his mates, because he had just joined Newcastle's centre of excellence and he had been given a couple of tickets.

Clark was the most coveted player in the region at the time.

When he was nine, all that mattered was catching a glimpse of Keegan.

'I think I went to my first game in 1980 with my brother and some of his mates,' he says. 'It was a case of pick where you want to stand against the old concrete barriers in the Gallowgate End. Even though I was little, you could get a good view, I think Bill McGarry was the manager.

'You fast-forward two years and it's pandemonium. It's the summer and there's talk of Keegan in the local press and you think it's rubbish. You hear your dad and his mates talking and you think it's just press stuff.

'That first game, it was absolutely crazy. I was in the paddocks watching it. You've got the best British player of his time, the European Footballer of the Year, and he's playing for us, in the Second Division.

'I was behind the home dugout. I was with a few mates. I was just getting into the centre of excellence and we got issued a few tickets off the club.

'It was just unbelievable. It was something we hadn't experienced before, a full house, squashed up against the wall at the front, just trying to get a glimpse.

'I remember when he first came running out, just before kick-off, you'd never experienced noise like it at St James' Park. I hadn't.

'Kevin scoring? That was the dream, and then he did. I went flying. When everyone had finally calmed down, there were loads of older fellas picking us bairns up, splattered everywhere, making sure we were sorted, putting us back on the concrete barriers so we could sit and have a view above people. That's the way it was then.

'It was fantastic. It was mind-boggling. Kevin Keegan at Newcastle? Anything was possible after he signed for the club.'

Clark was from the East End of Newcastle. He went to St Anthony's and when he was six he got picked for the school team after the PE teacher saw him kicking a ball around the playground.

He was spotted by Brian Clark, a scout for Newcastle who worked for Wallsend Boys Club, playing against St Vincent's. He went to Wallsend. They didn't know he was six.

When he was twelve, Tottenham, Manchester United and Ipswich came calling. His dad, Robert, kept answering the door. 'He would say, "It's Lee's career, he will decide,"' adds Clark. 'Well, everyone knew there was only one place I was going to end up.'

He signed forms at Newcastle when he was fourteen, captained England Schoolboys and scored a hat-trick at Wembley against Italy in a game for the national side that was televised.

Gordon McKeag, the Newcastle chairman at the time, called his parents to the boardroom at St James' and Clark says he told them there had been a £250,000 offer from Liverpool. It was declined.

As he took the step from the juniors to the reserves to the first team, Newcastle appointed Jim Smith, were relegated, lost in the play-offs, sacked Jim Smith and appointed Ossie Ardiles. There was also a battle for control of the club.

'It was a lot of pressure on a kid,' he adds. 'It made it difficult.' Clark made his debut at Bristol City when he was seventeen. 'What was it like? It was daunting. Afterwards I was like, wow, I've just played for Newcastle United.'

He was not involved in the play-offs.

'I remember them,' he adds. 'We got a great result across at Roker Park. John Burridge saved a penalty and got whacked off Paul Hardyman. I watched the second leg from the terraces. Gabbiadini and Gates were unplayable that night. It was awful.

'It's bad enough losing in the play-offs but losing to Sunderland was crushing.

'There was rebuilding going on afterwards. Ossie was the catalyst for us all. I will never forget it. His first game was at home to Bristol Rovers at St James' Park. On the morning we were playing a Northern Intermediate game at Benwell and he came to watch us.

'I think we won by a big score and the following weekend we [the first team] were away at Notts County and about nine of the squad of sixteen that travelled were from the juniors. We all got an opportunity over the period to play in the team. He gave us great belief. He let us express ourselves. He was a manager who never put us under any pressure.

'In his first season we had some good results and it looked like an exciting season. There was optimism. Looking back, Ossie's way was brilliant for us but we were so naive. We would dominate teams for an hour.

'At home to Charlton we were unplayable in the first half. We went three-nil up and we lost four-three at St James' Park.

'Pardew? He scored the winner! Fucking hell! Wow, that's scary. Jesus. That game summed up the Ossie era.'

Then Keegan returned. It was not plain sailing for Clark. Ardiles had loved him. He was the centre of his plans.

'We had a training session at St James' and then we had an eleven-v-eleven,' he adds. 'As a young player I was frustrated because I'd lost someone who had great belief in me in Ossie.

'During the game I lashed out at Alan Neilson. I've since found out Kevin turned to the staff and said, "He's a very good player but I'm not sure how his mentality is." I didn't start the first game. I was on the bench. I didn't start a lot of games.'

Clark had become peripheral. He did, however, understand more than most what relegation would have meant. 'As a local lad, going down to the Third Division would have been horrific.'

Clark watched in the summer as Keegan's future was determined.

'All of a sudden they cleared everything up and he stayed and he started a revolution,' he adds. 'His favourite saying was, "It's a roller coaster, get on it."'

Clark was back in the front seat. He started every game. Newcastle won the division. The Geordie midfielder scored nine times.

'We went to St Andrews that season and Sir John Hall came into the dressing room and he was trying to keep the football up with his suit on. He was jovial. I think he'd had one or two vinos. That was the camaraderie at the club, all the way down from the chairman to the manager to his staff through to the players. Every player will say it, at any age, Kevin made you feel so important to the team.'

Clark remained key in the Premiership after promotion. Then he was substituted during a game at Southampton that was being televised.

'I couldn't hide my emotions and there have been times he left me out and the next couple of days in training I've tried to kick him,' he admits.

'He knew it was because I cared and I wanted to play. I was a young lad so I did some silly things. At Southampton I kicked the bucket after I was taken off.

'That was awful. We had to travel back on the bus. Kevin gave me an absolute ear-bashing at the end. He talked about what I'd done, and rightly so. We had a bus journey back from Southampton that took seven or eight hours.

'As we approached the training ground, Terry Mac came down the bus to tell me the manager wanted me to play in the reserves at Leicester the next night.

'I'd just played an hour at Southampton. The next day I went in to have a chat with him and he said he wasn't prepared to talk to me.

'He said to go and play for the reserves and show as good an attitude as normal. I'd obviously made the mistake in the public domain so I decided the only way I could change things was to apologise in the public domain.

'The manager said that was important and if I did that he would be prepared to welcome me back. I did a press release for the TV and the written media and we got back on track.'

Keegan did not take well to insubordination. It was born from how close he was to the players.

'It was never in doubt the respect I had for him,' adds Clark. 'It is enormous, he knew everything. He took time out to know about our wives, our girlfriends, our mums, our dads, our kids, whenever we had them he knew straight away.

'It was a jovial place to be, you loved it, you wanted to stay there. We didn't have brilliant facilities at Maiden Castle but you never wanted to leave. You weren't desperate to get off the training pitch.

'In school holidays there were thousands coming down. It was crazy times. Kevin was a man of the people and a brilliant person with the supporters. He had time for everybody. He made sure that we all followed suit.

'In school holidays you'd be at training and then you'd be out there for hours making sure you did autographs or photographs for everyone who wanted them. He instilled that in the whole group.

'In the Premiership we kicked on and it was crazy, Peter Beardsley was coming to the fore, Peter was a player who was your hero, then he re-signs and you've got the chance to play with him.

'Before Peter, towards the end of the Championship season, we were going down to Swindon, Kevin said, "I've got a surprise for you, your mate's coming to sign." He meant Coley, because me and Andy had quite a strong relationship going when we met up with England.

'The standard of training was going up. Nobody was guaranteed a place in the team. I never remember him or any of his coaches having to stop a session because of the quality or the attitude or the temperament.

'He got culture into the club by his standards but also by the quality of player he kept bringing in. He made sure that we knew training was very important to him and how we trained would give him an indication of whether we deserved a place in the team.

'After we'd trained we weren't into gambling or snooker so we'd pop back to the stadium and hang around there and have a laugh and a joke.

'Kevin's office used to be in the foyer at the entrance to the Milburn Stand near the reception. He'd see us about and he'd say, "In you come, lads, have a drink out of the fridge, do you want a Coke or a bar of chocolate?" We'd sit watching the telly with him and we'd have chats with him.

'He'd be like, "How's things, you OK?" It was that type of relationship.

'We knew he was the boss and we had unbelievable amounts of respect for him but he made you feel at ease, even the young players. He looked after us so well.'

The Entertainers came third in the first season back in the top flight. Then Keegan sold Clark's big mate. There had been a suggestion in the run-up to the sale that Cole was not enjoying life in the north-east.

'We were really close,' Clark says. 'When he said, "I've moved into a new place," I said, "I'll come and see you, where have you moved to?"

'He said, "Crook." I said, "I don't know where the fuck that is. I'm from the north-east and I haven't got a clue where you've moved to."

'He was miles out of the way, he hadn't realised where he was moving to. I think Freddy [Shepherd] got him back into Jesmond. He ended up living over the road from me.

'We used to go to training together and it was his turn to take me in and I was sitting waiting and I thought, it's not like him, he's usually on time.

'I tried to ring him and his phone was off. I had to jump in my car so I wasn't late for training. He returns a call and I had to keep it secret but he said, "I'm down in Manchester and I'm signing for Man United."

'I said to him, "If I get fined, you're paying! You've got a big signing-on fee from Man U!"

'What a move for him, but it was gutting for us.

'Kevin went and got Ginola and Les Ferdinand. I would think most of the lads didn't know too much about David Ginola at the time.

'Then we saw this player in training and it was like, "Fuckin' hell! Wow, what have we got here?" Without the ball he wasn't great, but because he was so good with it the rest of us decided to do a bit of extra to cover for his defensive deficiencies.

'I've always said the best I've ever played with was Peter but for the first six months David just went to a new level. He was unplayable.'

Newcastle fans had never had it so good.

'We probably provided, over a consistent period of time, the club's best period in the modern era of football,' he adds.

'The run was awesome. Everywhere you walked people wanted to know what was going to happen, what was happening next. It was the best part of my career. The best. It was unique. It was all a bit of a dream really, and the way we did it as well.

'It was quite simple to play in that team as a central-midfield player. You either gave the ball to David's feet for him to do some dribbling, or you pinged the ball over the other full-back for Keith with his electrifying pace, or you gave it to Peter, who would produce a bit of magic, or you'd put it over the top for Les and his power.

'The manner we played and how we did it and the players we brought in – exciting players, and better with each signing – who bought into the Newcastle United way as well. I'm not saying there is a certain way of playing but we had a style.

'Because we're so far north, people think foreign players and lads who have played in London can't be attracted up here. That wasn't the case. We attracted some of the best players in Britain and from abroad to come and play for us, and that was down to the manager.

'It was also down to the players he bought and the way he had us playing and the lads that were there. Not one signing didn't come into the club and didn't buy what we were about, both on and off the pitch. We had a great chemistry between us all, a great respect between each other, for how we played and also how the type of guys we were. It was unbelievable.'

Clark played when Newcastle marched to the top of the Premiership, in his new role. He started 22 games and Newcastle lost four times. Then, following the draw at Manchester City, he was replaced by David Batty. There were eleven games to go and Newcastle were four points clear at the top.

By the time Newcastle arrived at Nottingham Forest, on a bus that Keegan made drive around the city because they were early with a driver who did not know the area and was terrified of getting lost, Clark had not started another game.

'From a personal point of view that was tough,' he says. 'I'd changed my role in the team. I'd been predominantly an attacking midfielder who would create a lot of chances for the forwards.

'In the summer leading up to that the manager was signing players and he was asking if I'd be interested and have a think about playing as a more defensive-minded midfielder.

'That pre-season we worked on it. Kevin said, "You've had a terrific pre-season, you're going to start the season in that role, you'll play at Spurs and we'll go from there."

'It felt brilliant. I'd reinvented myself into a different type of midfield player. During training sessions I played in that position.

'I think up until David Batty coming I only missed one game through injury. Then my last game was the three-three at Maine Road. The famous Man United game was after that when we lost one-nil and it was David's debut.

'It was devastating. Listen, David was a fantastic player in that role. There'd been talk of Paul Ince coming in that role but we signed David and he was great. There was two quality players for each position.

'It was nothing against David. It wasn't as if I'd been replaced by someone inadequate, but at the same time I was very, very frustrated. I worked as hard as I had been; try and be ready for when the manager wants me.'

Clark was on the bench at the City Ground when, just past the half-hour mark, Beardsley set off on a mesmeric run and smashed a left-foot shot into the top corner. Newcastle were back level with Manchester United at the top of the table, albeit with an inferior goal difference.

With fifteen minutes to go, Batty missed a through ball. It ended up at the feet of Ian Woan, forty yards from the Newcastle goal. It still didn't look particularly dangerous, until Woan went another ten yards and smashed a left-foot rocket into the top corner of Shaka Hislop's goal. Hislop barely moved.

Three minutes later Keegan turned to Clark and gave him the nod.

In the final minute, with Newcastle laying siege to the Forest goal, Albert hit a shot that clipped the top of Crossley's crossbar. There would be no winning goal. For the first time since a ball had been kicked in the entire season, it was not in Newcastle's hands.

Still, they had taken it to the final game of the season. Realistically Newcastle had to win and Manchester United had to lose (although a seven-goal victory and a Man United draw would also do it). The race, despite the disappointment, had not been lost. There were things to cling to, for those in the dressing room and for those readying themselves for a 170-mile trip home.

You looked around the Bridgford Stand and there was disappointment, bewilderment even, but not complete and utter dejection. It was a longer shot but that it was still a possibility, four years after oblivion beckoned, was huge.

On the final day of the season, Newcastle could be champions of England. It had not been like this since 1927. Deep down people recognised that. It was an inescapable truth. Lee Clark had been brought up in the East End of Newcastle. He knew too.

'It was still possible going into the last game,' he adds. 'We didn't think it was over.

'We came off the pitch and we were obviously disappointed, of course we were, you could see it, but we knew we could still win it. There were four Geordies in the team when we went back into the dressing room.

'We could win it because we knew how tough away games were in the Premiership.

'Man United had to win, away from home, at Middlesbrough, and they were a decent team, especially at the Riverside.

'I thought, "Nah, this isn't over."'

PETER BEARDSLEY – TIGHTROPE

'SPOTLAND. SPOTLAND. DON'T TELL ME. I KNOW THIS.'

The 18.05 train from Crewe to Manchester Piccadilly was a good place to be. Newcastle had won at Port Vale. It was 1992. Steve Watson had scored. He was 17.

Steve (not Watson) and Keith were sitting with a small group of Newcastle fans when I met them. There are hours to fill travelling around the country on away days.

'I can't get it,' Steve said again. 'Just tell me.'

'It's Rochdale, Whitley Bay were there in the FA Cup. 1990.'

'Bollocks! Rochdale.'

Friendships start that quickly.

'Right, next one. Football players with rude names.'

'Got one,' came a reply. 'Manchester City midfielder.'

'Who?'

'Fanny Lee.'

This is how travelling football fans fill their hours. And their souls.

On Sunday, 5 May, Tyneside basked in glorious sunshine. Outside the Three Bulls, the pub where Pavel Srnicek had been serenaded by a chorus of drunks, Keith Barrett flew his giant flag. All around the city there was nervous tension.

On the final day of a football season, for the first time in 69 years, Newcastle were still in with a chance of becoming the champions of England. There had been no time to think during the week. It had been too hectic, all sense of overview lost in the maelstrom of potential delirium or despair.

From Tyneside to Yorkshire, through Keegan's anger, to the East Midlands and back. Three games in six games, Friday and Saturday to recover and then hope – but then, Newcastle fans had a back catalogue of hope, it was a condition of following the club.

All around the city, as the time ticked towards four o'clock, grew a growing sense of possibility. It was unlikely; Manchester United had just to draw at Middlesbrough, who were now managed by their former great captain Bryan Robson, and Newcastle had to beat Tottenham, but mathematically it could be done.

Exactly four years earlier, on the final day of the season, Newcastle could, mathematically, have been relegated to the third tier of English football. Now they were within touching distance of the domestic throne.

Grey's Monument stands 130 feet tall. It was built in 1838 to acclaim Earl Grey, who had been born in Northumberland in 1764. By the age of 22 he was elected to parliament for the Northumberland constituency.

In 1830 he became prime minister; he passed the Great Reform Act in 1832 and oversaw the abolition of slavery throughout the British Empire the following year. In the shadow of Grey's Monument is the Theatre Royal and opposite one of its side entrances, on Shakespeare Street, is a pub that in 1996 was called the Adelphi.

By three o'clock in that bar, as was happening all over the city, belief had returned. At that point Steve went and sat on the pavement, leaning against the wall of the Theatre Royal. He had barely missed a match in ten years. He took his pint with him and no one followed. He was there for half an hour. He didn't touch his drink.

That lonely vigil said much: that this might be it, that Newcastle might become champions of England, or that this would be as close as they would ever come again.

In the ninety minutes of football that would follow lay so many answers. It was impossible not to feel the enormity of the occasion, of winning the title and of not winning the title.

The answer was in two dressing rooms, around 35 miles apart. One in a new stadium, with a team full of belief. The other at the heart of a ground that had housed Newcastle United since 1892. At the heart of a city.

'Did we think we could win the title? Absolutely,' says Peter Beardsley. 'They were going to Middlesbrough. We thought in a funny sort of way Middlesbrough would never throw the towel in, and they didn't.

'It was hope rather than expecting. We still had to do our job. We knew what was happening down the road.'

That there were two Geordies leading the two sides vying for the title that afternoon merely added to the theatre.

Steve Bruce and Peter Beardsley had known each other for twenty years, since they were teenagers at Wallsend Boys Club.

Now these two decorated sons of the region had to summon one final push from their men.

'I think there was a little bit of apprehension in the dressing room at Middlesbrough but we'd been on such a good run that we expected to win,' says Bruce. 'We'd only lost once in sixteen games. There was a steely confidence.

'We'd overturned them and all the momentum was with us. Newcastle still had to beat Tottenham as well. There was a resolve in the dressing room. Yeah, we'd fucked up the year before but we're not going to let that happen again. That was the feeling. The manager was very, very calm.'

Manchester United had blown it on the final day of the season twelve months previous. Then they had to beat West Ham and hope that Blackburn, led by Alan Shearer, did not win at Anfield. Blackburn lost 2–1, but Bruce, Alex Ferguson and their men could not find victory at Upton Park. Cole had missed a hatful of chances. Eric Cantona had sat out through his suspension.

For thirteen minutes those nerves returned. For thirteen minutes Newcastle had every right to believe they could follow the side of 1927 and become the champions of England. Two minutes had not passed when Juninho went past Denis Irwin, his cross came back to him and the second one picked out Neil Cox, six yards from goal. At that moment, it was alive. Cox had been tortured in the fourth game of the season, when David Ginola announced his arrival in England. That night felt a lifetime ago, when the ball fell to Cox, less than six yards from goal. Somehow he shot wide. The fragility of Newcastle's hopes were exposed rather than cemented.

Word spread around St James' Park of Cox's chance. There was renewed hope. Manchester United had not settled. Middlesbrough were making tackles.

Then, in the fourteenth minute, Ryan Giggs took a corner from the right and David May rose and headed it into the Middlesbrough goal, past Branco, who was on the goal-line.

News of the goal swept around St James' Park. It froze your soul. You knew then. You knew what had been gnawing at your insides for weeks was true; it was not going to happen, it was not meant to be.

Nick Barmby was presented with the chance to equalise and make it game on again, but he blazed his shot wide. Then, in the space of three minutes, early in the second half, came the undeniable evidence that it was done: Cole scored for Manchester United and Jason Dozzell scored for Spurs.

Newcastle equalised through Les Ferdinand, his 29th goal of the season. Somehow, at the end of all those turns, it was nothing more than consolation. Giggs would score at the Riverside Stadium with nine minutes remaining.

It was over.

Manchester United were champions. Newcastle had finished second. There would be no title, no trophy, no open-top bus parade. The dream was over.

Keegan remained extraordinary.

'KK went into the dressing room first,' adds Beardsley. 'He was so positive. He went, "I'm so proud of you, look at where we've come from. We signed four new players in the summer, it's incredible what we've done. Every one of you deserves a huge pat on the back."

'He was amazing. He showed no sign of being deflated, not in the dressing room. He may well have been devastated but he grabbed you and rubbed his head against your face and he did that to every one of us.

'He went round the dressing room and he was in your face in a nice way. He said, "What you've done is incredible." Inside he must have been so disappointed but the way he reacted you'd have thought we'd won the league. There was real pride, no negativity in his voice or his emotions. It was incredible.

'We almost felt guilty we had let the fans down. They were probably more exhausted than we were. I felt really bad. I've had laps of honour before and since; that was the worst. It really felt bad. The fans were devastated. There were people crying in the crowd. They were distraught.

'That for me was really hard to take. I felt really sorry for them. 1983/84 was the best lap of honour ever. That was the worst.'

It was slow and procession-like. Keegan had to be coerced to bring his players back to salute the supporters. No one had left the stadium.

By the time he reached the corner that linked the Leazes End and the Milburn Stand the pain looked like it was seeping through. Keegan put his hands to his mouth to blow a kiss and it took a fraction too long. Keegan would not show hurt, and that was heroic.

The distance a football club and a city had travelled in such a short space of time was truly exceptional. There was pride but there was pain. People knew, deep down, that it might never come around in their lifetime again.

It had been brilliant and it had been breathtaking. At times the city of Newcastle was simply overwhelmed with the drama.

The pain and the hurt and the questioning was part of a process, but the Newcastle team of that season will live longer in the memory and in the heart than some who have finished higher in the cold harsh reality of a league table.

The way Newcastle were that season was the way every football fan dreamed their team would one day play.

One minute it was there and in the blink of an eye the title had gone.

By the time you realised it could happen, it was sliding through your fingers, like the finest sand, and the tighter you grasped, the less you held.

Every Newcastle fan was left to imagine how magical the celebration would have been.

Those players told me they still see it sometimes, when they see a different finale, where Manchester United didn't finish like an express train. Heard melodies are sweet but those unheard are sweeter. It offers solace, now, at least.

It didn't then. It took years to watch the Premiership's greatest ever game, at least it did if your team was playing in black and white that night.

The lack of the crown has not dimmed the feeling for that side. That says much. The individuality and its impact remain as strong as ever.

Nothing about the side was predictable. You had to watch them.

Two decades on, there has not been another team like Kevin Keegan's Entertainers.

'You'd see us play and you'd think, "Anything could happen here",' adds Beardsley. 'That's probably what made us the way we were in terms of how much people liked watching us. We were The Entertainers.

'It was shit or bust. I mean that in the nicest possible way. That was what made us special. That is why people still talk about us now. I look at people who are thirty years old and they say they will never forget those days.

'I know it's easy to say, and I know people say of course you would, but I wouldn't change anything. I was lucky because I'd already won the league with Liverpool. Because of that, playing the way we did, nah, I wouldn't alter it. I was very proud to be part of that Newcastle team, entertaining the public. I was one of them. I know what they enjoy watching. They still talk about that team.

'I think Newcastle fans talk more about the team we had than about one that might have won being negative and playing boring football, one hundred per cent. They loved those days. They loved it. We were everybody's favourite second team.

'It was the legacy of 83/84. They were brought up on that kind of football. KK used to talk about how that season was one of his best years in football. He said that to me.

'He won the European Cup. He did what he did at Hamburg, twice European Footballer of the Year, but to do what he did as a player for Newcastle was special to him.

'He lifted the club, he lifted the city, he lifted everybody – that made him feel very proud and I know that's what he wanted to do, as a manager.'

Kevin Keegan did that all right.

HOW WAS IT FOR YOU?

'DO I THINK ABOUT WHAT IT WOULD HAVE BEEN LIKE IF WE'D WON the league?' said Warren Barton. He was in America when we spoke, several time zones from the north-east when he repeated the question I had asked. 'Every day. I think about it every day.'

*

IT IS TWO DECADES SINCE NEWCASTLE CAME WITHIN TOUCHING distance of being the champions of England. That it last happened in 1927 gives perspective to what the team Kevin Keegan assembled came so close to achieving.

This book was always intended to give a far broader picture of what happened that season, and indeed in the remarkable period when Keegan took a city and a football club on a quite wonderful adventure. It was intended to show a far greater complexity than the narrative that had been left behind.

History can be written very quickly, rightly or wrongly, and it was my opinion that the notion that a suspect defence had cost Newcastle the title, or the signing of Asprilla, or Ferguson's mind games, seemed an unfair and simplistic explanation of an incredible season. There was always much more to it than that. Hopefully Touching Distance shows the multitude of factors that meant Freddie Fletcher's planned open-top bus route was never used.

That everyone I spoke to from Newcastle in the period still felt regret was undeniable. 'You're making me depressed now,' said Darren Peacock when we touched on what might have been, in Lancaster.

Two decades on, the feelings are as raw for the players and management as they are for the folk of Tyneside. The 1995/96 season still stirs the men involved right to the core of their being. It is a time they still feel immense pride for being a part of. It is intertwined with tangible frustration.

The season The Entertainers came within touching distance of being the champions of England still rouses a myriad of emotions, but then Kevin Keegan and his group of players always did.

*

JOHN BERESFORD:

'I felt devastation. We had been built up for it. The lads on the pitch probably felt flat. I don't have regret. There is disappointment the silverware that would have put the icing on the cake did not come.

'To me, would you change it to win something but then be like the clubs I'd been at, with that training and everything? No chance, nowhere near. I'm telling you, I could not wait to get up in the morning and go training. I could not wait to get to that game and play.

'Sometimes at Portsmouth and Southampton it was a ball-ache. It was hard work. It was never like that at Newcastle. The adrenaline, the excitement and everything that went with it, it was just a special time.

'Keegan would go, "I need you out there, I want things to happen." He knew how he wanted me to play. It changes the game. If I bomb on and leave the gap they will attack that, the game will then get stretched but I will go again. The game automatically gets quicker. He knows that. If your full-backs go like that it influences the game.

'People are talking about full-backs bombing on now as if it's a revelation. We did it twenty years ago. I don't think he gets the recognition he deserves for what he did. I think Keegan was clever because he put the players together and he knew how he wanted them to play. He trusted us. "If you see it, do it, take responsibility." It was brilliant.'

*

WARREN BARTON:

'Every day. I think about it every day. Every morning I wake up and I go, "What if?"

If you ask anyone, it's the same, the fans as well. They were devastated as much as us.

'We never gave up. The last game Man United had to go to Middlesbrough and we knew it would be difficult.

'It was tough. Deep down, with about two days to go, we knew that they would not give up. They were relentless.'

*

ROBERT LEE:

'I regret not winning anything. You don't think about it until you retire. We'll win it next year. We'll win something next year.

'I don't regret anything about that season, no. I don't think I can change anything. Would I play a defensive team? No. We didn't have defensive players. Kevin was like a kid when he bought a player.

'On FIFA [FIFA Soccer – the video game] you buy exciting players, nobody buys defenders. Kevin was like that. Out of necessity I'll sign one, but I'll get attacking ones. That's the way his philosophy on football was, that's what I miss.

'I miss him not being in the game, not seeing his interviews, and his enthusiasm for Newcastle was amazing. His interviews were hilarious. His team talks were hilarious, he'd just make you feel at ease. When you feel at ease you play better.

'We knew we could win it. We knew we had the team capable of winning the Premiership.

'I think, as Kevin said at the time, the hardest one to win is the first one and you need a bit of luck. I don't think we got a lot of luck during that time.

'I personally think we were the better team. Take Schmeichel out of their side and I think we were better.

'We just kept coming in, "Cantona has scored, Schmeichel has been brilliant." That's exactly how it was. Every one of those games, even at home.

'We played them at home and we absolutely battered them. Ask their players, we annihilated them, Schmeichel was unbelievable.'

*

LES FERDINAND:

'I always say this, throughout any time in a season, there are big games that are momentum-changers. I honestly believe if we had won at Liverpool, we would have gone on to win the league; that was a pivotal one to lose.

'It would have given us a mentality and a belief that, "Yeah, we do belong, we can beat these good teams."

'We lost to Man United, Liverpool and Arsenal, our three rivals. Then it was perhaps we were not quite there yet. That might have been going through people's minds.

'I played against Schmeichel on many occasions. On some days I got the better of him and some days he got the better of me, like he did that day at St James'. I remember Philippe Albert hitting a free kick that hit the crossbar and he never saw it. It was one of those days. Ginola had chances, Albert had a chance at the end as well. We all had chances, the ball just wouldn't find the net for us.

'If I had my time again, would I want it to be as it was? No. Nah, nah, nah. Certain parts of it, yes.

'What I always said is I loved the football we played, free-flowing, attacking football.

'We had no structure to it. We didn't have a plan B. If you're all-out attack, great, but if we had a bit of structure to it, that may have given us the discipline to deal with that. Would it have taken away from the brand of football we played? That's the big question.

'I would risk it if it meant we had won the league.

'I still felt with the players we had we could play that attacking, flair football.

'We played a brand of football that everyone enjoyed watching. It was cavalier. Would I sacrifice being cavalier for winning the Premiership? I think all of us would have done. We were everybody's favourite second team but I would rather be champions.

'There is a pleasure to be part of that team. It was a great footballing, entertaining team. You didn't get that title for nothing.'

*

TERRY MCDERMOTT:

'Would I change something to win the league?

'No. If you change one thing you change it all. I wouldn't have changed it, no. It was too bloody entertaining not to play that away.

'You start tinkering with your defence and you will lose it somewhere else. Will you be as entertaining? Will you score as many goals? No, you can't, you can't change it.

'For the Geordie public not to have won that league when they should have done, I would have loved it, and I'm sounding like Kevin now, they deserved it.

'The players deserved it, the club deserved it and the fans certainly deserved it. We needed that bit of luck. For Man United to go on the run they went on, that's probably one of the best Man United teams ever.

'We were in such a position, with a bit more luck we might have won it and Man United wouldn't have missed one trophy, would they? One does make a big difference to us. It was sickening for us, it affected Kevin, not winning it when we should have done.

'I remember in the summertime, thinking, "What a season we had. We got beat by a better team only because they won the league." I thought we were the better, more entertaining team and we didn't get the luck we needed.

'We should have won it because we were the best team and it would have been deserved.'

*

DARREN PEACOCK:

'Do I look at it with regret or pride? A bit of both. It depends what mood I'm in.

'I'm sure the lads are the same as me, there are some games you think, I should have done better.

'There is frustration because with the brand of football we were playing, the title could have kicked us on.

'There is pride. The gaffer bought a lot of those players in from lesser, smaller clubs, for big fees, but at that time some players who were not established.

'The gaffer would have done homework on personalities, he knew what the atmosphere was like in Newcastle, he brought players in who could handle that situation. It is immense pride, first of all, playing for Newcastle.'

*

PAVEL SRNICEK:

'We would all have had the statue at St James' if we had won. It would have changed all our careers with the title. We would have stayed with Newcastle forever.

'I regret it because I could be the first Czech goalkeeper in history to win the championship in England, before Petr Cech. With the title, all of the things in your life changes. Life didn't change.

'Can I imagine life without Newcastle? I miss the banter, everything that there was. You can't have that again. I do miss it. Of course I do. I go there for five days a year but it is not enough. The city is in my heart. You cannot put it anywhere else.'

*

STEVE HOWEY:

'Would I change it? I think so, probably. It would have been absolutely perfect to play the way we did and win it. It didn't quite happen. We were nearly, nearly there, but at the same time, for the sake of just shutting up shop in a couple of games and win the Premiership . . . But then you would have to change the training and everything.

'Would I change it, then? Nah. Would you really want to change the way we played, the way the dressing room was? No. I wouldn't change that for the world. It was just a special time with unbelievable people and players.'

*

LEE CLARK:

'Would I change things to win the title? Aye. Yeah, I would.

'I know, sitting here years later and we're talking about the year we won the Premier League, people wouldn't be talking about some days where we had boring training sessions.

'As a professional, you would love to be sitting with your kids now and in another fifteen years with your grandchildren and you're watching the Premier League and show them you have one of them medals.

'Unfortunately the dust has settled on that part of the mantelpiece, because I did make a space for it, but it wasn't to be. You still have the memories. You still have the things you can talk about.

'Of course I still think about not winning it. Whenever you sit and watch live football and the Premier League you think, "We could have been one of the few who have done it." It is a select few.

'What does wind me up and rile me about our era was the perception that we were poor defensively. That was absolute nonsense.

'We had one of the best defensive records in the division. The other one was that the manager wasn't tactically aware. You don't take your team close to winning the title just on being exciting footballers and trying to score more than the opposition. He was tactically very, very aware.

'Those two things are said about the era and it's total fodder in my opinion.'

*

SIR JOHN HALL:

'Yes, we had an open-top bus parade planned. We were twelve points in the lead. We sat down. You have to plan ahead. Freddie Fletcher worked on the route. It was going to leave from the Gosforth Park Hotel.

'It just disappeared before our eyes. Never count your chickens.

'We kept believing. Just win a couple of games and we're home. It's mixed emotions. You've got to win. You keep on going. When it goes from you it is a drain and it takes some picking up because you've been so close. It happens with everything.

'If we had've won, it would have lifted up the whole city, and the club.

'Once you start to believe in yourself you can achieve anything. That's what Keegan gave the football club and everyone in the football club, to believe in themselves. He motivated them. They believed in themselves. You can do anything.

'It's over. It was part of the past. You have to feel some disappointment. We were nearly there but you cannot live in the past. If you live in the past you die in the past. You have to move on.'

*

STEVE WATSON:

'I've had a good career but I haven't got anything to show for it and that was the only thing I wanted. I will never get over it.

'I think about it more than I should probably. You can't do anything about it. How often do you get that close to being Newcastle's youngest player and winning the title with them?

'The squad of players we had was brilliant and you'll never take away the memories of what we had then. I suppose in hindsight, would you do anything differently on the training pitch? If you can't win a game just don't lose, or if you get a lead it's that important to hang on to it, I don't know. That might have taken something away from what was going on at the other end.

'We ended up being the second best team in the league and probably everybody's favourite team, but ultimately we were second.

'Yeah, it means something being so favourably remembered. We did a lot of things right. We played football in the right way and football people enjoyed.

'Just the fact that so many people who had no affiliation with us were complimenting us was good to hear. So many people around the country were saying, "We hope you win the league."

'Other teams from Christmas onwards, when it was the reality we had a chance, players you've known through the game, not mates, you've played against a dozen times, going, "Fuck me, I hope you go and win this." Other managers, other fans, it felt nice but ultimately we failed.

'But then, was it my happiest football time? Without a doubt.'

*

DAVID GINOLA:

'After Liverpool I was very frustrated because we were very good, scoring three goals at Anfield, it was like, for me, in my mind, 20 minutes to go, I thought, "We are going to beat Liverpool at Liverpool, wow, great!"

'When we concede all these goals, it was massive frustration. I couldn't express it. It was how we did it. This is not as a team, it's not only the defenders. We didn't manage to get the result. It was the end of the dream. Like a wake-up call in the last 20 minutes. We realised we weren't good enough to get the results.

'At the end, it is about frustration, it is not good to finish second. It was a shame in the South of France to look back to the games and the points and you just realise, no.'

*

ROBBIE ELLIOTT:

'Do I think about that season? Yes, I think about, "What if?"

'You can't even imagine what would have happened to the area. It's one of them, "What if?" I think it's what is on everyone's minds, what would have happened? Where would we have gone? Would we have continued to progress?

'What it would have meant and how the whole area would have kicked on is what I think about.

'When the team is doing well there is nowhere better to be than Newcastle. When you've spoken to the lads about this, the team spirit we had, it was a little bit special.

'On the team bus there used to be me, Steve Howey, Rob Lee and Bez. Bez and Rob would say to us, "This isn't normal. This is special, enjoy it." We would say,

"This is Newcastle, this is normal."

'Looking back, they were just spot on. It was something. Ask any of us in our career what our best time was and I'd be very surprised if anyone says it wasn't that period at Newcastle.

'It's just a shame we couldn't have got that extra couple of points. Who knows what would have happened?'

*

PHILIPPE ALBERT:

'If I go back to Newcastle, I am so well received. That is what I am proud of. I am more proud of this than the trophies. It means something for me. It means I gave something always to the team.

'When you give pleasure to your fans, that is the most important to me. Kevin and I, we had exactly the same visions of football. I prefer talking about the good memories more than the bad ones. It was the best period of my life football-wise and human-wise at Newcastle.

'Every time I go back it's fantastic, anywhere in the town. I can go anywhere in the town and people are talking about football, and the Keegan years. We were the best team in England with Man U, which is something we can be proud of. They were one of the best teams in the world.

'I would not change anything about that period, even if it meant we won the title.

'No. I don't know if other players would answer something else. I wouldn't change it. That was the way our boss wanted us to play football. He is the boss and we have to follow his instructions. I'm sure he's proud of us even if we finished second because we had a fantastic season. It is an absolute pleasure to talk about football and Newcastle.'

*

KEITH GILLESPIE:

'In four years it was a giant leap. We were one game away from winning the Premiership, the biggest thing that would have happened to Newcastle for so many years.

'It was an incredible season.

'I always remember the scenes after the last game, walking round the pitch, you'd have thought we won it. It was incredible. That night out in the town was the same, it was like we had won the league. I think the supporters realised, although we fell a little bit short, they realised what an incredible year it had been. There had been ups and downs, but so many more ups than downs.

'You think of the downs, Liverpool away and Blackburn. Then the ups far outweigh them. It was the emotion for everyone that season. We got so close, the fans realised they had seen a pretty good team.

'If we'd won, they'd still be partying. That was the real disappointment. That was Newcastle's real chance to break through. Every Newcastle fan goes, "Flip, I wish it was twenty years ago."

'Rewind twenty years and it's great you can look back with such fondness about being part of such a great side.

'Oh yeah, I think, "What if?" Without a doubt. It's a real big regret that we just fell that wee bit short. I think it's the same for most of the players. Man United probably just handled it, the run-in, a little bit better than us. None of the players had really been in that position before of winning leagues, apart from Peter and Batts.

'Man United had been winning leagues already so they were used to that. They handled that a bit better than us.

'It was my best season, without a doubt, an incredible time to be around this city. When the football team is doing well and driving forward, the city is buzzing. It's a magical place to be.'

*

FAUSTINO ASPRILLA:

'We deserved to be champions. What left me really sad – because I was brought in to win the Premiership – was that we ended up coming second. It was a very disappointing way for the season to finish.

'It was hard when we lost against Liverpool but we only have ourselves to blame. You can't blame anyone else.

'I arrived with about fifteen league games to go. Normally players need time to adapt. I think I adapted quite quickly. One thing was that I don't think we got together as a team enough.

'We lacked responsibility. I don't mean getting together in the bars, but in the hotels. In Parma, if we were playing at home on a Sunday, on the Saturday we'd all stay at a hotel. In Newcastle we stayed at home and then went straight to the stadium. I wasn't happy at home, I was restless, opening the fridge, going up the stairs. I'm not a fan of get-togethers but they do work.

'It is a shame because we should have won the league. When I think about that season I can't sleep because of how huge the sadness I have at not winning it.'

*

KEVIN KEEGAN:

'I never thought we had the title won.

'The incredible thing I remember about that season more than anything else was we were getting clapped on to grounds away from home. At Leeds, Newcastle were clapped on. It was the same at Notts Forest. We were the home side when we came out.

'Although they didn't give us anything, as results will prove, especially the Nottingham Forest one, deep down, everyone wanted us to win the league.

'For a side that played like we did, that wasn't one of the big teams for a long while, we were everyone's favourite second team. That is the title we have to accept, and I think it's not a bad title.

'We didn't win the league but we were everyone's second team, everyone, wherever we went. I remember Arsenal fans coming up saying, "If you were on the television on a Monday night, I'd tell the missus, we aren't going out tonight."

'Oh yeah, I felt the pride the region had in the team.

'We were together, weren't we? When we went down to games, that's the thing about Newcastle . . . you have this whole support; buses on buses on buses, and the double whammy of when you're down in the Midlands you have second-generation Geordies whose dads moved down in the pits, like my dad. All the way back, you have toots, and people waving their scarves and hanging out the car, that was incredible.

'It was a great period but it's gone.

'If you go for the moon and you hit the stars and you miss the moon, at least you got pretty near. That was my theory. We knew we could challenge the Man Uniteds. We didn't know we could ever get an eight or ten-point lead.

'There's two schools of thought in life, there's the guys who say, 'We want to, but don't say anything because it'll put everyone under pressure.' Then there's the others who say, 'What's wrong with saying what you want?'

'In my notes in my last programme before we came up I said, 'Watch out, Alex, we're after your title!' People said, 'What you writing that for?'

'I'm sure if you talk to everyone they will have different reasons. If you talk to

John Beresford he will have a different reason to Darren Peacock. Darren Peacock would say we could have done with another defender in the side, gaffer, there's only me!

'Then, Rob Lee might say something else and the fans might say, 'Why did you buy Asprilla?' The truth is, we all didn't know how to get over the line.

'We had a lot of players in the team who were excellent players but they'd never really won much or knew how to win. Once you've won a league once, it's not a problem. They had a manager who had built everything on optimism and on painting pictures for people that said, 'Why can't we?'

'There's games I look back to, Man United at home, where Schmeichel was unbelievable. Cantona bobbled one in. You can't look back. What you have to look at, at the end of the day, is Man United were the better team. At the end of the day they went from Christmas, right to the end of the season, I think losing one game. We couldn't do that. We didn't have the consistency they found.

'They had a lot of players who knew how to win things. They'd done it before so they knew how to do it. Maybe that was the difference, they had a manager who knew how to win things. They had a manager who knew how to get it over the line. Had we won it, who knows, we might have changed football forever.

'We'll never know.'

EPILOGUE

THE BOEING 747 FROM HEATHROW TO THAILAND WAS GOING through its final checks. It was July, there was a thirteen-hour flight ahead and the entire Newcastle first-team squad were making adjustments for a trip that would take them to Thailand, Singapore and Japan.

There had been jokes, a few digs and the scars of the previous season's disappointment were not in evidence. It was the same group of men who had come so close to glory – no one had been sold.

Kevin Keegan was sat with Terry McDermott at the head of the Newcastle contingent when the bat phone rang. Keegan fumbled in his pocket before answering. There was a quick conversation, then he turned to McDermott and whispered, 'It's the big one, we've got the big one. Don't tell them until you're in the air.'

He pressed a button above his head and a stewardess came over. There was a quick explanation, he undid his seat belt and his bag was retrieved from an overhead locker.

Keegan stood up and walked off the plane. By now, his players were watching. McDermott told them not to worry.

When the doors were shut and all mobile phones had been switched off, he turned and addressed them.

'We're signing Alan Shearer . . .'

APPENDIX: WHAT HAPPENED NEXT

Pavel Srnicek:

Left Newcastle in 1998 and spent time with Sheffield Wednesday, Portsmouth and West Ham. Returned to Newcastle in 2006 as cover for Shay Given, came on as substitute against Tottenham to a tremendous ovation. Currently goalkeeper coach at Sparta Prague.

Warren Barton:

Moved to Derby after seven years with Newcastle, then briefly to Queens Park Rangers and Wimbledon before a spell coaching with Dagenham and Redbridge. Currently works for Fox Sports 1 as a TV pundit.

John Beresford:

Left Newcastle in 1998 and moved to Southampton for three years but struggled with injury and retired. Stayed in the media in the North east and is currently a TV pundit.

Steve Watson:

Was sold by Ruud Gullit to Aston Villa in 1998. Moved onto Everton, West Brom and then Sheffield Wednesday. Has held coaching roles with Huddersfield and Birmingham and created @ProSportApps.

Darren Peacock:

Moved to Blackburn in 1998 and was there for two seasons. Damaged the vertebrae in his neck in a game agains Fulham. Took over as manager of non-league Lancaster City in 2013.

Steve Howey:

Was sold to Manchester City in 2000 for £2 million. Moved to Leicester three years later. Had a spell in charge of non-league team Crook. Currently does television work with Sky and coaches for the Premier League.

Philippe Albert:

Moved to Fulham on loan in 1998 and then returned to Charleroi in Belgium in 1999 before retiring. Currently works on Belgian TV as a pundit and is also involved in a fruit and vegetable company.

Keith Gillespie:

Left Newcastle in 1998 when he moved to Blackburn in for £2.5 million. Went onto play for Leicester, Sheffield United, Glentoran and Longford Town. Retired in 2013 . Was capped 86 times for Northern ireland. Works in television and is also an after dinner speaker.

Robbie Elliott:

Elliott was sold to Bolton by Kenny Dalglish in 1997 for £2.5 million. Returned to St James' Park four years later and left in 2006. Finished his career at Hartlepool. Currently works in Nike sports research lab in America.

Kevin Keegan:

Left Newcastle in 1996 because of the share flotation. Went on to manage Fulham, England and Manchester City. Returned to manage Newcastle in 2008 but was undermined by the new owner Mike Ashley and successfully sued the club for unfair dismissal in 2009. Currently a television summariser.

Terry McDermott:

Stayed at Newcastle in his role as assistant manager when Kevin Keegan left and Kenny Dalglish took over. Left when Rudd Gullit took over but returned as part of Graeme Souness' management team at St James' Park and worked under Glenn Roeder, Sam Allardyce and Keegan for his second spell. Worked as number two for Lee Clark at Huddersfield and Birmingham and currently working as a media pundit.

David Kelly:

Was sold to Wolves for £900,000 after helping Newcastle gain promotion to the Premiership. Moved to Sunderland, then Tranmere and Sheffield United before ending his career at Derry. Has worked as number two at Preston, Derby and Notts Forest and currently assistant manager at Scunthorpe.

Sir John Hall:

Stood down as Newcastle chairman in 1997 but his family retained majority shareholding in the club. Sold the 41.6 per cent holding to Mike Ashley for £55 million in 2007. Still an active businessman in the north east and has just completed the second stage of developing the gardens of Wynyard Hall.

Graham Fenton:

Left Blackburn in 1997 to go to Leicester for £1.1 million. Had loan spells at Walsall and Stoke before going to St Mirren and then Blackpool. Made over 100 appearances for Blyth Spartans. Currently managing North Shields in the Northern League. Led them to the 2015 FA Vase. Also works as a coach at Monkseaton Academy.

Brian Kilcline:

Left Newcastle in 1994 and moved to Swindon. Lived in a barge for a spell before moving to Mansfield. Finished his career at Halifax. Backpacked around the world with his wife Lynn and continues to combine travel and the life of a landlord who repairs his own properties.

Steve Harmison:

Was released by Newcastle in his teens but was then spotted by Geoff Cook playing cricket for Northumberland against Durham Under-16s. Went on to play first class cricket for Durham and represented England in 63 test matches and 58 one day internationals. Currently back in football as manager of Northern League side Ashington.

Les Ferdinand:

Left Newcastle in the summer for 1997, joining Spurs for £6 million, after scoring 41 goals in 68 games. Had spells at West Ham, Leicester, Bolton and Reading, and won 17 caps for England. Was number two to Tim Sherwood at Tottenham and is currently working at Queens Park Rangers as director of football.

David Ginola:

Ginola moved to Tottenham for £2.5 million in 1997, sold by Kenny Dalglish. Two years later he was named PFA Players' player of the year. In 2000 he moved to Aston Villa for £3 million and ended his career at Everton. Ginola has been involved in acting, wine making and TV punditry since and in 2015 made a failed attempt for the presidency of FIFA.

Rob Lee:

Was handed a testimonial by Newcastle in 2002 when Newcastle faced Atletico Bilbao. Played more than 300 games for Newcastle and scored in an FA Cup semi-final at Wembley against Chelsea. Moved to Derby for £250,000 and went onto West Ham and Wycombe. Played 21 times for England and currently works as a TV pundit.

Peter Beardsley:

Beardsley left Newcastle in 1997, moving to Bolton for £500,000. He went to Manchester City before linking up with Kevin Keegan again at Fulham. He went to Hartlepool and had a brief period with Melbroune Knights. He was capped 59 times for England and scored nine goals. He returned to Newcastle as an academy coach in 2009 and is currently the football development manager.

Lee Clark:

Clark left Newcastle in 1997 and moved to Sunderland for £2.5 million. He would score 16 goals in 74 games and helped take the club into the Premiership. He joined Fulham in 1999 and was there for six years before returning to Newcastle for a season. He moved into management and has been in charge of Huddersfield, Birmingham and Blackpool.

Steve Bruce:

Bruce left Manchester United at the end of the 1995-96 season and moved to Birmingham for two seasons before a brief spell at Sheffield United. He took over as manager at Bramall Lane and has been in charge at Huddersfield, Crystal Palace, Birmingham Wigan, Sunderland and is currently in charge at Hull. Bruce came close to becoming Newcastle manager in 2006.

Alan Shearer:

Shearer signed for Newcastle in the summer of 1996 for a then world record fee of £15 million from Blackburn. He went onto break Jackie Milburn's goalscoring record for the club, scoring 206 goals in 10 seasons. His testimonial was marked with a farewell game against Celtic. He returned for brief spell to manage the club and currently works for Match of the Day.

Alan Pardew:

Briefly went to Spurs on loan after leaving Charlton in 1995 before ending his career with Barnet. Started in management with Reading, before having spells at West Ham, Charlton, Southampton before he took over at Newcastle in 2010. Left in 2014 to take over at Crystal Palace.

Stephen Miller:

After Stephen won gold at the club throw at the 1996 Paralympic Games in Atlanta, he repeated the feat at the 2000 games in Sydney and the 2004 games in Athens (where he set a world record). He was selected as captain of the men's athletics squad for Great Britain at the 2012 summer paralympics. He still has a season ticket at St James' Park.

Faustino Asprilla:

Asprilla would go onto score a famous hat-trick against Barcelona in the Champions League at St James' Park. He was sold by Kenny Dalglish for £6 million in 1997 back to Parma. He then moved to Palmeiras, Fluminese, Atlante and Universidad de Chile. Asprilla player 57 times for his country, scoring 20 goals. He came close to joining Darlington in 2002. Has been involved in the running of a small football academy in Colombia.

Andy Cole:

Cole went on to win five Premier League titles with Manchester United, he also won the Champions League and the FA Cup. In 2001 he moved to Blackburn for £8 million and then spent a season at Fulham and a season at Manchester City. Brief spells followed at Birmingham, Sunderland, Burnley and finally Notts Forest. Currently a TV summariser.

ACKNOWLEDGEMENTS

'I'VE HAD AN IDEA FOR A BOOK.' MICHAEL BOLAM, WHO RUNS THE excellent website www.nufc.com, will probably rue the day I ever said that in his company. The developing thought for *Touching Distance* had been in my mind for quite a while before I said those words. I could still not have envisaged how much work it would entail and quite how enjoyable and tiring an experience it would be. Through it all Biffa (M Bolam) proved a priceless friend, through proof reading, stats, facts, advice and help. I can't say a big enough thank you.

"The interviews will be the best bit." Michael Walker was halfway through the excellent *Up There* when he made that prediction after I told him of my plan. Michael was similarly hugely supportive to the endless conversations that such a project entails. He was also right about the interviews, they have created memories I will never forget.

It is impossible to say which was the best one, as I often get asked, but having a beer with Philippe Albert and his friends in Belgium and seeing Pavel Srnicek amongst my friends in Prague were highlights, of which there were many.

I would like to thank all of those who gave me so much time to talk so openly about the period this book covers, Terry McDermott and Peter Beardsley willingly gave up afternoons to chat to me and it was a great moment to speak to Kevin Keegan about the unforgettable football team he created.

To Graham Fenton, John Beresford, Les Ferdinand, Philippe, Pav, Terry, Peter, Kevin, Sir John Hall, Steve Watson, Darren Peacock, Warren Barton, Steve Howey, Robbie Elliott, Keith Gillespie, Rob Lee, Lee Clark, Alan Shearer, Faustino Asprilla, Alan Pardew, Steve Harmison, Steve Bruce, David Kelly, Brian Kilcline, Stephen

Miller and to Joan Bradshaw, my aunty, for such an emotional interview, I would also like to say a huge thank you.

That similar goes to James Corbett, the owner of deCoubertin Books, who heard my pitch about an idea to tell the unique story of a period of Newcastle's history and bought into it immediately. It was a big show of faith, and I will always be grateful.

Steve Brown, another journalist and a great friend, was similarly an endless supplier of support and possible contacts. Thanks also go to Melissa Chappell, Mark Davis, Barclays and their Spirit of the Game campaign and Ian Skinner for help on that front. Thanks also to Aidan Magee with additional research and the excellent statistics at www.nufc.com and www.statto.com.

I would also like to thank Amy Lawrence, author of *Invincible: Inside Arsenal's Unbeaten 2003-04 Season*, who offered advice and encouragement towards the book's finish.

Steve Wraith and Mick Speight also proved invaluable as I worked through an at times endless list of people to see. Thanks also go to Newcastle United for their help for photographs from the period, as it does to the photographer Ian Horrocks, whose work is featured in this book.

Writing *Touching Distance* was an incredibly rewarding experience, one I will never forget, and it was an exhausting one as well. To my family, to Matthew and to Jane, to my dad and his endless ideas, to my mam and my sister, thanks for all your support. Similar thanks go to those who endured and continue to endure my company on a Sunday evening. There was the need for the occasional escape.

And once more to Matthew, whose face was priceless when he saw first Peter Beardsley and then Les Ferdinand's name flash up on my phone within the space of five minutes one afternoon on the way to play football, at which point he discovered what his dad was doing (and kept quiet until I went public on the idea), this book's for you son.

BIBLIOGRAPHY

BOOKS

Batty, David: The Autobiography (*Headline Book Publishing, 2001*)

Beardsley, Peter: My Life Story (*HarperCollins Willow, 1996*)

Bolam, Mike: The Newcastle Miscellany (*Vision Sports Publishing, 2007*)

Cantona, Eric and Flynn Alex: Cantona on Cantona (*Manchester United Books 1996*)

Cantona, Eric: Cantona: My Story by Eric Cantona (*Headline Book Publishing, 1994*)

Ferdinand, Les: Sir Les: The Autobiography of Les Ferdinand (*Headline Book Publishing, 1997*).

Ferguson, Alex: Managing My Life (*Hodder and Stoughton, 1999*)

Gillespie, Keith: How Not to be a Millionaire (*Sports Media, 2014*)

Ginola, David: From St Tropez to St James' (*Headline Book Publishing, 1996*)

Hardisty, Tony: Peter Beardsley, Proud to be a Geordie (*Knight Fletcher print, 1986*)

Harrison, David: Alan Shearer: My Story so Far (*Hodder and Stoughton, 1998*)

Joannou, Paul: Newcastle United, A Complete Record 1982-1986 (*Breedon Books, 1986*)

Joannou, Paul: Newcastle United: the Ultimate Who's Who 1881-2014: An Official Publication (*N Publishing 2014*)

Keegan, Kevin: My Autobiography (*Little, Brown and Company 1998*)

Lee, Rob: Come in Number 37 (*Collins Willow, 2000*)

Milburn, Jackie: Jackie Milburn's Newcastle United Scrapbook (*Souvenir Press, 1981*)

Ridley, Ian, Cantona: The Red and the Black (*Victor Gollancz, 1995*)

Walker, Michael: Up There: The North East, Football, Boom & Bust (*deCoubertin Books, 2014*)

ARTICLES:

The Independent, Aug 4, 1996: Profile of Sir John Hall, Ruthless Pursuit of a Goal.

The Independent, Nov 1, 1995: Sir John Hall's zeal is opening up the North-east frontier.

The Shields Gazette, various cuttings from March 1983.

The Guardian, Faustino Asprilla interview, by Michael Walker, 1997.

Newcastle Evening Chronicle, April 11, 2103, Paralympian Stephen Miller takes first step to a new life.

Newcastle Sunday Sun, Sep 25, 1994, Keegan's Test of Strength, by Brian McNally.

The Independent, April 17, 1994, the Other Side of Eric Cantona, Richard Williams.

MAGAZINES:

Auf Wiedersehen Kev,' special tribute brochure for Kevin Keegan's farewell appearance for Newcastle United, v Liverpool.

FourFourTwo, November 1995, David Ginola interview, with Amy Lawrence.

When Saturday Comes, Weekly Howl 04-0-9-09, Touching the Stars, feature on Darren Peacock.

Life after Football (Dutch Magazine), Faustino Asprilla interview, by Michael Walker, 2013.

Black and White Summer Special, 1995-96, the Offical Magazine of Newcastle United

TELEVISUAL:

Charlton Athletic 1991-92 season review.

Newcastle United 1991-92 season review

Andy Cole, Sports Life Stories, ITV 4.

Sporting Heroes: Steve Harmison interviews Kevin Keegan, Sky Sports.

Time of our Lives, Sky Sports, with John Beresford, Steve Howey and David Ginola.

Schmeichel: Football's Greatest, Sky Sports.

Manchester United Review 1996-97.

PL Legends: Schmeichel, Sky Sports.

So Close! Newcastle United - End of Season Official Review 1995/96

Going Up; Tyne Tees documentary of Newcastle promotion season, 1994

OTHERS:

statto.com Numerous historic league tables

www.stephenjamesmiller.co.uk

Eric Cantona's kung-fu kick: The moment that shocked football, BBC Radio 5 Live programme, Jan 22, 2015.

INDEX